Mel Hantz (Satoru)

A Way To Love

Laugh

(The Secret of Life)

Life is action books and **A Way To** is a series of books that give insight and perspective to live a more stimulating and significant existence. The books are a combination of Zen outlooks, eclectic wisdom gleaned over several lifetimes, stories of inspiration, opinions and sayings that stimulate fresh thoughts, and advice on making meaningful decisions that improve self-authenticity without regard to time or sequence.

Summary

A Way to Love - Laugh. Is a series of original stories about a flawed older man with prescience, filled with dichotomies, seeking a lifetime love and companion. The personal narratives are infused with wisdom and humor gleaned from a lifetime of searching for a loving woman. Mike's philosophy is that "Anything worth doing is worth overdoing." "Do anything you want, with style, as long as you don't hurt anyone," and that, "Life is too important to be taken seriously, so a sense of humor is the most important aspect of any successful, loving relationship."
These accounts also read as "recipes" to find true love by inducing the experience of new thoughts and actions in the reader and demonstrating what to do and what not to do when interacting with your perspective love partner. There are also many interesting examples of the way a culture thinks about itself and suggests solutions for some of the problems that shape these transitional times. This book is the antithesis of The Rules, a dating manual that asserted archaic and ineffectual central tenets of not responding to overtures, written by two women who eventually got dire guys, unhappy marriages and rancid reputations.
The book is sprinkled with Zen philosophy, novel short stories, strong viewpoints, jokes, parables, anecdotes, aphorisms, personal encounters, entertaining Emails, dates, expressions, and a varied cornucopia of loving lessons to be learned. There is little competition in the book market for A Way to Love – Laugh because the book is a manual on how to find more essence in your existence through emotional expression, growth, Zen, and humor. This book comes with a Trigger Warning.

Trigger Warning. This is a preemptive alert, issued by a professor or institution, indicating that material presented in class or the textbook might be sufficiency graphic to spark symptoms of stress, trauma or disorder. This teacher, and his course, A Way to Live – Zen, asserts that there is no trigger warning for living your life. Zen gives expression to many discomfiting and challenging ideas to enlarge a person's comprehension and experience without care for the greater cultural preoccupation of achieving safety. Consciousness raising requires dispelling ignorant ideas, expanding ones' reference's, gaining a rejuvenating awareness of your physical body, and changing your perspectives.

Sense of Humor

Exercise probably helps to sustain your life more than any other factor. It allows us to have more focus, energy, and relaxation because it reduces stress. The second most important factor in prolonging your life is probably a sense of humor. Laughing also deactivates stress hormones and aids the immune system. People with a developed sense of humor tend to be more creative and more adept at solving the many problems that life gives us. It improves many cognitive functions. Most of all, it helps people get along with others. Two people sharing lives together, who both have a good sense of humor, are significantly happier than those couples with a poor sense of humor. Humor can act as an emotional release thereby releasing anxiety and promoting longevity. It also allows us to cultivate and keep friends, support groups, and perhaps even love, and love heals. You want to be with someone who makes you smile and laugh. To me, **a sense of humor is the definitive personally trait that makes being with someone over time possible.**

Laugh and the world laughs with you; "Weep, and you weep alone; For the sad old earth, must borrow its mirth, but has trouble enough of its own." Solitude by Ella Wheeler Wilcox

"This novel is both entertaining and a serious study for women and men. It elaborates many aspects about women's struggle to create and control their own identity in contemporary society, and in doing so shape their relationships with men, expressed by a sensitive male chauvinist." Gloria Steinman

"If I read this book when I was a girl twenty years ago, by now I would be a queen or at very least an empress." Newel the JAP

"Mel Hantz's book, and his multiple interactions reveal that unfortunately the newly liberated women are off time confused, defensive, and hypersensitive to anything that defines their status. But his evocative insights give hope and information on overcoming some of these problems. This humorous psychological novel enters the deep consciousness and sensibility of an individual's mind forever." Sigmund Freudly, Psychoanalyst.

"Evolutionary processes give rise to diversity at every level of biological organization, including species, individual organisms and molecules such as DNA and proteins. This book is a testament to the fact that women are a few million years more evolved than men." Charley Darwin

"A Way To Love – Laugh, is a modern, intellectual, evocative, iconoclastically humorous, personal, Poor Richards Almanac about relationships and change. The book should be read very slowly and referred to often. It demonstrates how, paradoxitly, a person can hold two opposite thoughts about a given situation, and consider them resolved even when introducing more variables." Al Enstein

Hantz's book sings the song of the modern mans dilemmas. The tiger was running wild and free. From his cage he said, "They clip your claws, cut your hair, and make a pussy cat out of you. It's one step from the jungle to the zoo." Dr. Hook

"A man stood in the street trying to give away a gold ingot. He had no success. Teaching Zen and reading this book is a bit like that. Why were so many of those old Zen masters so grumpy? Zen has plenty of room for laughter. People persist in wanting things they can't have, even though they already have everything." Satoru

"This book is like drinking an iced cold drink when you are really thirsty. It contains the condensed wisdom of a lifetime of learning and relationships." Rick Mavrovich

"I laughed so much my stomach hurt. Mikes storytelling strategy is a most impressive achievement, as is his synopsis of centuries old wisdom, and the conflicts facing the sexes in finding an emotionally fulfilling relationship." Dr. Maggie Cooper

When I was fourteen, I had a very sexually precocious girlfriend. Doing what came naturally, I focused all of my attention and energies on sex. I did terribly in high school, because of this distraction and a lack of concentration on studying. Years passed, and the beast subdued slightly. After a hitch in the army, I returned to civilization and felt a strong need to overcompensate for my inadequate education. I read for six hours a day and matriculated in two different universities. I fed my brain and became smarter. After years of being emerged in study, I became brilliant, developed an unusual prescience, and knew everything. Lamentably, I went into the educational system and became a teacher and educator. I lost hundreds of words from my vocabulary, dumbed down my quick thinking, had political hacks for supervisors, and became brain damaged. Such is the price for peaking early. Now, after many years of living, reading and experience, although still drain bamaged, I occasionally get a glimpse of wisdom. Unfortunately, by the time I get home, I forget the brilliance. Every few months for a few seconds, a thought that seems significant suggest itself to me. This book is an attempt to record some of these Zen existential moments and sexual realities without regard to time sequence, linear order, or politically correct language.

Everyone in town is at least a little crazy, and all the woman I met are idiosyncratic. When I meet the next woman on a blind date or one who answers my ad, I'm going to dress up like the hunchback of Notre Dame, but with dark glasses and a white cane, like a blind Quasimodo. I will fill my mouth with green rubber bands. When I first speak, they will spill out like worms.

What a great filtering device. Maybe since so many people are meeting on the Internet, I'll put the personal ad on some of the dating sites and see how many and what kind of women will go for a hunchback with bad teeth and special needs. Surely, I will get a lady with a sense of humor. But will she be oral and into necrophilia? You think that she is too good for me? Was Esmeralda too good for Quasimodo?

All the books in the series A Way To, on Kindle, are sold for eight dollars and eighty-eight cents ($8.88) because; the number eight is symbolic of rebirth and life after death.

In music composition, every eighth note, an octave that is composed of eight notes, merges in unison and resonates with its counterparts. In numerology, eight represents a new existence or a new period. A master Yoga gave eight gifts that instilled a new consciousness to rise above the level of reality. Eight is the first cube number and is a new dimension in mathematics. Man, has seven orifices, but a woman has an eighth and sacred opening from which we are born into this world. Eight is a maximum number for our memories and total recall for short-term memory. Finally, the number eight when turned on its side represents infinity.

ISBN 978-0985407841

Printed in the United States of America.
Registration Certificate Case # 1-2128053648

Book Cover, layout, and illustrations by www.seheenal.com

A Way To LOVE Laugh
(The Secret of Life)
by Mel Hantz

Table of Contents

Tax Audit

Russ & Daughters was my first stop today. The store was in the opposite direction of where I wanted to go, but I had a plan.

"Good morning Nikki. How have you been? May I have six slices of smoked sturgeon and six slices of sable? I'd like two plain bagels and a small container of cream cheese with chives."

"Sure, Mike. Everything's good. Are you still the last single man in New York who's not gay?" she laughingly asked.

Nikki said something to the counterman, and he packed everything like a present. I hailed a cab to take me to the Federal building near City Hall. I got off a block from the Fed, went into a good coffee shop and ordered two cappuccinos and a green tea.

The security checkpoint inside the Federal building was as inconvenient as it is at the airport. There were two machines to walk through, but redundantly, after passing through the scanners, the agents still took their time using their wands. In this case, however, it seemed reasonable since people probably hated the Internal Revenue Service more than any other branch of the government, even the phone companies.

I asked for an eleven o'clock appointment, reasoning that if I brought the auditor lunch, he would be more relaxed since he did not have to hassle with the twelve o'clock lunch crowd. He also had an hour off and might appreciate the gesture if done surreptitiously. I took the elevator upstairs and reported for my IRS audit.

"Hi," I said to the secretary. "I have an appointment with Mr. Adam Gottlieb for a tax audit."

"You're a little early, let me see if he's ready for you. All right, go right in."

"Good morning Mr. Gottlieb... Please don't put me in jail. I didn't do it.

It was someone else's fault. I wasn't there. I didn't hear anyone; I didn't see anything. And if I was there, I was sleeping."

He smiled in a business-like way, gestured for me to sit down, and said, "Put your stuff on the big table and hang your coat up."

I unpacked the shoebox that I was carrying, taking out the papers, notebooks, and my cell phone. As I emptied the bag of fish, bagels, and cappuccinos, I said, "I hope you don't mind me eating something, but I'm hypoglycemic, and I didn't get a chance to have breakfast. And please join me."

He lifted his nose slightly and smelled the fish like a sommelier with an excellent wine, took one look at the bagels and sturgeon and grinned like a fat kid in a candy store. My plan was working. Even if I would have to pay, it was going to be less, and I would make it up next year with what I learned from this professional man today. Or was I being too optimistic?

While we were eating, Gottlieb, the auditor told me the problem. "Your entertainment, especially your dinner expenses are out of sight. Even if you made more money with your book sales, you can't deduct your entire dating expenses. Also, you have enough audio equipment deductions to be an agent for the CIA."

"But Mr. Gottlieb, these are legitimate operating and research costs, and most of the research is done over dinner. I even have recordings to help me to remember the conversations."

"I'm the last single man, in my age group, in New York City, who's not gay. I'm writing a book called, A Way to Love - Laugh. It's about all the women I meet, how they span the entire range of incompatibility, and what they have to do to change their behavior to bond with a man."

He took an extended look at me over his glasses, brushed back his thinning hair over his balding head and said, "Either you're totally legit, or the biggest bullshit artist to hit this office in months."

"Mr. Gottlieb I'll make you a bet. I'll play two of the recordings for you and show you some stories to read. If you don't laugh so hard you feel like peeing in your pants, you don't validate my expenses. But, if you believe my research, then you give me a break. I can make this bet because you will hear that I can't make this stuff up. May I plug my phone?"

He turned his desk chair to one side, sat back and relaxed, supporting his cheek with one hand and slowly munching on the sturgeon and bagel with the other. Intermittingly, he savored the aroma of his cappuccino, taking tiny sips. Looking at me incredulously and totally in charge he said, "This is going to be one for the books."

A secret recording of an onboard plane conversation.

I boarded the airplane and settled in. The speaker was right over my head and too loud. I wasn't paying attention but I still heard the announcement. "Thank you for flying with us. We hope you enjoyed giving us the business as much as we enjoyed taking you for a ride."

I took one of the earpieces from my IPhone out of my ear.

"Welcome aboard. To operate your seat belt, insert the metal tab into the buckle, and pull tight. It works just like every other seat belt; and, if you don't know how to operate one, you probably shouldn't be out in public unsupervised."

I took the other earpiece from my ear.

"In the event of a sudden loss of cabin pressure, masks will descend from the ceiling. Stop screaming, grab the mask, and pull it over your face. If you have a small child travelling with you, secure your mask before assisting with theirs. If you are travelling with more than one small child, pick your favorite. Thank you, enjoy your flight, I hope I don't get fired for my creative announcements"

The cabin exploded with applause.

Glancing up, I saw a beautiful woman coming down the aisle and looking around. I soon realized that she was heading straight toward my row of seats. I put my earpieces back in and relaxed. Moments later, she took the seat right next to me. Not wanting to seem too obvious, I just smiled at her as she made herself comfortable and I went back to my reading. She seemed eager to strike up a conversation. Smiling, she turned her body slightly to me and asked, "Business trip or vacation?"

"I guess a little of both. And you?"

"I'm going to the annual Nymphomaniac Convention in Miami."

"Sure."

"No, really."

"You're not putting me on?"

"No," she said, a pleasant smile rising to her lips.

"And what is your business role at this convention?" I asked, expecting to be told some funny punch line.

"Well, I'm a doctor and lecturer," she said, "I use my experience to debunk some of the myths about sexuality."

"Brains and beauty. And what myths are those?"

"Well," she explained, "One popular myth is that African-American men are the most well-endowed, when in fact, it's the Native American Indian who is the most likely to possess that trait. Another popular myth is that french men are the best lovers when it is the man of Jewish descent. However, we have found that the best potential lover in all categories is the Southern redneck."

At this point in the conversation, I knew she was just playing with my head, but I could not think of anything witty enough to say to her as a retort. So, I played it as a straight man and said, "Fascinating. And what are some other myths?"

Suddenly, she became a little uncomfortable and blushed.

"I'm sorry," she said, "I shouldn't be discussing this with you. I don't even know your name!"

"Tonto," I said, "Tonto Goldstein. But my friends call me Bubba."

Her mouth opened wide, showing a lovely set of white teeth as she chortled uncontrollably. "I can't believe you said that," she told me, unable to stop laughing. "I thought I had you."

"Well, if you want to have me I guess you really can."

Conversation recorded in a sophisticated uptown bar.

I was in a splendid mood. I was killing two birds with one stone. I was out hunting for a new honey, and at the same time, getting notes and dialogue for my book. I picked this very expensive Manhattan bar that has a reputation for beautiful, smart women.

She had perfect eyelashes, but her eyes were pools of deep hurt. When I said a simple "Hello," she waved me off with a brush of her hand, as if shoeing some invisible insect.

"Are you ready?" I said.

She turned and looked at me skeptically.

"If you had one wish, anything except money, what would you wish for?"

"I don't understand." She answered.

"Too late" I replied, "Your time is up."

"But you didn't give me time to answer your question."

"You did answer. You said you didn't understand."

"So, you were just playing with me?"

"I didn't lay a hand on you."

"So you were teasing or testing?"

"Yes. I wanted to see if you knew what you wanted."

"Good test. I'll have to steal it from you. But the answer to my wish would be another good man."

"Good, you proved my point." I said sarcastically, "Women relate to men like monkeys."

"That's because men are like tiles."

"What?"

"Pardon me."

"Yes," I said. "Monkeys don't let go of one branch, until they have a firm grip or until they grasp another."

"Because men are like tiles. If you lay them right the first time, you can walk on them forever."

We both stopped, and there was an enjoyable pregnant pause.

She looked me in the eyes, straightened up, crossed her legs, and said, "I hate you with a passion you can only dream of."

"You despise me, don't you?"

"I would if I gave you thought."

"I only came here for the water. "

"There is no water. This is a desert."

"I was misinformed, like when I went to the air & space museum but nothing was there."

"You're just impressed with any girl who can walk and talk and has a beautiful body."

"Who said walk and talk? I think you are a truly beautiful, loquacious, witty, and liberated woman."

"You are an extraordinary verbally quick man and an excellent judge of character."

"Never interrupt when you are being flattered. So, are you looking for Mr. Right?"

"No, Mr. Big, I'm still hot, it just comes in flashes now."

"Well, a clear conscience is the sign of a fuzzy memory."

I was having a good time and judging by her beaming demeanor, so was she.

I smiled and sipped my full-bodied Merlot. She smoothed back her hair and adjusted her shoulders to turn more of her body to me. I anticipated getting lucky.

"I can't believe what a smooth feline move you just made."

"Oh, now you're calling me a cat?"

"Well, not just you, but... Cats do what they want when they want. They rarely listen to you. They're totally unpredictable, and they whine when they are not happy. When you want to play, they want to be alone. When you want to be alone, they want to play. They expect you to cater to their every whim. They are moody. They leave hair everywhere. They drive you nuts. Which admittedly for me is more like a short walk than a long drive. And so, the conclusion is that cats are like little tiny women in inexpensive fur coats."

"Wow, you are so damn verbal and glib. You must be a lawyer. What do you do?"

"The best I can, and I wrote the book. But, I think that I'm just putty in your hands."

She replied, "In my hands, nothing turns to putty."

"I can barely believe your retorts are so excellent. But, remember that Lilith was evil and independent and would not lie beneath him and so she was cast out."

"You're just saying that because I'm celibate. I sell a bit and give a little bit away."

"Ouch, I may have spoken too soon. That's like me saying: "It's a gala day for me and that's all I can handle is a gal a day." However, I will always cherish the initial misconceptions I had about you."

"Where are you from?"

"My mother."

"Is that phone recorder on?"

"Yes."

"Goodbye."

As she gathered her things just before she was leaving, I asked her if she was penile psychic.

"Penile psychic? What's that?

"You know when something is up."

It takes two

Mercedes was young, slim, beautiful, Columbian and sexy. We lived together for a few years until she left me... thank God. When she first moved in with me, because she had a fire in her apartment, and perhaps in her crotch, she only had one suitcase of clothing. As I moved my things around, or threw them out, giving her more space, she filled the spaces with shoes, extra kitchen things, an extraordinary number of shampoos, lotions, creams, things for the hair paraphernalia, nail maintaining devices, books, more shoes, and new clothing. Even though Mercedes continually had more space for her stuff, it was never enough and most of the time she left stuff out all around the apartment. I should have been alerted to the future when she complained that she was deprived because there was not enough room to display the new three dozen shoes that she brought since she moved in.

All the furniture in my apartment was custom made and designed for aesthetics and efficiency. So, it was irritating when she left draws and closet doors ajar or open. She had little awareness of the objects in the physical world of the apartment and continually broke, burnt, scarred, water-soaked, misplaced, and abused the everyday accouterments. For example, she wrenched free the handles on the sink, shower, and toilet. She broke the handles on the stove and sprung the dishwasher door. She bleached out my soft colored towels and broke crystal glasses. When she cooked, she never covered the frying pans, so in a short time, the entire kitchen, walls ceiling, floor, and closets, were covered in oil.

As if devastating my apartment was not enough, over the years, although she was always lovely and energetic, she became less sexual, talked continually, stopped cleaning after herself or the apartment, even though the housekeeper did almost everything, and she rarely cooked or did a laundry. It was as if she believed that being lovely was all she had to be. She didn't get it, that living together is a partnership and both have to help each other carry the load.

Over the years her laziness took on a new dimension for me when she stopped cleaning up the dishes after I cooked our meals. This cleaning only consisted of her rinsing the dishes and putting them in the dishwasher. She became a spoiled high maintenance lady that would never make my life easier. When it ended, I said to her, "Mercedes, you've never had it so good, and I've never had it so bad." It was a little strange sleeping alone, but the quiet was peaceful and after so many years of constant companionship, I found the solitude exhilarating and felt like I was on vacation.

My relationship of the last few years was over and the high maintenance that I had to perform was gone. My life was now a lot simpler. Everything in my life was changing and I was changing everything in my life.

Alone is also All One

I was looking for a new honey. I wanted someone not too spoiled, attractive, as nurturing as I was, and able to give, love and fulfillment. Most of all I wanted someone who would not make my life harder. I needed someone who knew how to be alone with someone and themselves and would value the interaction with an aware, continually self-improving, person. For me, romance still counts, but the world is not a romantic place anymore and the women I met lacked trust, enthusiasm, and passion. Was I yearning for something that was long gone but still within reach?

I resolved to find a woman and to work at trying to have a real deep relationship. I asked my friends to fix me up with their best shot. I told them that this was not going to be a habit. They had just one chance to introduce me to someone of quality and substance. Little did I know to what I was going to be exposed.

I live in New York City, which has an enormous single population. This book documents some of my search for a woman and some interesting dates. It is also a portrait of how some modern urbanites strive and fail to connect, why they do not succeed and suggests some ideas, tactics, and strategies to remedy this situation. The philosophies promulgated herein are strictly my own. They are asserted totally from a male's viewpoint to counteract some of the ridiculous "Rules" and other "How to Find a Good Man" books written by women. This is a manual for both women and men. I suggest some contemporary thoughts and actions. If you have always done the same thing and action, then you will always get the same results. I know the hardest thing to do is change. But, maybe a different way of thinking and acting can bring you a fresh existence. This book is a recount of some of these dates and experiences. Hopefully, you can learn from my mistakes, hard-earned lessons, and save years of frustration and regrets.

I Love HeadlineS.

A Piece of Ass.

The Pastor entered his donkey in a race, and it won. The Pastor was so pleased with the donkey that he entered it in the race again and it won again. The local paper read:

PASTOR'S ASS OUT FRONT.

The Bishop was so upset with this kind of publicity that he ordered the Pastor not to enter the donkey in another race.

The next day the local paper headline read BISHOP SCRATCHES PASTOR'S ASS.

This was too much for the Bishop, so he ordered the Pastor to get rid of the donkey. The Pastor decided to give it to a Nun in a nearby convent. The local paper, hearing of the news, posted the following headline the next day: NUN HAS BEST ASS IN TOWN.

The Bishop fainted. He informed the Nun that she would have to get rid of the donkey, so she sold it to a farmer for $10. The next day the paper read: NUN SELLS ASS FOR $10...

This was too much for the Bishop so he ordered the Nun to buy back the donkey and lead it to the plains where it could run wild.

The next day the headlines read: NUN ANNOUNCES HER ASS IS WILD AND FREE.

The Bishop went to his physician the next day. The moral of the story is, being concerned about public opinion can bring you much grief and misery, even shorten your life. So be yourself and enjoy life. Stop worrying about everyone else's ass, and you'll be a lot happier and live longer!

"I want a man who is kind, sensitive, generous, attentive, smart, rich, healthy, big, perceptive, oral, beautiful, sexual and funny."

"If I had all
those qualities,
why would I be with you?"

The Jewish American Princess

High maintenance, low return

Ade'lie was the woman that all the people who wrote humor about the Jewish American Princess or JAP had in mind when they wrote the jokes. She was the penultimate personification.

"Mike, meet me downtown. I want to pick up something on West Broadway and then we can have some brunch."

"All right Ade'lie, my gallery is on that street so I can get some business done before we meet."

We met at a jewelry store where Ade'lie was buying a necklace that consisted of three big diamonds strung on a monofilament fishing line. The rocks appeared to float on her neck since the transparent fishing line was almost invisible. She was also looking at an obscenely fat, clumsy gold bracelet that had a thick jewel placed on it. I wondered how someone's taste could have such a huge range, from the delicate necklace to the lumpish bracelet.

"Do you like the bracelet, Mike?"

"No, it's too big on your wrist."

Reaching out and touching the bracelet, I asked, "Is the gold supposed to rub off?"

We walked out of the store and into the bright sunlight. For an older woman, Ade'lie looked remarkably good. She has amazing high cheekbones that keep her face youthful and possesses a Mephistophelian glamor that made her initially charismatic. She worked out at a gym with a personal trainer. She spared no expense on herself and lived a good life. She also had no inhibitions about telling you so.

The problem with Ade'lie was that aside from being totally spoiled and self-centered, she had a big mouth. She would shoot from the hip, alienate people immediately and start fights without provocation. It was as if the words short-circuited from her mind and came straight from her ass, an anal-cranial inversion. Her sharp tongue could injure someone's feeling easily, and she always believed that she was in the right. I would usually bait her to get her started if she said something to me that I did not like.

"Mike, tell me about that book, Dead Man's Float, that you have written."

"Well, it's a non-fiction event that happened to me in the Bahamas. I was on vacation where I was grabbed, tied up and thrown into the ocean to drown. They confused me with my brother, the detective Supercop. The book also predicts the terrorist attacks."

"Oh, I don't believe you. Anyone who is tied up in the water dies."

"Ade'lie, sometimes you are like a woman that has PMS and ESP at the same time."

"What do you mean?"

"A bitch that knows everything."

Ade'lie was aware of the fact that she was of royal birth. Like so many middle-class women in America, who believed what their mothers told them, nothing was too good for her, and no one could do enough to compensate for the fact that unfortunately she had been switched at birth through some hospital mix-up, and should be eternally compensated. Her misguided sense of entitlement sometimes made dealing with her an ordeal, but she compensated for it by switching to a sweet, nurturing, gregarious women, when it pleased her. She once confided in me that, "I married my husband because I thought it would be a great way to meet guys."

"I can't decide whether to buy that bracelet or a gold necklace."

"Ade'lie, don't you have enough jewelry by now? You must have boxes full, and you can't wear it all. Do you know the difference between a Spanish American princess and a Jewish American princess?"

"All right. Let's hear your filthy male chauvinist joke."

I interjected, "remember honey, it's harder for a woman, she has a double standard to live up to. A Spanish American princess has fake jewelry and real orgasms, but a Jewish American princess has real jewelry, etc. Let's go up to the country next week to see the changing trees."

"Oh, what a good idea! It will give us some time to talk."

"Are you sure you just want to go for a walk in the country? It might change your entire perspective and bring you down to earth."

"No, it's a great thing to do to change my vision, since everything I do is so ritzy. I have such a good life. I even belong to a gourmet club."

"But, you just told me how you go to the gym and how you are trying to lose weight? Isn't that a bit of an incongruity?"

"Don't be silly. Half of all the uptown society goes to gourmet dinners in the evening and works out in the daytime."

"I guess I don't know what I'm missing."

"I'm so busy I don't have time to keep in touch, with my friends, so I'm going to have a birthday party at a restaurant, so I can interact with my friends and not have to do any work."

"What a good idea."

"And I don't want you telling anyone my age. I know you, and a very few people know, so don't say anything."

"Does this mean I'm invited? Do you believe that no one can guess your age at your birthday party? And what can I possibly give to a woman who has everything?"

"Diamonds."

"Anything else?"

"One of your sculptures?"

"Right. Did you like that thirty-year-old balsamic vinegar I bought you last time?"

"Oh, it was good, but I have so many of them."

The balsamic vinegar that I bought Ade'lie was a tiny bottle of the best sipping vinegar in the world. Its' cost was excessive and was a wonderful dinner gift because everyone I gave it to loved the vinegar. Since it was only half the size of a bottle of wine, it was much easier to carry. I found it consistent that Ade'lie would not be impressed, or even thank me for the present. What could I get her that would satisfy the gift giving ritual, establish that it was expensive and still get her goat at the same time? I'd have to think about it.

The party was very well done, with some new friends, good food, and good company.

Ade'lie and I went together for a while. I liked her style and Joie de vivre and her assertiveness. Her assertiveness was more like her proclivity for total control over everything in all situations. She gathered people around her whom she could control, or who thought of her as the princess or great queen. After a brief affair, together, it was evident that I could not support her in the style that she would like to be accustomed to and that she was too provoking. Instead of parting, we became party acquaintances and interacted over dinners and affairs. After a while, she found another man, Martin, who was able to provide her with everything she wanted. Martin wanted a shiksa blonde wasp mistress who would take care of him. Even though Ade'lie was Jewish, she fulfilled the role, and they both were happy with each other. We would call each other often. Since we had nothing to hide because we had already been to bed with each other, we relaxed and spoke freely and personally. Martin did not mind our now friendly interaction since he was brilliant and secure, and the three of us became fast friends.

"Mike, we're going out to dinner after a movie in Soho. Like to join us?"

“Ok, I’ll meet you at the restaurant. What time?”

“Seven o’clock.”

“Good, see you then.”

I arrived at the restaurant a little early and looked over the tables.

“How many please?” the headwaiter asked.

“Three or four,” I replied.

“Would you like that table?”

“No, it’s too much in the traffic.”

“How about the table in the corner?”

“No, someone will be facing the wall.”

“How about if we put those two tables together near the center of the room?”

“That sounds good.”

I sat down at the two nice sized tables and made myself comfortable in the chair facing the entrance. The waiter approached and asked, “Would you like”?

“Definitely,” I answered before he finished his sentence.

“Would you like a wine or a… ”

“What is your best red bar wine?”

“We have a nice Merlot or a Chianti. The Chianti has more… ”

“The Chianti reserve with the full body will be all right.”

“Thank you.”

“Thank you.”

Playing with the Piranha.

New Yorkers can and do talk and listen at the same time. As the waiter set the glass down, and as I picked up the glass to smell the bouquet of the wine, Ade'lie waltzed in and surveyed the room, followed by Martin and an impeccably dressed woman.

"That table near the window is much better and more private." She said to me as she approached.

"But this one has much more room and someone will have to sit facing the window at the other one."

"I'll sit facing the window."

"All right, as long as I can see the entranceway. Tell me we're both not too idiosyncratic."

"No, I just know restaurants, it's my thing." She said as she handed me some Time magazines with the top one earmarked to photos of past New York mayors. The four of us sat down.

"This is my friend."

Ade'lie introduced me to her friend who was a writer and public speaker trainer. She was quiet but secure. Somehow, I instantly forgot her name.

Shaking Ade'lie's friends hand, I said, "Do you think I could sit in one of your assertiveness training courses; it's just what I need."

Ade'lie and Martin laughed setting the mood for the evening.

Ade'lie said, "Yes, you need that course as much as former mayor Giuliani or Attila the Hun."

"Don't say anything negative about the Fuhrer," I retorted. "He still may make a comeback in 2017, after all the orangutan won the election. Remember Rudolph Giuliani made the trains run on time." (Interestingly when I referenced the Fuhrer in the reference dictionary or thesaurus in German, on my three-terabyte Mac Pro, no results were found.)

"Yes, but he handled that shooting situation so poorly. The Blacks all voted against him. He was just a little insensitive."

"A little insensitive? Let me write that down," I said, as I took a few index cards and pen from my pocket. "Ex-Mayor Giuliani is a little insensitive." I wrote.

"Oh, stop being so obnoxious. You know what I mean. The Blacks all voted against him, even blacks who never voted before defeated him."

"No, I don't. You have to be incredibly naive and politically unsophisticated to think that he gave a damn about the black vote. He could not care less, and he never had the black or Puerto Rican vote. His power base was the white upstate vote. People whose lives he improved through paying less tax and city people who feel that the streets are safer."

"Look, I know what I'm talking about. I read all the papers... you don't know what you're talking about."

"Well, if I agreed with you, we'd both be wrong."

Ade'lie knew a little about everything and tried to assert that she was very well informed about many different topics. In truth, she was simply assertive, totally opinionated, and disliked being proven wrong or bested in an argument. When she was losing an argument, she would resort to name calling or put-downs. I knew it was wrong to tease and bait her, but I could not help it. It was as if I posseted my personal, more verbal, Gracey Alan and I could be George Burns getting fed all the great lines.

"And do you think Hillary had a chance against Obama?" Said the quiet public speaker sitting next to me.

"Not if anyone remembers the meaning of carpet bagger, and all she had to do was make Bernie the vice president and she would have won. But she didn't want to share the power," I answered.

Martin chimed in. "Hillary was insulated in the White House by a diplomatic Washington press corps. The New York and national press have no respect for anyone. They were like a pack of hyenas after a bone-they tore her up and gave the unqualified the edge."

Ade'lie argued back. "The woman is smart and classy. She parried the press as good as Trump."

"But, Trump is a thick-skinned junkyard dog compared to her..."

"No, no, Martin you're wrong..."

"All right." I said, "I have to interject something. Hillary may have been the most qualified candidate but she was irresponsible and almost caused the downfall of the free world. She knew her man. She was the first lady. She did not give him the BJ's that he needed, so he had to go elsewhere. I want Martin to be the arbitrator. What do you think Martin"?

"Good point Mike, but people only care about the issues that affect them directly. Obama tried to fixed the infrastructure, cleaned up the cities, lowered crime to make people feel safer. That's why Barrack Obama won after eight years of a retard. And his health plan is..."

"Oh, what do you know?" Ade'lie said, "You only read one newspaper."

I tried to lighten up the conversation, but could not help myself when I said, "Ade'lie, what is your position?"

She answered with her best attempt at levity that evening.

"I'm Jewish. I just lay there."

Martin turned his chair sideways, crossed his legs, and settling into the authoritative pose of a senior banker, filled in the pause, "This man walks into a bar. With him, are a cat and an ostrich. The man orders a beer; the ostrich requests a scotch. "And what will you have?" asks the bartender of the cat. The cat replies, "I'll have some milk, but I'm not going to pay for it."

The bartender says, "That will be sixteen seventy-five."

The man reaches into his pocket and pulls out exactly sixteen seventy-five and gives it to the barkeep. Ten minutes later, the man asks for another beer. "This time, make it a bottle of imported beer please, and a double scotch for my friend, the ostrich."

"And what will you have?" The bartender asks the cat.

"I'll have a double cold milk, but I'm not going to pay for it."

"That will be eighteen sixty," says the bartender.

The man digs into his pocket and pulls out eighteen sixty correctly and hands it to the bartender.

"Wait a minute," the bartender says, "How come you always have the exact amount in your pocket?"

"Well," the man answers, "I was on the beach and found a magic bottle with a genie in it. The genie gave me two wishes. My first wish was that I would always have the right amount of money in my pocket to pay for what I bought. The second wish was for a tall chick with a tight pussy."

Ade'lie scolded Martin. "That's such a male chauvinist pig joke."

The quiet public speaker said, "But why are we talking about such an old political topic when current events are ripe for discussion?"

"That's an easy question." I answered "It takes time for Martin to think of and memorize the jokes that will antagonize Ade'lie. For instance, take the stock market."

Martin cued in immediately with, "It was a Monica Lewinsky stock market week. It kept going down."

I said, "That's because Monica came out with a new line of pants, they have built in kneepads."

Martin took a sip of wine, smiled, and was off. He liked playing with the Piranha. "Is sex a high crime and misdemeanor? The natural lubricant of the Millennium will be the scandal, talk, unplanned chastity, money and sex. Sexual McCarthyism allowed the Republican Party to allow a blow-job to bring down the President. So, Clinton was caught between a rock and a hard-on. The atmosphere was so cold in Washington that Clinton had the intern blow on his hands. He should know when he was licked. The secret service, when they see the President being serviced, they are supposed to keep it a secret. Monica was in Kinko's photographing- copying herself on the machine without underwear. She was just copying her resume. She was going to become the spokesperson for weight watchers because husbands love the Monica Lewinsky diet."

I chimed in, "That, by the way, produces a superb relationship and happy marriage. Mike Tyson and Monica Lewinsky have one expression in common. Can you guess? If you can't beat them, eat them."

Martin, never to be outdone answered, "The Lewinsky story poses some stiff questions. It's a fascinating oral history. Clinton is glad to get rid of his suit. Still, the lower his pants, the higher his ratings and he took a licking and keeps on ticking."

I parried with, "And the government has a new, The Monica Lewinsky stamp that licks you back. Monica has given new meaning to the phrase, close but no cigar. I met her at the gym. She said, "I go to the gym almost every day. I'm trying to slim down my love handles." So, I asked her, "But how can you reduce your ears?" "And remember: a little fat once in a while might be good for you." And Bill said to Hillary "See."

Ade'lie was ticked off as usual and just glared at both of us while the quiet public speaker, who was thoroughly entertained, just kept up a rolling laugh. We ordered a salad for the table and took turns telling what we did today. Although I thought the salad was nothing out of the ordinary, everyone else expressed that they thought it was great to excellent.

"Shall we order some wine?" Martin asked me.

"Absolutely, the bar wine isn't that good."

"Shall we order a split or a full bottle?"

"I could drink three glasses tonight, so order a regular one."

"Oh no," Ade'lie said. If you order a large one, I'm not driving home with you, and I will take a cab."

"Ade'lie" Martin said, "Mike said he could drink three glasses."

"I'm not driving home with you."

The expression "Pussy whipped" came to mind as I said, "Just order a split, Martin."

I always liked Martin. He was honest, sophisticated, and smart. He had a way of approaching life from two different directions at the same time. He was always involved, yet, at the same time observing the situation from the outside. He liked interacting with me, and our harmony of repartee. He enjoyed my teasing of Ade'lie because, he was secure, and I said things that he could not get away with.

Martin replied, "And to elaborate on a split I have an illustration of President Obama's health plan and the changes the Republicans want to make. A woman walks into a hospital to which she is going to donate money. An administrator gives her a tour. As she passes through a ward, she sees, through an opening in a drawn curtain, a nurse masturbating a male patient. She asks the administrator, "What's going on?" The director says that the man is suffering from prostrate problems and his testicles are filled with fluid, so the nurse is relieving him. They pass through the ward into a corridor of private rooms. In one of the rooms, the woman observes a nurse giving her patient a blowjob. The woman asks the administrator, "What's going on?" The administrator answers, "It's the same problem as the previous patient we observed, but this patient has a better health plan."

This time, I was ready for Ade'lie's criticism of Martin and in unison Ade'lie, and I said, "Martin, -you're–such-a-pig."

And the quiet speaker's laughter was out of control, as she held her stomach and stared at us with tears in her eyes.

"Let that be a lesson to you," I said to her. People at the tables around us leaned in the better to hear the jokes. I didn't care, I was on a roll and wanted to continue the lesson and said, "The Republican Party announced today that it is changing its emblem from an elephant to a condom because it more clearly reflects the Republicans party's position on the major issues facing America. A condom accepts inflation, halts production, destroys the next generation, protects a bunch of pricks, and gives you a sense of security while you're actually getting screwed.

A young man is talking to his father and said, 'Dad, I'm considering a career in organized crime.' The father asks, 'In the government or the private sector?'

A woman was in an elevator with a rattlesnake, an Islamic terrorist, and President Donald Trump. She only had two bullets. So, she shot Trump twice. By the way, Trumps 'draining the swamp' has resulted in the wealthiest cabinet in the history of the US."

We ordered three main courses and Ade'lie got up to speak to the waiter. "Make sure the pasta is al dente," she said, "I hate overcooked pasta."

"Ade'lie," I said, as she seated herself, "don't you think they know how to cook pasta in a good Italian restaurant?"

"I just wanted to make sure."

"Why are you guys always arguing?" Martin asked.

"They're not arguing" the public speaker lady interjected, "They're New Yorkers. That's how they talk."

Changing the topic, I said, "Ade'lie, tell us about the trip Martin, and you are taking to Morocco."

"Did you ever go there?" She asked.

"A long time ago, I was living with a French nurse in Porte Santa Maria Cadiz, in Southern Spain. She was going back to France for a few months, and some of her friends were going to Agadir and Marrakech, Morocco. So, I went with them and spent a few months there."

"What was it like, what was the architecture like?"

"Are you kidding Ade'lie? First of all, take some surgical masks so that you can breathe, because the dust blows continually. And make sure you only drink sealed bottled water, don't buy anything on the streets and bring some soft toilet paper."

"Toilet paper? We are going to a five-star hotel that costs twelve hundred dollars a day. For that much money, they wipe your ass for you.

We are going to see the country and the gardens from a chauffeur-driven Mercedes."

"How are you going to get a feel of the country and how will you get into the enclosed courtyards?"

Martin interjected, "It's a small Mercedes."

"You know Ade'lie; I read an article by Todd Kliman. He said, "You need to become a traveler, not a tourist. After all, the visitor is led the traveler seeks. The tourist demands certainty; the traveler leaves the sure thing to the unadventurous and seeks out raw, unadulterated experience. Sure, it takes a little time to research the..."

Ade'lie waved off my comment like she was shooing a fly from her nose and said, "Mike, darling, I think we travel differently. But what was the country like and where did you live?"

"I'll tell you that in a moment, but first an observation. Place and time have become vague concepts to travelers. The experience of travel used to mean exploring and being emerged in the countries culture. Now it's all illusion without adventure, with instant gratification, and no inconvenience.

But, to get back to your question, Ade'lie, my dear, I don't think you understand the time in which I traveled. This was in the early seventies, and the world was safer and less crazy, and the world's heads roamed with lots of freedom.

Let me give you some idea of the ambiance. My most vivid memory was entering an old house that had a huge courtyard room piled high with ripe marijuana plants. In the middle of the room was a big cage made of chicken wire with cheesecloth covering the inside and outside of the cage. Everyone was wearing a dust mask. Inside the cage, a young man was shaking the marijuana branches, and the pollen from the flowers filled the air with fragrant golden pollen dust. The most potent powder was the lightest and floated to the top of the cheesecloth. The pollen was scraped into a box, dumped into a silk cloth and slowly roasted over a small fire outside the house. While it was heated, it was squeezed and compressed to make extremely potent hashish.

So, all I remember about the months in Marrakech was the open faucets of hot and cold running women and the best and the strongest hashish I ever smoked. I was so stoned that I missed it. You remember I told you; I was only high once in my life... for ten years."

The evening passed quickly, as we ate and drank too much. The goodbyes were friendly. I could not help myself from baiting Ade'lie one more time. "Ade'lie I forgot to tell you that you have to be aware of the Lewinsky Virus. It sucks all the memory out of your computer and then e-mails everyone about what it did."

The fresh air on my walk home was invigorating.

Two days later the phone rang. I monitored the call through the answering machine.

"Mike, oh Mike-ee. My God, we can never get to speak to each other, you're never there."

I picked up. "Hello, Ade'lie, How ya doin?"

"Mike, I have a problem that I know you can help me with."

"Yes."

"My gun doesn't work, and I need you to... "

"What's wrong with it? What type of gun is it?"

"Well, it's a Smith and Western."

"No, I mean is it an automatic or a... "

"It's an automatic."

"Is it jammed? Is it loaded?

"I don't know!"

"Can you remove the clip?"

"I don't know how."

"All right. Wrap the gun in a towel and handle it very very carefully as if it was loaded and could go off easily. Don't point it at anyone or anything and treat it gently and if you know how to put the safety on, make sure it's on. Bring it to me, and I'll take care of it and show you how to use it."

"OK, and after drinks and fixing the gun, we can have dinner?"

"Sure."

A few days later, Ade'lie and Martin came over, holding the towel wrapped up pistol outright, like a gift to the king. I took out the clip and unfortunately saw that there was a cartridge in the chamber. I taped some thick rubber to the wall and smacked the slide with a leather hammer. The gun fired into the rubber and into the plaster wall. I sprayed the mechanism with silicone, slide the breach back and forth a few times, and gave it back.

We took the car to Chinatown because Ade'lie wanted to have Chinese food. She knew that I was familiar with the restaurants, but it was always a hassle finding one that would please her. This was understandable, but still difficult. I like to eat esoterically since I live just a few blocks from the hundreds of Asian restaurants. Ade'lie, on the other hand, always conveyed the predisposition that no restaurant was good enough for her. To say she was spoiled would be a monumental understatement.

"I can give you a choice of about six different types of Asian food, depending on what you would like."

"Well, maybe we should have Italian instead?"

"Ade'lie, make up your mind. We're walking in the wrong direction if you want to eat Italian."

"Well, I want some vegetables and greens."

"I think I can accommodate you on that one. I can probably order some greens that you have never tasted before."

"Oh really?"

"Yesss, really."

"I have two really great places, but it's a holiday, so I'm not sure exactly what we will encounter. Do you think you might like Da Been Low? That's a place where you cook your own food in a communal boiling pot of chicken broth in the center of the table."

"Why would I want to go out to cook my own food? If I want to do that, I'd stay home."

"No, no, this is a place that has a huge selection of different foods, and you bring them to our table to cook them exactly how you desire. But, never mind, you have to be famished to eat in this style since it a high Prix fixed price."

"I don't like small places or small tables."

"I understand that perfectly. I hate when they try to give me a postage stamp sized table for two, on a banquette, between two other couples, on an isle that has continual traffic. Usually, I just walk out."

We walked for a block, or two and I decided to take them to a seafood restaurant on Mott Street. This place was huge and only had tables for twelve. When we entered, I said, "Don't let the waiter seat us."

"This way please," the waiter said, as we entered and as usual, Ade'lie paid no attention to what I said. We were seated at a table near the kitchen so that the waiters would not have to walk to the other end of the restaurant, which was the quieter spot I had selected. Instead, we were seated at a table surrounded by three other tables, for twelve, fully packed with entire families out for a holiday meal.

"Do you have enough room?" I said to Martin and Ade'lie, as the waiter seated us at a huge round table with fourteen seats.

"I can't believe he is seating us at a table this size. It's hysterical. It's a good thing we're not going to stay here too long. It's so noisy."

"That's why I like this place, intimate dining. It will get quieter when one of the tables leaves. Why didn't you listen to me, when I said don't let the waiter seat us?"

Ignoring my question, she said, "Oh, I must have some vegetables.

Would you like some fish? I think I'm going to have some dumplings. What are you having?" My wrinkles have more depth than Ade'lie's.

Martin was deeply in love with Ade'lie. When she spoke, he thought he heard bells, as if she were a garbage truck backing up. He fell for her like his heart was a mob informant, and she was the East River. She was as easy as the TV Guide crossword. She had a mind like a steel trap that had been left out too long and rusted shut. She was changing her last name to right, and her first name to always. Her scope was limited to the extent that she truly believed that shopping was a worthwhile and significant activity. She contributed nothing to the society or the concept of free enterprise but was the typical high-end consumer. She hoped to option class by buying expensive clothing. Ade'lie prepared food with rubber gloves on, so she would not ruin her manicure, and never bought packaged food because it was not good enough. She never took a subway or bus but would take a cab rather than walk a few blocks. The ideas of the times, considering she was so self-possessed and spoiled, passed over her like a moonbeam on the surface of a pool, without ever warming the depths below.

"Stop talking like one of my patients."

"You're what?"

"Please, you're an idiot."

"If you can't be kind Ade'lie, at least have the decency to be vague. Why do you pretend to be a doctor?"

"I don't."

"Certainly you do. I'll bet that you don't even tell your patients that you're under-qualified."

"You don't know what you're talking about."

"Ade'lie, you got your degree in social work and just took a year of internship treating mentally ill patients. The internship was not with an accredited university or hospital. So, in essence, with my two masters, I'm more or just as qualified to hang out a shingle.

"I don't want to talk to you. You're an idiot."

Martin chimed in and said, "Let's change the subject."

Poor Ade'lie, she never had to struggle in her entire life and so has never known failure. She has always been outrageously outspoken and not particularly bright. Most of the time, her outlandish comments are amusing, and there have been no consequences for her being that way or any incentive for her to change or grow. Unfortunately, she could be cruel and wrong without ever realizing it. She was so emasculating and aggravating to her male friends that eventually they all deserted her after she showed them little respect, insulted them and never possessed the maturity to apologize. The best apology she could muster was, "Oh, stop being such a girl."

One of the last things Ade'lie did before she alienated me with her incredibly disrespectful behavior, was to fix me up with a woman named Arlene.

"This isn't one of your "patients," is it Ade'lie?"

"Don't be stupid; I would never do that."

"Where did you meet her?"

"It was at a very expensive wine tasting, and she was wearing very expensive clothes."

"How do you know she wants to meet someone?"

"She sat next to me and asked me if I knew any winners to fix her up with."

"What was her definition of winners?"

"She wanted someone rich, in good shape, educated and big."

"Clearly, three out of four ain't bad. Big in a sense like when I asked a woman at a party if she was looking for Mr. Right and she answered, "No, I'm looking for Mr. Big."

"I think she was talking about tall and not a little guy, but there is usually a correlation."

The strange thing was that with all Ade'lie's faults I still liked her so much. I could tolerate almost all her nonsense except her disrespect.

A few days later I received a call from Arlene.

"Hi Mike, Ade'lie gave me your number. I'm going to a party on Saturday night in a lovely home in Jersey. Are you free and would you like to go with me?"

"I'm free and meeting you sounds great, but I don't have a car."

"I do, I'll pick you up."

On Saturday night, Arlene picked me up in a big Lexus town car. She was wearing Italian black high heels, and a remarkably beautiful black designer dress topped off with a strand of eye-wateringly expensive black pearls. The beads probably cost as much as the car. She wore two diamond rings on her hands that completed the paraphernalia of her posted understated opulence. She started asking questions immediately to ascertain how wealthy I was. I felt like asking her if she would like to see my bankbook and portfolio. Instead, I asked her, "Arlene, if you were a poor working girl, I could understand your curiosity. But, you seem to have adequate resources, and I'm sure Ade'lie told you that I'm financially independent."

"I just wanted to know if you were going to be busy with work all the time or if we could go to my other home in Florida and play golf."

"You move right along, don't you? Why don't we see how the evening goes, meet again for dinner and take it from there?"

"You seem to be so orderly Mike, especially when I ask you a question, what about some spontaneity?"

"You're absolutely on the mark Arlene, very perceptive of you. But, it's just a way of thinking in a linear fashion to find the right answer. Yes, I'm a planner. But, I can plan to be spontaneous tomorrow."

I leaned back and relaxed transported by thinking of what song would accompany this journey. It was an easy choice.

"Putting on the agony, putting on the style.

That's what all the women are doing all the while.

And as I look around me I'm very apt to smile.

To see all the women putting on the style."

She was a good driver, although a little too fast for my taste. We got out to Jersey in record time. By the time we pulled into the driveway, I had learned that Arlene was divorced, spoiled, and a little strange. Like most of the women I was meeting, she was also unskilled in the art of compatibility and on an impossible search for the perfect man.

The party was well done. The food was delicious, the wine excellent. Arlene was a little ostentatious in that she was never without a wine glass in her hand and she continually rotated the wine in the glass to open it up. She sniffed and drank, swirled, sniffed and drank in an entirely affected manner. After about two hours, she asked me if I wanted to leave.

"Sure, why not? Do you want me to drive back?"

"Did you drink as much as I did?"

"I don't know. I didn't keep track of how much either of us drank."

"No thanks then, I know the car, so I'm all right."

We drove for about ten minutes and talked about some of the people we met at the party. Suddenly, the expression on her face changed and she said, "Dammit, I have to pee."

"We're only ten minutes away. Let's go back, and you can pee."

"No, I have to go now."

She pulled off the main street and onto a residential street with some cars parked on one side. She got out, and lifting her dress high up, squatted and peed between two vehicles. She came back to the car, said, "That's better," and drove off.

"Why are you looking at me like that?" she said.

"Because you're the only other person in the car," I smiled.

My real thought was that there is not necessarily a correlation between wealth, good taste or even consideration. And I thought, Ade'lie personified the Jewish princess, but she has competition.

The expression on her face turned sour as she became defensive and said, "What can I say, I'm down to earth, and maybe you're uptight?"

Trying to alleviate the tension of the situation, I set up a joke and answered, "Isn't that a direct quote from Mein Kampf? And that's once."

"Listen," she said...

"That's once," I replied, unhappy with her inappropriateness and overbearing demeanor.

"What do you mean? That's once."

"Didn't you ever hear the story about... A man who was strangely competent and a gentleman farmer marries a woman he meets in the city. She is a real estate agent, aggressive, self- possessed, loving, and all knowing. He picks her up at the train station in a horse and buggy. He kisses her passionately upon meeting her again, takes her luggage and loads it into the back of the buggy, tells her how happy he is to see her, and helps her up onto the buggy seat.

She looks at his strong, handsome face, tells him how happy she is to be married to him and how she is looking forward to seeing his estate. He takes the reins in hand and slowly pulls out of the station. Cantering slowly down a field, the horse bolts and rears up. The horse then trots and stops and rears up again. The man ties the reins back, gets out of the buggy, confronts the horse straight in the eye and says 'that's once."

He gets back in the buggy and continues the trip talking pleasantly about the farm and the new lake he had dredged on the property. The horse now bolts from a snake going across the road. He canters and gallops almost pulling the reins from the man's hand. The man gets out of the buggy, confronts the horse and looking at it straight in the eye says 'that's twice." He gets back in the buggy, and the journey continues until passing through the massive main gate. They are just several hundred feet from the magnificent farmhouse.

The horse now acts up and bolts again for no apparent reason. The man gets out of the buggy, takes a pistol from his belt and putting the gun next to the horse's head, blows its brains out. He then tells his new wife, "Just take a small bag with what you need and the farm hands will take everything up to the house."

"Why did you shoot the horse?" his new wife scolds. "It's not the horse's fault that he was scared. That's his nature. Now, we have to walk all the way up to the house and carry some luggage. That was a foolish thing to do, and horses are expensive."

The man answered, "That's once."

Icily and defensively, Arlene asked, "Is that joke supposed to teach me something?"

Arlene wasn't just thin-skinned and self-absorbed. She rejected any criticism or suggestion for self-improvement, and she was pathologically narcissus.

"You know Arlene, getting through to you is like taking the panties off a virgin... it can take days. When you talk to someone who is open to interacting with you, perhaps you should try a little tenderness, if only as a relief from chic transgressiveness." I said as I shake my head in disgust. "Arlene, didn't you read that book written by two divorced women, The Rules? It expressly states that you're not supposed to pee between two parked cars in a public street on the first date. I don't think I'm a prude and it's not that you peed between two vehicles in the street. It's the fact that it was done on the first date. Usually, people are a little shy and on their best behavior when they first met someone. I realize that everyone seems normal when you first met them, and until you get to know them, but this seems really too uninhibited to me. I've had an absolutely wonderful evening, but this wasn't it."

There is power and force. I learned the difference from my, imbued with integrity, friend Rick. For many years, I just used force by asserting myself and occasionally going ballistic. Since I now have the power, I find it much easier to use it quietly. It gets the same results without using as much energy, and I can speak softly.

Some people never want to improve for the simple reason that they think of themselves as perfect; their vanity is stronger than their misery.

It didn't matter what was said or done at this point in our meeting. Perhaps my standards were too high, but I wanted a woman with a little more class. And I reasoned: if this woman was peeing between cars on a first date, what was she capable of after the tenth time we were together?

When I told Ade'lie about the date, she defended Arlene. I asked her, "Is this women a good friend of yours? She must go through men like I go through tissue paper. She is never going to find a man to stay with her."

"Well, she said you're very inhibited and not sexy enough for her."

"OK, Ade'lie, Arlene must be right."

"She would slip into bitch-mode at the slightest provocation."

Swing hard in case you hit it.

Say little. But when you speak, utter gentle words that touch the heart. Be truthful. Express kindness. Abstain from vanity. This is the way.

The first sin or original sin was the knowledge of good and evil. We have forgotten that the second sin is speaking clearly. These are man's affronts against God, the child against the parent and the citizen against the state. This is why, when as a human Adam commits these sins, he is punished. Such is the price for being civilized and communicating. Is there any doubt that if Jesus came to earth again and preached we would first put him on television and then, after he established himself as a leader, either assassinate or crucify him again?

Our consequence for being civilized is to allow a multiplicity of controls to be placed on us. Our task is to assert our individualism and evolve while dovetailing into our society, an almost Sisyphusian task.

The difference between "I like you." and "I love you." When you like a flower you pick it, when you love a flower you water it every day. If you understand this, you comprehend life and relationships.

You are always one decision away from a totally different life.

Ships do not sink because of the water around them. Ships sink because of the water that gets into them. Don't let what's happening around you get inside you and weigh you down.

"Haven't we met before?"

"Yes, I'm the receptionist at the VD clinic."

My Yamahama Mama

I first saw Na Ho May on the beach. She had long black hair down to her tiny waist and a blinding smile. She was carrying a lovely small child that I later learned belonged to her best friend. When she walked past my beach blanket, on the way to the water, I asked her, "Would you like to sell that baby." Instead of walking by, she stopped and asked, "How much."

"That depends. Let me talk to the baby."

She placed the baby on my blanket and sat down.

I said to the child, "Would you like to come home with me and I will buy you a pony and take you swimming every day."

The baby shook its head yes. Na Ho May laughed, showing her Hollywood smile that made the angels dance and looked me straight on with a lively expression.

I continued talking to the child and asked, "Will you help clean the house and do you do windows?"

The baby naturally was perplexed, but my future wife cracked up. We spent the rest of the day talking and getting to know each other. She was very smart, aggressive, and possessed a vitality that radiated. The hook was in. When we walked off the beach, she got on a green Yamaha motorcycle, having given the baby back to her friend, and roared off into the evening.

I called her often for the next week, but the phone just rang. A few days later she called me and said she had a motorcycle accident and was in the hospital. I visited her every day. It was the beginning of a deep, young infatuation that lasted. Two years later, both in our mid-twenties, we married, much too young, and without any substantial resources. In retrospect, I should have taken my mother's advice to, "Shop around." The Vietnam War was heating up. A year after we married in my third year of college, I was drafted.

I returned to New York after spending several years in the army and Alaska. I stayed in Alaska to develop the land, on which I was homesteading, a one hundred and sixty-acre plot on the side of a mountain overlooking the Chena River. I also dreamt of making a chunk of money that would pull me out of poverty and save my marriage. I married to get Na Ho May out of her home since her father beat her. I knew that soon after being drafted I would be shipped to Vietnam. On route to the war, I was diverted to an Alaskan headquarters company where I remained for my hardship tour of duty. It was a tough choice whether to face bullets or cold, so I flipped a coin.

Leaving a young wife for several years was not the best way to ensure a marriage, but, drafted, the government gave me little choice. By the time I returned, my wife was involved with someone else. I could not blame her. Our relationship, at that young age, was like sliding down the razor blade of life. When it ended, she caught it by the handle but I caught it by the blade. Also, my young Polynesian/Russian princess went from the hundred and eighteen-pound beauty that she was when I first meet her, to a one hundred and eighty pound Yamahama Mama. Poor Na Ho May had genes that would cause her to blow up all her life. It was only a matter of time until we were going to part. The story of my Yamahama mama might have a significant meaning to the women who marry and do not take care of themselves after their marriage. But, at this point in time, this woman was out of my control, and I was already moving on to another chapter, jumping out of the frying pan into the fires of life.

After I returned from Alaska, while the relationship was deteriorating, I worked days in construction and went back to The Cooper Union at night. In one of my classes, there was a slim Irish woman who moved like a greased eel. She was a dancer with sturdy legs and a long neck. I was instantly and powerfully attracted to her. When we, at last, touched I knew I found a woman, that in my adult life, to whom I could again try to commit myself. I was completely in love with her and dreamt every night of touching her. Her skin was like no other women I ever felt, soft, smooth, hard and mysterious and lit me up like fireworks.

I felt that she saved me. She gave me hope that in a short time, after I divorced Na Ho May, that I would find happiness and joy living with her. She was equally attracted to me. However, her biological clock exploded, and the overwhelming desire in her life was to have children. When her old boyfriend returned from Germany, asked her to marry him and have a child, she reconsidered our relationship. She confessed that she did not love this other man, but with him, she could fulfill the desire she wanted most in life and have a child. I told her that in just six months I would be divorced and I would marry her and start a family. I begged her not to leave me. Unfortunately, she did not believe that I was going to divorce my wife, tragic for me but understandable. She left me and married her dark-haired, brown-eyed boyfriend.

I was heartbroken that I lost her. Six months later, I divorced my wife, who subsequently married the man she had seen while I was in Alaska. Still thinking of our time together, I contacted my magic dancer. It turned out that her husband had a low sperm count and was not able to impregnate a woman. We thought about having a child together, but my blond hair and blue eyes would be too much of a difference from her husband's features.

We saw each other when we could, but it was always a combination of ecstasy and frustration. Her Catholic upbringing would not allow her to be divorced and soon we slipped apart. I'd see her for an afternoon ever few months, and we talked about how our lives would have been so different, and how much happier we both would be if we were together.

The Zen Pill

In this modern age, the Bushido code of Justice and Compassion means that the warrior and Zen Buddhist support women's rights and their way toward physical and mental health.

I like to kept the quotes that I glean from other writers very short, and just to emphasis a point. But in time magazines, Milestones, Letty Pogrebin, in her writing about the death of Carl Djerassi, a creator of the birth control pill, wonderfully summed up the entire abortion and birth control problem. She writes: Djerassi's pill gave women more freedom than the Declaration of Independence. "Unless a woman is free inside her own skin, not subject to involuntary pregnancy, it is difficult if not imposable for her to exercise personal liberty or enjoy the pursuit of happiness. By giving us control of our bodies and reproductive decisions, the Pill has revolutionized our economic, political and sexual lives and enabled us to bear children whom we are financially prepared to support and emotionally committed to nurture and love."

After twenty years of terminating unwanted pregnancies and its corollary lower crime rates, legal challenges to Roe v. Wade are rampant. Ohio Governor John Kasich signed a bill banning abortions after twenty weeks and a newly appointed conservative supreme court justice has raised fears among abortion rights advocates.

Dear power and money seeking politician, Stay the hell out of my bedroom and keep your outmoded religious mind and dirty little hands off my worldly body and rights.

If you close one door, open another.

"I am going to make you the
happiest woman in the world."

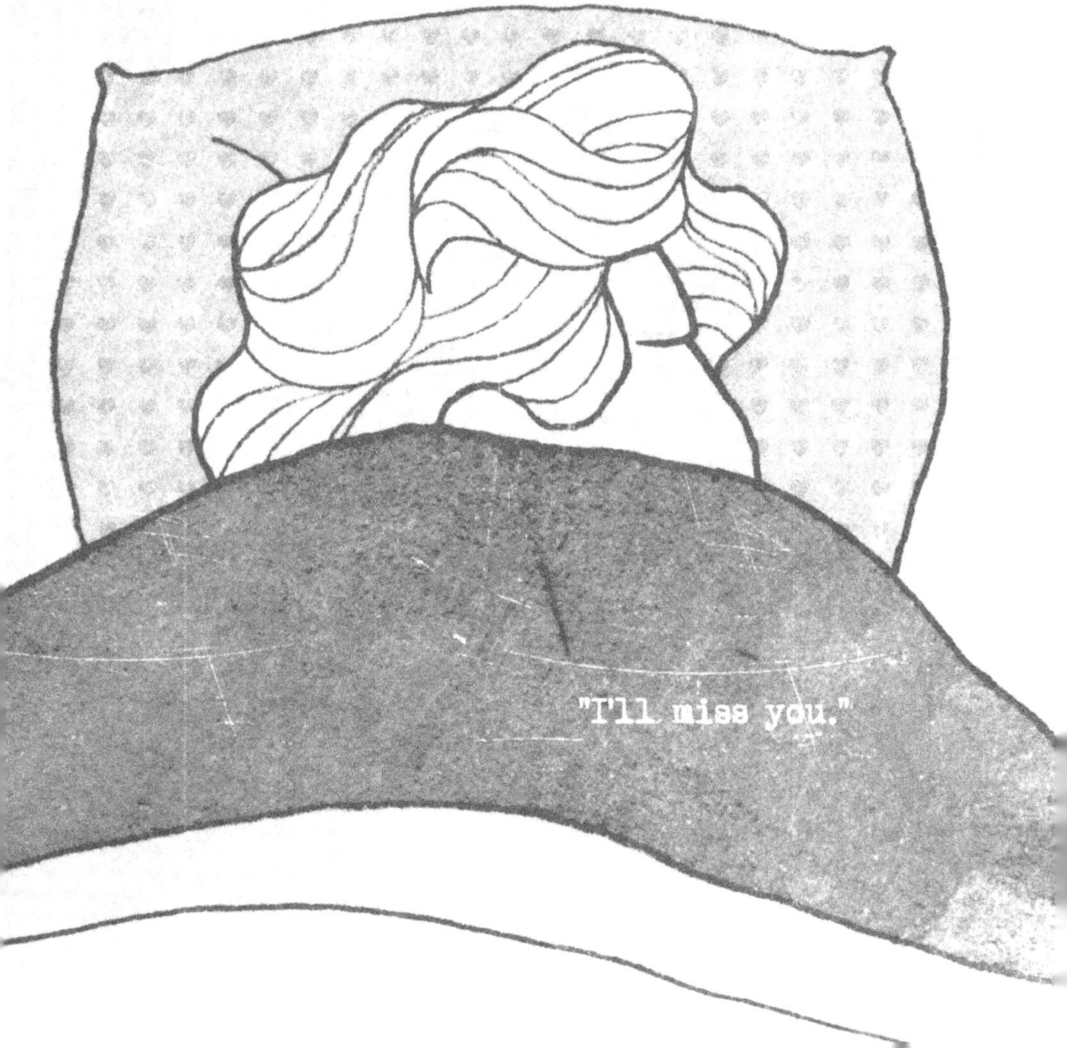
"I'll miss you."

Marriage

If the knot fits, tie it.

In Zen Buddhism all actions and knowledge is connected. Jumping to seemingly non-connected, unrelated expressions, is intentional and a way to force a readjustment and flexibility in your thinking. This device is used throughout this book.

Q: What do you call an intelligent, good-looking, sensitive, single man?

A: A rumor.

Everything I have and can give is all that my lover requires.

Q: How do you keep your husband from reading your e-mail?

A: Rename the email folder 'Instruction Manuals.'

Women will never be equal to men until they can walk down the street with a baldhead and a beer belly, and still think they are sexy.

My wife was hinting about what she wanted for our upcoming anniversary. She said, "I want something shiny that goes from 0 to 150 in about 3 seconds."

I bought her a scale.

We all have our cross to bear, but for me, she keeps changing her name.

In an exchange between Churchill & Lady Astor: She said, "If you were my husband I'd give you poison." He said, "If you were my wife, I'd drink it."

Q: What does it mean when a man is in your bed gasping for breath and calling your name?

A: You did not hold the pillow down long enough.

MINT CONDITION:

Male, 1932 model, high mileage, good condition, some hair, many new parts including hip, knee, cornea. Isn't in running condition, but walks well. (Who says seniors don't have a sense of humor?)

Do not regret growing older. It is a privilege denied to many.

Boots and Vladimir's ex-wife

Women love shoes and men love boots

I was drafted out of my last year of The Cooper Union College and my first year of a good marriage, so I was not happy being in the army. Although willing to serve my country, I was reticent, objective, and iconoclastic. The army was another planet; an organization where alcoholism and machismo ran rampant but were communication and smoking of marijuana was perverted. I was out of the civilian world, a free spirit, to be indoctrinated into a total institution.

The captain drawled, "Boy, yawl must think that we're not too smart down here, but my mother drowned all the dumb ones and yawl got a northern Jew boy attitude."

I answered, "Yes sir, that's called intelligence."

The sergeant had already asked me to put it in more succinct terms. I complied with his request.

He said, "Boy, with an attitude like that, we gonna ship your ass to Korea and put you on the front line of the DMZ, so you can fight that bat shit crazy, dear leader."

I decided that I was better off going to Korea than to Fort Benning, Georgia, our next post. We referred to that base as, The Armpit of the World. All the training was Gung-Ho, follow-me stuff. I told the sergeant "Anything would be better than the South's Fort Benning"; I was off to a great army start.

Before being drafted, I held various jobs in the construction industry and attended college at night. I was in great shape and used to working very hard. The army, by contrast, was a bit of a joke. As most total institutions are, it was devoid of character and the indoctrination was transparent. Two weeks later, I was on my way to Korea, via Alaska, Japan, and Southeast Asia.

During basic training, being restricted to the base, the army library was one of the only distractions. It was poorly stocked and censored with few interesting books. Hungry for reading, I perused books of army regulations. I looked for codes that allowed me to use or continue my college education. Arriving in Alaska, on route to Korea, I used information I chanced upon in the army regulations. If you fulfilled a military occupational specialty or job, on a base, while you were in transit, the government saved money by not having to transport you any further.

The Military Occupational Specialty's (MOS), were all listed on a huge bulletin board outside the main mess hall. One open job was Cold Weather Survival Expert Light Equipment Field Maintenance Specialist. I flipped a coin. Let's see, cold or bullets, cold or bullets? Cold was safer than bullets. Korea was always heating up with Chinas support, and encouraging the puppet regime to poke its finger in Americas eye. I didn't know then that this MOS was designated as a hardship tour because the job included months of winter, at an average temperature of forty below zero, in the field. The tiny base was also far away from the main base so no one volunteered. I took the job and was reassigned to Headquarters and Headquarters Company, Yukon Command, Alaska.

I liked the hard winters and living in the cold. The outdoor life appealed to me, and the Alaskan air was so oxygenated and clean that I needed less sleep and woke up clear headed. The remoteness and hardship of living outdoors, in a large well-equipped tent, also left little time for anyone to bother with picayune or army nonsense. I also learned a rugged lifestyle, appealing for a city boy, living alfresco, self-sufficient and ecologically sound. Outdoors was dusky dark, forty below zero, and tunnel vision with no peripheral view due to parka hoods. We trained in the extreme cold for a few hours a day acclimating to the dry arctic air and frozen landscape. At night, the winters was spent indoors and "cabin fever" was rampant. In the spring, we moved into the main base.

Summers were wonderfully expanding. It was light twenty-four hours a day, the sun revolving low on the horizon, but never setting. It rained briefly every day, but the ground dried afterward and rainbows filled the sky. It was a warm eighty degrees, and the mosquitoes were so big men went on assignments two at a time. If the mosquitoes attacked, the other man could grab his legs; they weren't big enough to carry two men. Sometimes mosquitoes landed on the airfield and were refueled before they realized they weren't planes.

Hunting was an excuse to walk the mountains, a hundred miles and never hit a fence. A hunting license cost hundreds and a homestead license much less. With a government homestead, you hunted on your own land, one hundred and sixty acres. I picked a plot, in a remote area, from a map in the survey office. With no settlement near, I'd have the side of a mountain in which to hunt. My farmstead was a few miles from a town called Nanana, fifty miles from Fairbanks with seventy Inuit's as the occupants.

I was in Headquarters Company that ran the base for eighteen thousand men by coordinating the other companies and supplying maintenance, quartermaster, and officer services, so I had a typical officer's class A pass. This meant that except for regular work hours, I was free to spend weekends on my land. A small shelter, an old surplus tent on top a wooden platform, was all I needed. The winters were interesting but boring, and summers were fun for the feeble-minded. Fortunately, the army was kind enough to supply me with a distraction that took up my time for the summer weeks.

The diversion was assigning me to an unusual detail, the running of a test machine. The mechanism, as big as two eighteen-wheeler trucks, was used to verify vapor barrier boots. The working temperature of the vapor barrier, when mist freezes, is forty degrees below zero- Fahrenheit. The boots the army issued cost the government hundreds of dollars a pair and was supposed to keep feet warm at forty below. The boots, either completely black or all white, consisted of several layers of felt sandwiched between layers of rubber. To help them fit, they had blow-up valves that inflated to make the boot tighter, and the air provided additional insulation. The problem was that the boots didn't work. At twenty degrees, your feet got cold, and several GIs (government issues,) in the skiing combat companies got frostbitten toes. The army blamed the manufacturer of the boots. The makers gave the military a snow job and rejected the obvious, stating the boots were abused and didn't work because they were punctured. It was a typical bureaucratic situation in which no one wanted to be held accountable.

Whether the boots were perfect or not, they never worked, and someone was getting rich at the taxpayer's expense, what's new? Since covering your behind was a standard Army policy, the boots had to be tested for leaks.

Men stationed from all over the bases marked their boots and sent them to a massive hangar at Fort Wainwright where the testing machine was assembled. The trial detail consisted of six men and a mountain of boots. Submerging them upside down in a tank of special water, over an imitation metal foot, tested the boots. When bubbles appeared, the boots were defective. When they were submerged names and information on the marker tags were obscured, then, not being waterproof, the tags shriveled up and disintegrated. The testing detail became the personification of the service cliché that there are three ways of doing things, the right way, the wrong way, and the army way.

The size of the boots was embossed on its heel. After a pair was tested, if one leaked and the other was not defective, I had them placed in two different piles. Since the boots were now nameless, none could be returned to their original owners. The defective boots were going to be sold at the surplus depot on the Air Force Base. This was not smart since water would penetrate the boot and freeze the owner's feet. They should have been shipped back to the manufacturer, but these were problems not under my control.

After working for several days testing, sorting and creating new combinations of pairs of good boots, I was told that I was doing the job wrong. I should reject the pair of boots even if only one were defective. Considering the boots had just been issued and were new, this logic seemed foolish. We had already labeled and filled cartons with different sizes. The detail was saving about half the stock by matching good single boots, making a usable pair. What sense was their testing them, if we rejected the sound and the defective? I told my sergeant, a man named Levinsky, that since I was put in charge of the detail, to do the job differently, that is, wastefully and without thinking, I wanted written orders on exactly what I was to do. If not, I could be held responsible for rejecting all the good boots. Specifically, I wanted orders in writing that I was to reject the thousands of boots by the pair and not individually. After all, it was standard Army procedure to cover your ass. I also protested, for the sake of the detail, that the water be heated. It was uncomfortable for the soldiers to have their hands in water all day, but cold water was an unnecessary torture.

In charge of this detail, was a second lieutenant named Grahik, who had a personality you could store meat in. The officer, a boy, given a little power, came into the hangar and gave me a direct order.

“Specialist- Lance, I’m- giving- you- a- direct- order- to reject both boots, if one is defective.”

He spoke army, and I could hardly understand him.

“I’m not sure of what you’re saying, sir, although It sounds like English. Would you mind repeating what you mumbled?” He did. I asked him why. He didn’t know.

“I’m sorry Sir. But I’m responsible for the detail since I was made Non-Commissioned Officer in Charge. As N.C.O.I.C it is in my province to ask for an order in writing.”

He said, “If you make me put that order in writing I’m going to give you an unsatisfactory rating and take you off the detail.”

The vapor barrier machine tester was complicated. It took me days to set things up and read the manual of instructions for the machine. No one was going to walk in and operate this complex model. The reason they gave me the job was that no one wanted to take the time to read. The lifers were aware I had a brain. And there was the danger of grounding the mechanisms correctly since water and electricity make for a volatile combination. I had proven myself all winter in field assignments that I could handle responsibility. Now I was getting conflicting cues.

I went back to the barracks annoyed at myself for not knowing how to handle the duty. I talked the circumstances over with Vladimir, the company clerk. Vladimir was a music aficionado and had dozens of classical recordings. Most of Vladimir's hobbies and time were spent alone, probably because he was so ugly. His face was full of bumps and his skin scarred with holes. He had narrow dark eyes and an evil permanent smile. He was relatively short, and his body was shaped like a lumpy potato. Vladimir overcompensated by allowing his best assets, caustic wit, acute timing, and a distorted sense of humor, to project in conversations and smokescreen his appearance. It worked. I took him to parties, and he was grateful. I never told him that his friendship saved me, starving for intellectual stimulation and humor, which he provided unceasingly. I did tell him that he was a giant among pygmies. As the Company Clerk Vladimir had one of the few private rooms on the base. It was exceptionally kind of him to give me a key to his kingdom, unusual to have some privacy, and I could listen to his music. We became good friends. Vladimir had an exasperating, but amusing habit of continually interjecting non-sequitur jokes into a conversation, usually about his ex-wife or marriage. He referred to his ex-wife as the classic queen bitch of the universe or she who must be obeyed.

"Vladimir, I'm disgusted."

"You're disgusted. I'm so miserable without my wife; it's just like having her around. I told her 'If you don't leave, I'm going to find someone who will.' She was so emasculating that she would keep an armrest in bed with us. But, all seriousness aside Mike, what happened?"

"Oh, it's so trivial, but..."

"I'm listening."

"Well, Levinsky called me into his office, told me we're transferring out of Headquarters into the Maintenance Detachment for the summer. This is after I busted my hump in the field all winter and trained two dozen troops. He handed out the clearance papers and written on it is the rating for conduct and efficiency. Do you know what that punk gave me? In place of the top rating, he gave me, "poor."

"So, big deal. Do you want to hear high rating? My wife would always close her eyes when we had sex; she hated to see me have fun. She used to say, 'What's the good of happiness if you can't buy money with it?' The top rating was our foreplay. It consisted of one hour of me begging, and sometimes my wife would fake foreplay."

"No, Vladimir, you don't get it. He gave some guys excellent. Do you know the difference between poor and excellent?"

"Yeah, the Good Conduct Medal, right? Mike, you must remember that medals are like hemorrhoids, sooner or later every asshole gets one. What the hell are you going to do with the Good Boy Medal? Do you want to hear about good conduct? My wife went in for a beauty treatment, a mudpack, she looked good for two days, then the mud fell off. She came into the room after the mud fell off and I yelled, take her away I'm turning to stone."

"That's not the point. It's the principle. Levinsky was told to give me the lower rating, because of the testing fiasco."

"Mike, talk about principle. We had a principal in our Intermediate School, Bowman Dong. He had such a demeanor they named the Dong Computer Virus after him. When the Dong Virus gets into the system, it wipes out all the excellence. And the Chinese government named a missile after him because everything he touched blew up. I don't know how you do it. I don't understand how you get involved in these petty issues. I just get involved in pretty tissues."

Vladimir was referring to his warped sense of humor. He kept putting pink toilet tissue in Lieutenant Grahik's bathroom, and once he substituted a roll of steel wool.

"Talk about petty issues, my wife used foam as a birth control method, but it made me look like a wild dog. And speak of a dog, I took my wife to a dog show, and she won. I took her to a plastic surgeon, and they added a tail. She got so fat that when she walked backward, she started peeping. I'm getting a little older though and having sex gets me out of breath, especially when it takes me twenty minutes to blow up the rubber doll. And I have arthritis, I get stiff every place, but where I need it."

"Look, it's not petty. Anything less than the best rating bears with it the connotation of a goof-off. Levinsky's just a nothing. Anyway, who is he to rate my work?"

“But he’s in charge. The Army regulation states that he gives you your rating. There’s nothing you can do about it. Talk about ratings; my wife said to me, ‘Vladimir, you are a lousy lover’ I replied, “Ha, you can’t decide something like that in two minutes.”

“But Val, I have to try. The whole idea of rejecting the good boots is crazy. They took me off the detail, and the testing stopped.”

“You’re fighting the machine. It’s like when I said to my ex-wife, “Did you see the dead bird?” and she looks up. Mike, she was the type of woman that when she was walking in the forest a tree fell right in front of her and she didn’t hear it.”

“Vladimir, someone has to fight it. Look, it’s just a regulation. How can a rule give a man the knowledge to judge? Sure, it gives him the power, but not the smarts. Just because it’s there, it doesn’t mean it’s right. I’m going to the Inspector General.”

“Well, you have a big pair of chops. But, I don’t see the big deal. Now, sex with my wife was a big deal. She would get a headache walking through a mattress store. We had a waterbed; I called it the Dead Sea. We had a problem with sex and money. She always charged me too much.”

“All right, let me explain. I don’t do these things because I’m a nervy guy, it’s just part of my psyche. Every time I get close to some injustice, I get scared. I relate to it. Existentially, if you’re going to change the world, you have to start and take the first step. Once you give in to the control freaks or the incompetence, it becomes aggressive apathy, then capitulation, then cynicism and death. Do you see what I mean? I know it’s just chipping at a huge rock, but little chips make a difference. Exfoliation wears the mountain down eventually.

“Jesus Mike, you’re so fucking negative at times, and antigovernment, and anti-authority…”

“That because my generation grew up with Vietnam, the JFK assassination, were the dreams of a generation were buried that day, and the atomic bomb. And they were all human-made events. Imagine as a child having drills and hiding under wooden desks to escape the ten-thousand-degree nuclear fireball. That engenders trust in a government.

A military film titled The Big Picture was produced for the armed forces and the American people. It was to instruct soldiers before they participated in atomic maneuvers. The military Chaplin in the film calms and tells anxious soldiers what to expect. "No need to be worried the army has taken all possible precautions. First, you will see a bright light, then a shock wave follows. Then you look up and see the fireball ascending to the heavens with all the colors of the rainbow as it turns into a beautiful sight to behold, the mushroom cloud." The soldiers after witnessing the atomic explosion from as close as 3,000 yards from ground zero return to camp bleeding from their eyes, ears, nose, and mouth."

"Shut up. Shut up. You win. Are you sure you're only half Jewish? You'll never do it."

"I'll try."

"Talk about trying; I took this girl out, and she had a two-hour orgasm. I was going to marry her. Then I found out she was an epileptic. Talk about trying, every time I had an orgasm with my wife would say 'OK, I'm ready.' My wife had her unique method of birth control. She would point at my crotch and laugh."

"How can I get my statement typed up, Vladimir?"

"Well, you can't use the typewriter in the Orderly Room. That will get someone in trouble. The army has no procedures for this."

"You know Vladimir, sometimes you're a pain in the ass, trying to have a conversation with. All your jokes sound like they were swiped from a Henny Youngman joke book."

"You know Mike, since I was twelve, I carried a notebook to record the jokes I heard. If I didn't tell jokes, people would have time to stare at my face and count the holes. The only reason a girl ever spoke to me was to hear a joke so that she could laugh at it and me."

"Sorry, Vladimir, I guess I'm wired. But, no one cares what anyone looks like when they grow up, and you look as average as the next guy."

"Yeah Mike, that's why the women in town nicknamed me the "toad.'"

That night, I wrote out my statement and the next morning I delivered it to the Inspector General's office. He was out, and I made an appointment for tomorrow, a good idea to work up the chain of command. The next day, I walked the long way around the airfield and rambled into the I.G.'s office. The walls were painted white, the floor black, and against the one window, there was an insignificant desk. The starkness of the room jolted me into seriousness.

"Sergeant Cooper, may I see Major Baxter?"

"He's out right now."

"Can I see him if I come back later?"

"OK, you have an appointment in three hours."

I went back to the barracks and changed into starched fatigues, wondering why they call them fatigues. I shaved, dusted my boots that I paid someone to shine the night before, and headed to Headquarters' building.

"May I see Major Baxter, Sergeant Cooper?"

"Go in and report."

"Sir, Specialist Lance, Headquarters Yukon Command, reports."

"Sit down, Lance."

"Thank you, Sir. The problem is this, Sir. Lieutenant Grahik and Sergeant Levinsky gave me a lousy rating because of my insistence that I receive written orders on the boot testing detail. He knew nothing about that job, neither of them ever criticized me, and I've never criticized Levinsky or Grahik. I always do my work; both have never told me anything pertaining to my work being of poor quality. In the field base, where I was the NCO in charge of cold weather survival for twenty troops, it was evident to everyone that I was doing an excellent job."

"First of all, show the proper respect. It's Sergeant Levinsky and Lieutenant Grahik."

I thought, yeah, a worm and punk. If I were wrong, he would be ripping me apart by now. "Yes, Sir."

"Let me take a look at the army regulations."

Here we go. Spending a half-hour looking over the army regulations, the same ones I read in basic training, he decided I was within my rights to ask for a written order in a non-emergency situation. I was more justified than I thought. Hesitant to change the rating, the Major said he would get back to me with his decision.

What a day, perspiring I went back to the barracks office to Vladimir.

"Don't know, Vladimir, it's going slowly."

"Wait until the S-G-T. E-V-A-C-U-A-T-E-S," he spelled, as he clued me.

"Hi, Sergeant Levinsky. I didn't see you standing there."

"Hi, Lance. Is it true that you demanded hot water for your detail? This is the Army, not some pussy outfit."

"First Serge, I didn't demand anything. I requested the water be warmer, better for the men and the work's done faster. The big thing was I wanted the order in writing that I reject the boots. Do you remember a week ago when that Corporal lost his stripes? He was ordered to paint the outdoor tables, with the wind blowing, and dirt and leaves flying around. Everything stuck to the paint, and it took weeks to clean. He told his lieutenant it was a lousy idea, but he still lost his rank. I thought we were in the same Army, just because they're grunts doesn't mean we have to make it tough on them."

"It was still a pussy thing to do," Levinsky said, as he walked out of the room. "Hot water my ass."

This sergeant had an attitude implant probably surgically placed by a proctologist. I was setting a bad example.

"Rather lose an argument with a wise man than win one with a fool, I said to Vladimir."

"You sure know how to get yourself in hot water, Mike," He grinned with his evil permanent smile.

Bright Star

BY JOHN KEATS

Bright star, would I were steadfast as thou art—

Not in lone splendor hung aloft the night

And watching, with eternal lids apart,

Like nature's patient, sleepless Eremite,

The moving waters at their priest like task

Of pure ablution round earth's human shores,

Or gazing on the new soft-fallen mask

Of snow upon the mountains and the moors—

No—yet still steadfast, still unchangeable,

Pillow'd upon my fair love's ripening breast,

To feel for ever its soft fall and swell, Awake forever in a sweet unrest,

Still, still to hear her tender-taken breath,

And so live ever—or else swoon to death.

Addressed to a star (perhaps Polaris, around which the heavens appear to wheel), the sonnet expresses the poet's wish to be as constant as the star while he presses against his sleeping love. The use of the star imagery is unusual in that Keats dismisses many of its more apparent qualities, focusing on the star's steadfast and passively watchful nature.

Actual dating ad for seniors;

FOXY LADY:

Sexy, fashion-conscious blue-haired beauty,

80's, slim, 5'4' (used to be 5'6'),

Searching for sharp-looking,
sharp-dressing companion.

Matching white shoes and belt a plus.

Condoms don't guarantee safe sex anymore. A friend of mine was wearing one, when the woman's husband shot him.

Just got scammed out of $25. Bought Tiger Woods DVD entitled "My Favorite 18 Holes". Turns out it's about golf. Absolute waste of money! Pass this on so others don't get scammed.

After many years in prison, suffering incredible hardships, Nelson Mandela was finally released. But after only six months of a reunited marriage he stated, "I can't take it – I want a divorce."

At the wedding reception the D.J. yelled... "Would all married men please stand next to the one person who has made your life worth living."

The bartender was almost crushed to death.

Why are married women heavier than single women?

Single women come home, see what's in the fridge and go to bed.

Married women come home, see what's in bed and go to the fridge.

One spelling mistake can destroy your life!

A husband wrote a message to his wife on his business trip and forgot to add 'e' at the end of a word...

"I am having such a wonderful time! Wish you were her."

My wife was standing nude, looking in the bedroom mirror. She was not happy with what she saw and said to me, "I feel horrible; I look old, fat and ugly. I really need you to pay me a compliment.'

I replied, "Your eyesight's damn near perfect."

A physician asked a woman during an office visit
whether she was sexually
active and she said she was not. So he
was surprised when her pregnancy test came back
positive. She explained,
"Well we only do it once a week.
That's not very active."

Never thought that you would be, standing here so close to me. There's so much I feel that I should say, but words can wait until some other day. Kiss me once and kiss me twice and kiss me once again, it's been a long long time. (Lyrics from "It's Been a Long, Long Time" by Louis Armstrong.)

To wives and sweethearts-
may they never meet.

The Viagra Virus: Makes a new hard drive out of an old floppy. Viagra is like Disneyland. You take it, and you wait an hour for a ten-minute ride. I'm depressed. I went to my doctor today and he refused to write me a prescription for Viagra. He said it would be like putting a new flagpole, on a condemned building.

Some people wait all their lives for an opportunity that is sitting right in front of them but end up missing it because of fear and reluctance to take chances. They let their excess baggage get in the way. Remember that Zen perception is about living in the now of the present moment, as well as spontaneity and simplicity.

If you are depressed, you are living in the past.

If you are anxious, you are living in the future.

If you are at peace, you are living in the present.

Nostalgia isn't what it used to be.

The Pew Research Center recorded a record high in the ratio of American adults of age 25 and older who have never been married. The study attributes this trend to a multiplicity of factors including financial problems, marrying later in life and increasing cohabitation.

After retiring, I went to the Social Security office to apply for Social Security. The woman behind the counter asked me for my driver's License to verify my age. I looked in my pockets and realized I had left my wallet at home. I told the woman that I was very sorry, but I would have to go home and come back later. The woman said, 'Unbutton your shirt'. So I opened my shirt, revealing my curly silver hair. She said, 'That silver hair on your chest is proof enough for me' and she processed my Social Security application. When I got home, I excitedly told my wife about my experience at the Social Security office...

She said, "You should have dropped your pants. You might have gotten disability, too."

An old woman was sipping on a glass of wine while sitting on the patio with her husband. She says, "I love you so much, I don't know how I could ever live without you." Her husband asks, "Is that you or the wine talking?" She replies, "It's me... talking to the wine."

Many people get married for all the wrong reasons such as social pressure, to improve their status, economic improvement, and for sex, to name a few. Many women and men marry to satisfy their parents' desire for grandchildren. People, and especially parents of grown married children, want children for all the wrong reasons. Mostly it is a matter of ego and to relive our childhood through them. Sex is really a biological imperative and the byproduct is children. But most of all, the subliminal reason we have children is because of the awareness that, when we are forgotten we cease to exist. Children, or so our ego surmises, give us immortality. Instead of saying die we punch the ecclesiastical time clock to insure that our existence had a purpose and our lives were significance.

I asked my girlfriend if she knew why I called my penis Lazarus. She answered; it was because Jesus reconstructed Lazarus. I used to call my penis the sun, because it rose every morning but now I call it Lazarus because it rises from the dead. I told her that only Jesus had a Second Coming and that if she didn't get off this time, she'd have to wait for the next time. I said that a boxing round takes three minutes. A man can be knocked out in that time and that she would have to get knocked out and come in that time without getting knocked up. She said to me, "Why don't you take some Viagra?" I answered, "Viagra really does the job. The other day I had some. I had the papers in one hand, coffee in the other and six donuts. The first time I used Viagra, I didn't know how powerful it was and I hurt my wrist." She replied, "If you ever leave me... I'm going with you."

Does there come a time when a spouse-seeking woman needs to settle? Oh, yes. These girls are 34, -39 and they're not settling. "They're foolish." your instinct should tell you have to.

What part of your body goes to heaven first?

The nun teaching Sunday school was speaking to her class one morning and she asked the question, 'When you die and go to Heaven, which part of your body goes first?' Suzy raised her hand and said, 'I think it's your hands.' 'Why do you think it's your hands, Suzy?' Suzy replied, 'Because when you pray, you hold your hands together in front of you and God just takes your hands first.' 'What a wonderful answer!' the nun said. Little Johnny raised his hand and said, 'Sister, I think it's your feet.' The nun looked at him with the strangest look on her face. 'Now, Johnny, why do you think it would be your feet? Johnny said: 'Well, I walked into Mom and Dad's bedroom the other night. Mom had her legs straight up in the air and she was saying: 'Oh God! I'm coming!' If Dad hadn't pinned her down, we'd have lost her." The Nun fainted.

The mourning woman dressed in black cried out loud at the funeral. “At last they’re together, at last they’re together.” Another mourner asked,” But she was married three times and had so many lovers. Which one are you talking about? The woman in black answered, “Her legs.”

And another mourner said, ”She ought to have put her pussy in a box and buried it.”

“Why are Jewish men circumcised?”

“Because Jewish women won’t touch anything unless it is 20% off.”

Why are hurricanes usually named after women?

Because when they arrive, they’re wet and wild, but when they go, they take your house and car.

And God created woman and she had 3 breasts. He then asked the woman, "Is there anything you'd like to have changed?"

She replied, "Yes, could get rid of this middle breast?"

And so it was done, and it was good.

Then the woman exclaimed as she was holding that third breast in her hand, “What can be done with this useless boob?"

And God created man.

A senior citizen said to his eighty-year old buddy;

"So I hear you're getting married?"

"Yep!"

"Do I know her?"

"Nope!"

"This woman, is she good looking?"

"Not really."

"Is she a good cook?"

"Nah, she can't cook too well."

"Does she have lots of money?"

"Nope! Poor as a church mouse."

"Well then, is she good in bed?"

"I don't know."

"Why in the world do you want to marry her?"

"Because she can still drive!"

Q: What's the difference between the Pope and a spoiled woman?

A: The pope only expects you to kiss his ring.

Morris, an 82 year-old man, went to the doctor to get a physical. A few days later, the doctor saw Morris walking down the street with a gorgeous young woman on his arm. A couple of days later, the doctor spoke to Morris and said, "You're really doing great, aren't you?"

Morris replied, "Just doing what you said, Doc. 'Get a hot mamma and be cheerful.'"

The doctor said, "I didn't say that. I said, "You've got a heart murmur. Be careful.'"

The tiger was running wild and free. From his cage he said, "They clip your claws, cut your hair, and make a pussy cat out of you. It's one step from the jungle to the zoo." Dr. Hook

Why is it difficult to find men who are sensitive, caring and good looking?

They already have boyfriends.

And then the fight started...

My wife and I were sitting at a table at her high school reunion, and she kept staring at a drunken man swigging his drink as he sat alone at a nearby table. I asked her, "Do you know him?" "Yes", she sighed, "He's my old boyfriend... I understand he took to drinking right after we split up many years ago, and I hear he hasn't been sober since." "My God!" I said, "Who would think a person could go on celebrating that long?"

True and faults understatements.

To be happy with a man, you must first understand him a lot and love him a little. To be happy with a woman, you must love her a lot and not try to understand her at all.

A woman marries a man expecting him to change, but he doesn't. A man marries a woman expecting that she won't change and she does.

Married men live longer than single men do, but married men are a lot more willing to die.

A woman worries about the future until she gets a husband.

A man never worries about the future until he gets a wife.

A successful man is one who makes more money than his wife can spend.

A successful woman is one who can find such a man.

"It's just too hot to wear clothes today," Jack says as he stepped out of the shower. "Honey, what do you think the neighbors would think if I mowed the lawn like this?"

"Probably that I married you for your money," she replied.

"I know all about marriage and the equality of women," he said in a jocular spirit. "I have been married for forty years and I usually have the last two words:"

"Yes, dear.'"

There are 2 times when a man doesn't understand a woman.... before marriage and after marriage.

A dentist and a manicurist
married. They fought tooth and nail.

Death is a part of life.
Marriage is a part of death. We
must learn to live ith both finalities.

As the maxim goes, "When
a man marries his mistress,
he creates a job opening."

The difference between men and women in one paragraph;

A man is driving up a steep, narrow mountain road. A woman is driving down the same road. As they pass each other the woman leans out the window and yells: "PIG"

The man immediately leans out his window and replies: "BITCH"

They each continue on their way, and as the man rounds the next corner, he crashes into a pig in the middle of the road.

Success and Innovation

Choose your battles, lovers, and your company wisely. Life is all you ever see and touch so have some fun and relax. Life is about to get harder before it gets harder. Do not worry about what you should be doing and focus more on what you want. Doing something you love with passion makes work fun and gives you a life. Innovate, strategize, and try to understand human nature and yourself. There is always something you can succeed at, so always hope and do, do not just try-do it. Do not be afraid of failure, it is the best teacher and a key to success. If you want something you have never had before – then you must do something you have never done before. To achieve success, review the blogs on my site and apply them to your life. Satoru

Communication, perseverance, timing, and taking advantage of the prospect, combine uncompromisingly to give you success. Equally important is that you recognize that your luck is preparation meeting opportunity.

Beautiful people even if they are born with normal intelligence quickly realize that they do not have to fill their brains with unpleasant concepts. They know that they can get money by charging ugly people to look at them. This commerce takes many forms, including television, movies, love, and marriage.

Roses For Rose

Red roses were her favorites, and her name was also Rose. And every year her husband sent them, tied with pretty bows. The year he died, roses were delivered to her door. The card said, "Be my Valentine," like all the years before. Each year he sent her roses, and the note would always say, "I love you, even more, this year than last year on this day." "My love for you will always grow, with every passing year." She knew this was the last time that the roses would appear. She thought he ordered roses in advance before this day. Her loving husband did not know, that he would pass away. He always liked to do things early, way before the time. Then, if he got too busy, everything would work out fine. She trimmed the stems and placed them in a unique vase. Then, sat the vase beside the portrait of his smiling face. She would sit for hours, in her husband's favorite chair. While staring at his picture, and the roses sitting there. A year went by, and it was hard to live without her mate. With loneliness and solitude, that had become her lot. Then, the very hour, as on Valentines before, the doorbell rang, and there were roses, sitting by her door. She brought the roses in, and then just looked at them in shock. Then, went to get the telephone, to call the florist shop. The owner answered, and she asked him if he would explain, why would someone do this to her, causing her such pain? "I know your husband passed away, more than a year ago," The owner said, "I knew you'd call, and you would want to know." "The flowers you received today were paid for in advance." "Your husband always planned ahead, and he left nothing to chance." "There is a standing order, that I have on file down here, and he has paid, well in advance, you'll get them every year. There also is another thing, that I think you should know, He wrote a special little card...he did this years ago." "Then, should ever, I find out that he's no longer here, That's the card...that should be sent, to you the following year." She thanked him and hung up the phone, her tears now flowing hard. Her fingers were shaking, as she slowly reached to get the card. Inside the card, she saw that he had written her a note. She stared in silence, this is what he wrote. "Hello my love, I know it's been a year since I've been gone, I hope it hasn't been too hard for you to overcome." "I know it must be lonely, and the pain real. For if it was the other way, I know how I would feel. The love we shared made everything so beautiful in life. I loved you more than words can say; you were the perfect wife." "You were my friend and lover, and you fulfilled my every need. I know it's only been a year, but please try not to grieve. I want you to be happy, even when you shed your tears. That is why the roses will be sent to you for years." "When you get these roses, think of all the happiness, that we had together, and how both of us were blessed. I have always loved you, and I know I always will. But, my love, you must go on, you have some living still." "Please...try to find happiness, while living out your days. I know it is not easy, but I hope you find some ways. The roses will come every year, and they will only stop, when your doors not answered, when the florist stops to knock." "He will come five times that day, in case you have gone out. But after his last visit, he will know without a doubt, to take the roses to the place, where I've instructed him, and place the roses where we are, together once again." Author Unknown

Uncontaminate your heart. You have to give yourself what no one else can give you and what your parents never gave you.

The Coin Jar

When you first meet someone that you fall in love with and think you are going to marry, put a coin in a jar every time you have sex. After a few years, your jar is filled. After you marry, take a coin out every time you have sex. You will find that it takes twice as long to empty the jar of coins, as it was to fill it.

Is this an indictment of marriage? Considering that the divorce rate in the U.S. is about fifty percent, it might be. Perhaps the expectations for this institution are unrealistic, but only a cynic would enter into a marriage contract with the idea that if it does not work out, we can always part ways. Of course, an added factor contributing to late divorces is that we were never meant to last this long. Primal procreation was; we had children very early in life, lived some more years to take care of them, and then died. Nature was only concerned with the survival of the species, not with old age. Now, it is possible to stay together for what our ancient ancestors would have considered two lifetimes.

Of course, especially in this modern life, there are multiplicities of rational reasons for divorce. But, the most prevalent is that the marriage and relationship simply died, because not enough work or effort was put into keeping it viable. Also, because the infatuation and happiness derived from the marriage does not last, it must change into a deeper affection and genuine liking of the other person. This requires maturity, commitment, work, and most of all time to feel like kindred spirits. The flame and attraction that a relationship has at the beginning invariably cools. For the bonding to continue, it must mature, grow, and change into a caring, long lasting emotional trust. So, the passion must evolve into a companionship love for the togetherness to continue.

So, how do we keep love alive and viable? Here are some suggestions, words, and actions that can be put into practice to negate marital dissat-

isfaction and boredom. We have to move on and realize that what made us happy before will not necessarily keep us happy now.

Marriage, like a friendship, must be cultivated. This means stressing the positive aspects of the relationship and telling each other, openly and realistically, what you appreciate about them and the marriage. You have to make time to talk and listen to each other, and spend some quality time together. Resist taking the marriage for granted and add some spice by adding some calculated spontaneity. I am reminded of a quote by Aldous Huxley; he noticed, "Most human beings have an almost infinite capacity for taking things for granted." Surprise each other by doing something new, even if it is only a little step, like bringing home dinner instead of cooking, or vice versa. You can indeed express affection in a variety of ways from kissing a new spot, a different touch, a different present, and anything that is a little novel.

Variety is innately stimulating and rewarding and is a powerful aphrodisiac. Novelty and variety can stimulate a relationship and rejuvenate routines. Acquire and share some new friends, new activities, new music, and new skills. A favorite might be both getting bicycles or joining a gym, learning to swim, or even going out for a short jog. Also, touching more, non-sexually, science suggests, can rekindle some of those dying embers. All these things should be done long before the union is in trouble.

A positive attitude in life and your relationship will make it more mutually rewarding and elicit constructive emotions. Help your partner pursue their passion and support their dreams and goals. What can you do, and any simple action will do, to make their life better? Share your enthusiasm for your passion to encourage a flourishing relationship. Remember, positive energy motivates good behavior and positive verbal and emotional expressions toward one another.

Do not let life and your relationship just happen, make it happen.

King Arthur and the Witch

Young King Arthur was ambushed and imprisoned by the monarch of a neighboring kingdom. The monarch could have killed him but was moved by Arthur's youth and ideals. So, the monarch offered him his freedom, as long as he could answer a tough question. Arthur would have a year to figure out the answer. If after a year, he still had no answer, he would be put to death. The question? What do women really want? Such a question would perplex even the most knowledgeable man. To young Arthur, it seemed an impossible query. But, since it was better than death, he accepted the monarch's proposition to have an answer by year's end. He returned to his kingdom and began to poll everyone: the princess, the priests, the wise men and even the court jester. He spoke with everyone, but no one could give him a satisfactory answer. Many people advised him to consult the old witch, for only she would have the answer. The expense would be high, as the witch was famous throughout the kingdom for the exorbitant prices she charged. The last day of the year arrived, and Arthur had no choice but to talk to the witch.

She agreed to answer the question, but he would have to agree to her price first. The old witch wanted to marry Sir Lancelot, the noblest of the Knights of the Round Table and Arthur's closest friend! Young Arthur was horrified. She was hunchbacked and hideous, had only one tooth, smelled like sewage, made obscene noises, etc. He had never encountered such a repugnant creature in all his life. He refused to force his friend to marry her and endure such a terrible burden; but Lancelot, learning of the proposal, spoke with Arthur. He said nothing was too big of a sacrifice compared to Arthur's life and the preservation of the Round Table.

Hence, a wedding was proclaimed, and the witch answered Arthur's question thus: "What a woman really wants," she explained... "Is to be in charge of her own life." Everyone in the kingdom instantly knew that the witch had uttered a great truth and that Arthur's life would be spared. And so, it was, the neighboring monarch granted Arthur his freedom and

Lancelot and the witch had a wonderful wedding.

The honeymoon hour approached and Lancelot, steeling himself for a horrific experience, entered the bedroom. But, what a sight awaited him! The most beautiful woman he had ever seen. The astounded Lancelot asked what had happened. The beautiful witch beauty replied that since he had been so kind to her when she appeared as an ugly witch, she would henceforth be her horrible deformed self only half the time and the beautiful maiden the other half. Which would he prefer, beautiful during the day or night? Lancelot pondered the predicament, during the day, a beautiful woman to show off to his friends and enjoy looking at, but at night, in the privacy of his castle, an old witch? Or, would he prefer having a hideous witch during the day, but by night, a beautiful woman? What would YOU do? What Lancelot chose is written below. BUT... make YOUR choice before you scroll down.

OKAY? Noble Lancelot said that he would allow her to make the decision herself. Upon hearing this, she announced that she would be beautiful all the time because he had respected her enough to let her be in charge of her own life. What is the moral to this story? The moral is, if you don't let a woman have her own way, things are going to get ugly.

Positive Attitude

It was a busy morning, about 8:30, when an elderly gentleman in his 80's arrived to have stitches removed from his hand. He said he was in a hurry, as he had an appointment at 9:00 am. As the office nurse, I took his vital signs and had him take a seat, knowing it would be a half hour before the doctor would be able to see him. I saw him looking at his watch and decided since I was not busy with another patient, I would evaluate his wound.

On exam, it was well healed, so I talked to one of the doctors, got the needed supplies to remove his sutures and redress his wound. While taking care, I asked him if he had another doctor's appointment this morning, as he was in such a hurry. The gentleman told me no that he needed to go to the nursing home to eat breakfast with his wife. I inquired as to her health. He said that she had been there for a while and that she was a victim of Alzheimer's disease.

As we talked, I asked if she would be upset if he was a bit late. He replied that she no longer knew who he was, that she had not recognized him in five years. I was surprised, and asked him, "And you still go every morning, even though she doesn't know who you are?" He smiled as he patted my hand and said, "She doesn't know me, but I still know who she is."

I had goose bumps on my arm, and thought, "That is the kind of love I want in my life."

True love is neither physical nor romantic. **True love is an acceptance of all that is, has been, will be, and will not be.**

A precious gift

An old woman who lived in China lived a Zen-Tao centered life. One day, she came across a precious stone while sitting by the banks of a running stream in the mountains. She placed this highly valued item in her bag.

The very next day, a hungry traveler approached the woman and asked for something to eat. As she reached into her bag for a crust of bread, the traveler saw the precious stone and imagined how it would provide him with financial security for the remainder of his life. He asked the woman to give the treasure to him, and she did, along with some food. He left ecstatic over his good fortune and the knowledge that he was now secure.

A few days later, the traveler returned and handed back the stone to the wise woman. "I've been thinking," he told her. "Although I know how valuable this is, I'm returning it to you in the hopes that you could give me something even more precious."

"What would that be?" the woman inquired.

"Please give me what you have within yourself that enabled you to give me that stone."

Almost all societies frown upon unmarried women and proselytize traditional behavior to continue the family. They have not modernized enough to assimilate the fact that marriage is not a mandatory goal, it's not an accomplishment, it is an option, an elective, and a choice of lifestyles.

Futility

We live in an imperfect world, surrounded by imperfect people, with idealized preconceived judgements, time stressed schedules and digitally saturated lives. The idea of finding a perfect someone, a person that we can live happily ever after with, a soulmate, while romantic, is a misconception. This is a myth that has done incredible damage and continues to trick and keep people single, forever unfulfilled, and discontented. You have to create your ideal partner. A relationship, marriage, love, deep friendship, and soulmates, all take a commitment, time, patience, luck, and opportunity. But most of all it takes a realistic approach to the impossible-to-meet expectations that have been proselytized by religion, Hollywood, romantic writers and conservative societies.

You say you are seeking a soulmate or a friend. But then, you cannot be so self-centered, used to only receiving, negate reciprocity, and just talk without making a concerted effort to communicate, be responsive, be nurturing, sexual, positive, happy, and maintain the relationship. If you are alone, some of the above reasons are probably why.

Choosing a Wife

A man wanted to get married. He was having trouble choosing among three likely candidates. He gives each woman $5,000 and watches to see what she will do with the money. The first does a total makeover. She goes to a fancy beauty salon, gets her hair done, new makeup; buys several new outfits and dresses up very nicely for the man. She tells him that she has done this to be more attractive to him because she loves him so much. The man was impressed. The second goes shopping to buy the man gifts. She gets him a new set of golf clubs, some new gizmos for his computer, and some expensive clothes. As she presents these gifts, she tells him that she has spent all the money on him, because she loves him so much. Again, the man is impressed. The third invests the money in the stock market. She earns several times the $5,000. She gives him back his $5,000 and reinvests the remainder in a joint account. She tells him that she wants to save for their future because she loves him so much. Obviously, the man was impressed. The man thought for a long time about what each woman had done with the money he'd given her. Then he married the one with the biggest tits.

One way to be happy in life and in a relationship, is to lower your expectations. *This does not mean give up your realistic appraisal of the situation, however, high expectations usually lead to dissatisfaction. Instead, invest your emotions and time in making small improvements and rendering positive actions and completions.*

Flying Linda

Dreams that flew away

You can't keep a good Kamikaze down.

I dropped over Jeff Fox's house every few days for the last three weeks. He was never home, and his beach house was unoccupied and wide open. The two big sliding doors were slid back, and the entrance was a 12-foot wide portal into his living room. His theory was that the Bahamians would cause less damage when they burglarized his house if they didn't have to break into it and they just might think that someone was home. The television was always on, and I sat on the sofa when I visited his open house and watched the weather report before I left. The other side of his living room was all floor to ceiling glass doors that faced the open sea. Jeff's terrace had become the most exposed parapet on the beach since the last hurricane sent a surge of waves for six hours undermining his foundation as the sand was carried back into the sea. A share drop of 30 feet from his terrace to the beach made his balcony a wondrous pinnacle jutting out onto the beach and almost into the ocean. I left his house only to return the next evening. I spent too much time sitting in the golf cart and decided to take a walk before dinner and to see one last time if Jeff was home. Ten minutes later, I was at his house having walked rapidly down the road.

"Hello, hello, anybody home?"

"High Mike, perfect timing, I'm having a going away party."

"Great."

Jeff's guests arrived moments later. Heinrich from Hamburg Germany, a quiet man from England with a Scottish accent, and Phillip and Linda from Saint Tropez. The six of us sat around Jeff's kitchen, which was built like a bar, drank, got acquainted, and talked about the talent on the island. Philip had just quit his job after only two weeks. He was a painter and had several boxes of pictures of his work that he proudly showed. His originality was impressive, as were his sharp lines and images of reality and social criticism. One painting distinguished itself from the rest. It was a painting of six-sky diver's in an abrupt circle against a cloudy blue sky day. I asked him why skydivers bothered to wear safety helmets.

"We're going over to Spanish Wells tomorrow," Jeff said, "would you like to go?"

"That place is so strange. You can't get a beer anywhere on the island, and there are only three restaurants."

"And only five last names in the phone book," Jeff interjected.

We laughed and then explained the joke to the group. Jeff spoke about the movie Deliverance about the Appalachian people and compared it to the Spanish Wells individuals who had been marrying among themselves for decades. He told them about the scene about the banjo picking and the mentally disabled boy, and how when they went to the island they'd hum the tune.

Jeff was an excellent host and kept the dips and drinks flowing. The group was light, compatible and the rapport was funny. Philip was a sensitive, passionate artist with a warm disposition, and his woman Linda reminded me of a woman, coincidently with the same name, that I lived with years ago. Both women were not particularly well grounded but were still very sweet. We relaxed, drank and talked of beaches around the world and storms. Outside the warm breeze was blowing and pushing the running waves sideways as it blew diagonally to the beach.

"Jeff, do you mind if I open the terrace door a crack."

"That's what it's for. Let's all go out and feel the breeze."

I slid open the door, and the six of us strolled out onto the terrace. It was magic. The white sand folded along the shoreline and the black sea topped with white foam only fifty feet in front of us.

Phillips said, "That wind is coming from Africa, and if we can change the wind pattern going to farmers, all the crops would change."

"Yes, Jeff answered, and sometimes in April this sea turns brown with the dust off the Sahara and the island has a dust storm."

As he spoke, he turned toward the ladder used to climb to the overhead observation deck twelve feet above the lower terrace.

"It's fantastic up here. Come on up."

Everyone climbed the ladder and marveled at how strong the wind was and how exposed we all felt. Some of us leaned back on the slanted roof and others stood by the railing. Linda lay down on the top of the railing, and Phillip said to her, "You're not going to fall, are you? You can't fall unless there is wet concrete below to break your fall."

"I'm all right," Linda replied. We all went back to our conversations.

Suddenly, Linda was gone. She had fallen off the railing, landing fifteen feet onto the concrete tile deck below. Momentarily, everyone froze, the realization of what happened taking the time to sink in. I dove for the ladder, sliding down with my legs on the outside. I was thinking of the worst-case scenario, as I rushed inside banging into the closed terrace doors. I opened the door and got a pillow to put under her head, which if she had struck it on the hard tile would have cracked. She was lying on the terrace slightly stunned by conscience. I said to Philip "Don't move her."

I cautiously set the pillow under the back of her head and felt for bleeding. Miraculously, she had no bumps or bleeding.

"Can you move your hands and feet? Do you have any pain?"

I felt her legs and bones, and everything seemed intact.

I surmised that she fell just right and absorbed most of the impact in her hands, shoulders, and buttocks. Four men stood silently around her, apprehensive, relieved and traumatized.

"I'm okay. I'm all right," Linda said.

Philip helped her to her feet.

"Phil, see if she is swollen or bleeding at the base of the spine."

Phil ran his hands all over her and did not find anything broken. Flying Linda said that she was fine. We all looked at each other relieved, but still concerned. Some shook their heads in disbelief, and everyone was visibly shaken.

"We know you need attention Linda, but this is going too far."

"Don't do that again," I said.

"You know, no one is going to believe me if I tell them the story. They'll just say he's bullshitting us."

"You flew fifteen feet and landed on your back on concrete tile, and you didn't even bruise yourself? Where's your broomstick?"

"I just flew down on the wind from one terrace to the other." Linda said, "It was like flying, I just flew down."

We all had been drinking, but immediately cleared our heads in that state of shock. We were relieved that miraculously she did not hurt herself seriously. I believe that she was injured internally or spinally and that the others thought likewise but did not say anything. I was just happy that she did not bash open her head. She had missed death by absorbing the shock of the fall on other parts of her body.

We were all going to meet the next day for dinner. I thought it was not going to happen since Linda would not be in good shape. The next day Jeff and Hedrick dropped by to tell me that Linda was black and blue. She may have hurt her spine and that her ribs were bruised. I believed that she would have some repercussions and I was surprised and relieved that they appeared initially to be so slight.

Jeff, Heinrich, and I went out for drinks the next day. We went to a bar. If this drinking hole were in the city, I would not drink there on a bet. The place was rundown, dirty, and cramped for space. Several locals stayed close to us, to ease drop on our conversation. It was as if they saw some potential in interacting with us since we represented the outside world. They were desperate to link up with any of us interpreting our lives as a vehicle for them to get ahead. The myth of the millionaire white man runs rampant on the island, underlined by passive aggressive actions and feelings.

When I got back to New York, I thought about calling Linda, the women I lived with years ago. Flying Linda reminded me of my old flame, and I grew curious as to what she was up to nowadays. We had somehow managed to keep in touch, over the years, calling each other sporadically, whenever there was some news. I looked through my contacts that I recently updated and could not find her name. Other things had priority, and I forgot about getting in touch.

Coincidentally, a few days later Linda called. We arranged a quick stop by on an afternoon that I was in her neighborhood. I went into my bedroom and searched through a winter closet. Many years ago, Linda gave me a dark blue woolen hat that she brought home from Czechoslovakia. She said it was given to her by a freedom fighter, or maybe I just made that up- it was so long ago. I thought that she might enjoy getting the hat back since it was so unique with its wide, deep brim. I always wanted to have this hat manufactured in the city, but I never wanted to take it apart for the process because I loved wearing it. I called Linda the morning before we were going to meet and asked her if she 'd like the hat back. She said "yes, " and I told her I'd return it. When I got to her apartment, she was ill, supposedly from something she ate. She had stomach cramps and just wanted to lie down. We talked briefly. We spoke of getting together when she was well. I left the hat for her.

Several weeks passed, and she called.

"Mike, I've moved to a new apartment that I bought. Come over sometime and see it. I miss you and would love to see you again."

She spoke as if I had not dropped over to see her the last time. She sounded disoriented and far away. Linda over the years always appeared trapped in the past, a Woodstock type product.

"Linda, do you remember what happened the last time I saw you?"

She answered in her incredible deep throaty voice giving several different and conflicting explanations, as to why she didn't remember. Even after so much time had passed, she hadn't changed some aspects of her personality. That song, "Still crazy after all these years," played in my mind.

I arranged to meet with her, for a cappuccino, a few blocks from her home. Her beautiful long legs, large eyes, and fat lips still gave her an attractive appearance, but she had lost about fifteen pounds and was not as curvaceous. In fact, she was skinny, with a curious, offbeat, up-town chic, manner. We sat and talked.

"You know Mike; not many people keep in touch the way we do over so many years."

"Yes, I've always wondered why and been disappointed with so many relationships. One would think that after spending years, perhaps decades, in and out of love with someone that you'd want to touch base, at least to have a barometer of progress."

"Yes, but, there is too much pain most of the time. Although look how we have stayed in touch. One of the compensations about growing old is that time and some friend's move through time with you. We still have the music and the memories."

"Speaking of memories, I'm surprised you're not wearing the hat."

"I threw it away."

"You're kidding!"

"No."

"You threw a hat away that I saved for us for twenty years? Why?"

"Because you took it from me and wouldn't give it back."

"I don't remember that. I thought you gave it to me. You never asked for it back."

"No, you took it, and there was nothing I could do to get it back."

"But, now I gave it to you. It certainly had sentimental value to me, and I thought to us."

"No, it hurt me, so I got rid of it."

"I can't believe you did that. In this world, you don't turn down love, no matter what form it takes, if it's not destructive toward you. **To have a future with someone you have to give up your past."**

A wave of nostalgia passed over me, and I thought about all the women, over so many years, who I interacted with, that never kept in touch, even though I changed their lives significantly for the better. I sang to myself, "still crazy after all these years." I was sad but I realized that **no matter how complicated, great, or lousy today was, it will pass and tomorrow is a fresh start. A new tomorrow starts today** for me but even after all these years, Linda was still on another planet and that this relationship like our story stops too soon.

The foot of the candle is dark.

He yelled out to the woman who was walking on the other side of the river, "Pardon me for dreaming out loud, but I think I'm in love with you."

She replied, "Call me when you are not dreaming and sure."

"But I want to love you now. How can I get to the other side?"

"Fool, she answered, "You are already on the other side."

Do not search for a companion in some remote or exotic place. The easiest place to find love is where you are.

The big communication problem is that we do not listen to understand, we listen to reply.

Without communication, there is no relationship. Without respect, there is no love. Without trust, there is no reason to continue.

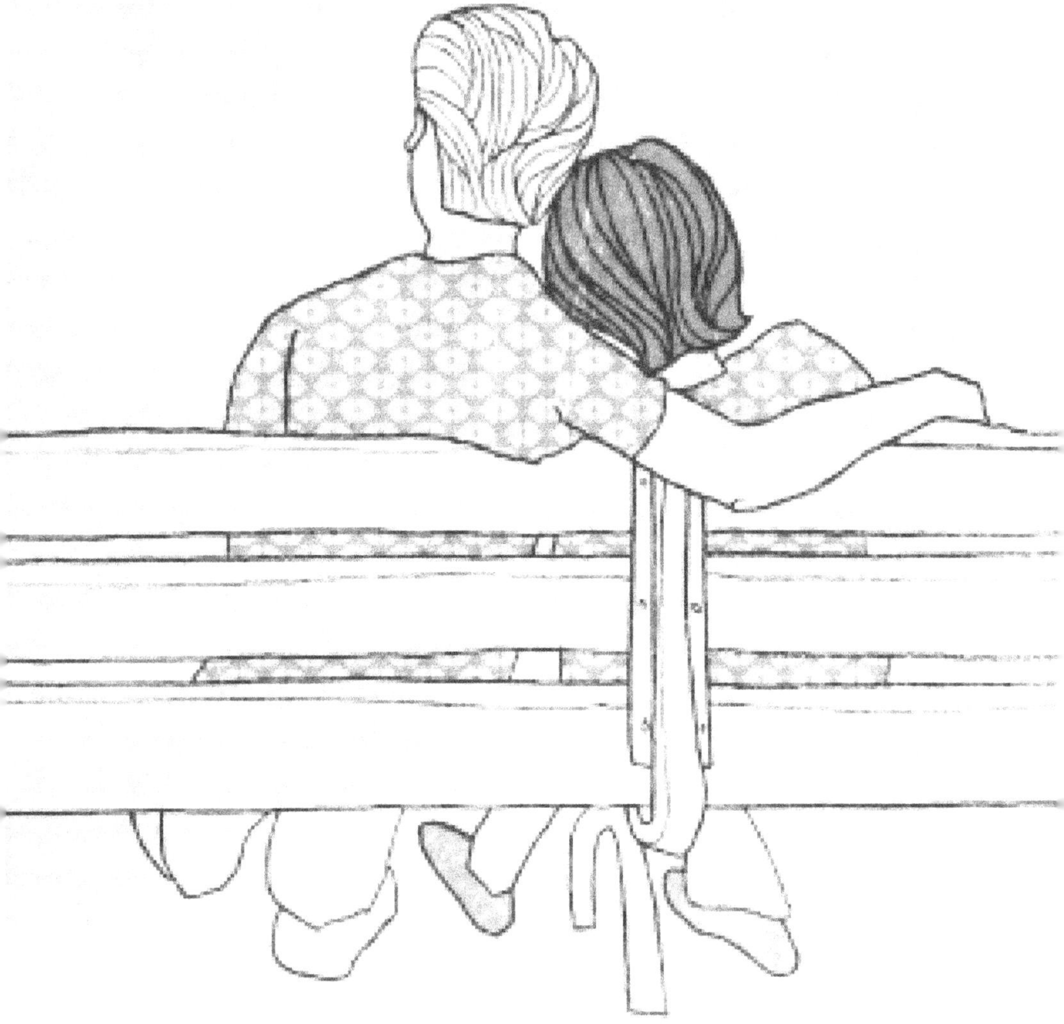

La Tulipe

(A chapter from Dead Man's Float. Soon To be published)

Love tossed me around like a mosquito in a hurricane.

Inviting Rita to the Caribbean with me was going to be an interesting test of our compatibility and perhaps clarify the conflicting perceptions I was receiving from her. On my secret island, living on what I affectionately call the last block on the edge of the world, because it is so remote, I have lots of anxiety about having an empty refrigerator. The security that a full freezer of fresh fish, lobster tails, and conch gives to me goes deep into my upbringing, which makes food one of the security blankets of life. Perhaps

the memory of being on my own when I was sixteen and never having money scared me more than I knew. At any rate, hunting, cooking and supplying my own fresh food from

the sea gives me an enormous amount of satisfaction. It is also true that the most expensive meal, at the best restaurant on the island, is barely passable compared to New York standards, which makes me appreciate the cities dining even more.

The antithesis of hunting for your own food has to be the cosmopolitan restaurant ceremony. Carried to extremes, the dining out experience can be the ultimate in role-playing and affectation. Sometimes the outrageous situations that evolve iconoclastically counteract the pompousness of the ritual.

I went out onto the terrace of my apartment and sat upon the hundred-year-old Doric capital that I use for a table. The capital was once on top of a massive, round, red, granite column. The polished pillar and capitals were part of a beautiful facade, in front of an ornate building decorated with ceramic reliefs, in lower Manhattan. For one hundred years, the twenty-four-inch diameter column was under compression and the weight of thousands of pounds of concrete, brick and stone attempted to compress the capitals into dust. The building that this structure was a part of was slated for demolition and destruction. When the demolition crew finished their shift one evening, with the help of two gorillas and a huge dolly, I moved the three intact capitals several city blocks into my top floor apartment and out onto my terrace. The Capitals possessed magical qualities since physiologically they had been compressed and under immense pressure for a century. I knew the stone had resisted the pressure and now the Capitals strained to expand and resume their original shape. There was Zen magic in meditating on them and sensing the power of the expanding stone.

I took a shower, put on a robe, slipped in a CD of Bach's Air on a G-string and went onto the terrace to allow my mind to shift thoughts and settle. I sat cross-legged on top of the column, my eyes half shut but gazing at the clouds and the skyline, half watching the pollution red sunset. When I look out from my terrace onto the metropolis, especially at dusk, as the light changes, it looks like OZ and always borders on the spectacular.

I have not stopped for weeks except for my interaction with Rita. I used to do my yoga and meditation every day, work out a few times a week, and have much less stress. Why was I driving myself? Was it because success breeds more success and my gallery sold so much of my inventory, and my writing was going so well? To think that I used to define success by never having to wear a suit: Probably living in Manhattan, where everyone and everything moves twice as fast, was responsible for it. Well, I rationalized; "at least you know you're alive." I resolved to try to **slow down and get back to more healthy pursuits.** Vowing to put my resolve into action, I planned a lovely relaxed evening. This was only our third going out date, but Rita, my Kamikaze, was taking me out to an excellent restaurant for my birthday. She was picking me up soon, and I took a few deep breaths more before going inside to get dressed. I put on my blue blazer and slipped a nail file into the pocket with a silver and black silk handkerchief. These days I didn't have time even to file my nails, and since my building has the slowest elevators in Manhattan, I developed a filing ritual in transit.

Since it was the first-time Rita was going to pick me up at my apartment, I told her to call me on her cell phone when she was close by so that I could give her directions and be on my way down if she could not park. She rang, and I went out to my terrace to see if there were any parking spaces on my Street so she could come up for a drink. I watched from my high perch as her old yellow Mercedes turned the far corner and pulled over. A small man in a large gray hat rambled out of her car and walked slowly up the block toward my building. I wondered who he was and why he was riding with Rita.

"I'm sorry Rita there are no spots to park, so I'm coming down. Pull up beside that little guard shack in the middle of the block."

As I exited from my building, holding the heavy outer door open for a slowly moving older woman to enter, Rita's yellow Mercedes, which resembled a toy car, pulled up in front of my building. There was no sign of the man in the gray hat.

"Hi, Mike."

"Hi, Kamikaze."

I got into the car, and the seat and the armrest were warm.

"Did you drive someone downtown? I asked.

"Yes, I gave a girlfriend a lift. How did you know? Do you want to drive?"

"Okay, because the seat is warm."

I registered the lie, without showing any reaction, building more pieces of her puzzle. The reason I nicknamed her kamikaze, as a joke, was because of the way she drove on our second date, skillfully but too fast for me. The trip took only twenty minutes, but at every red traffic light I looked at her. She was so pretty and dressed so brightly, her years of bicycling and working out with weights paid off because she radiated health and alertness. Her slim athletic body and narrow waist aided her classy projected image, which came to her naturally. I held her hand and got conflicting pictures of her. She liked me but was preoccupied; she enjoyed my company but was just biding her time. Well, my prescience was in transition and not accurate lately, so I will not force it. But why did she lie about the man in her car? Luckily we found a parking space and walked a block to the restaurant.

"So what are you working on this week my lovely?" I said to Rita as I took her hand.

"Well, I have a contract with IBM to do a five-part series called, "The Renaissance." I'm going to do some writing on it, as well as shoot three sections. And soon we go south to shoot a documentary on intern stress at a big hospital and university."

"Fantastic. What are the locations?"

"Europe. I have to go there about five times this year to shoot, probably in Italy and then Carolina."

"I don't know how you travel so much. That much sitting down on a plane makes me crazy."

"I love to read about designing, and I find the whole trip relaxing, that is until we start to work our fourteen-hour workdays."

I was unwinding and enjoying our repartee. Rita reached over and entwined my hand in both of hers as she spoke.

"I love being with you. I treasure your stories and sense of humor."

"I enjoy your company even more. You never bore me, and I think you're going to be one of the few people I know that I can relax with. How about starting a mutual admiration society?"

My Kamikaze had tried to reserve a corner table at La Tulipe but had been told it was impossible on a Saturday night. She decided to book there anyway and take a chance on getting a good table. It was one of the city's top restaurants, and she wanted to take us to a special place. She also reasoned, how bad could it be? When we arrived the Maitre D' Hotel escorted us, past opulently dressed diners and crystal chandeliers hung too low, to a table on the side of the room and pulled the table out for Rita. The table was too close to the other diners around us. We sat for a few moments, and we realized that our conversation was not going to be private. The waiter asked us if we would like a cocktail. We were being rushed. I always try to slow waiters down to a more controlling pace. I asked the waiter to send over the maitre d'. When he came to us, I requested another table.

"This one was a bit small and not very intimate," I told him.

The only other choice was a table for three across the way. It was near the kitchen entrance and a service station. It was isolated but not very appealing. The maitre d' said we could have that one, that it was more private and had more legroom. We changed tables and settled in. As soon as we were seated a waiter asked if we wanted a cocktail. He put the menus on the table with the wine list. The leisurely pace of dining had been violated by the waiter's insensitivity. Rita gives me an engaging, conspiratorial glance: and it was surprising how we were in synchronization with each other.

"Let's order a bottle of wine Mike. The wine list looks great."

Another waiter, more evenly paced, placed hot bread on our plates with much pomp and ceremony, and we began to feel catered to. The maitre d' approached us and apologized. He told us that he was unable to give us this table for three. Rita and I looked at each other.

"Where would you prefer us to sit?" I asked.

Looking around the room, it appeared that all the tables were postage stamp size or too close to other diners. On the other side of the room was another poorly situated table for two. By now it was the only one left. One side of this table was in the back of a serving station, and the other was right next to the corner table. Acquiescing, we stood near it while they set the table up.

"I suggest that we leave," Rita said, knowing that I was annoyed.

"Yes honey but I know that you are hungry and by now it would be difficult to get another reservation at any decent restaurant at the prime time."

"Alright, let's see how it goes, but I'm ready."

"Well, you always argue from a place of power, and you use it appropriately, but I seem to argue from a place of force. Maybe I can use the power this time."

We sat down and ordered a lovely red wine.

"Toasts," Rita said, "To new friends and old lovers, or if you prefer to new lovers and old friends. Or if we want to paraphrase a more contemporary, to banning pre-shredded cheese, to make America grate again."

"To wife's and lovers, may they never meet. Or, to this moment and to the moment next to come."

"Oh, that's so profound." Rita joked.

"Alright then, here's to swimen with bow legged woman and the Gods warped sense of humor." Looking up I said, "I'm only kidding."

I got up and walked into the bar area. The maitre d' was talking to the owner.

"Excuse me," I said.

"Yes sir," he answered, looking at me over his spectacles.

"Can you switch us to the corner table please?"

"That's impossible sir."

"It really isn't," I said. "I requested the table with my reservation, it's free, and I want it, and my table rocks and it is so diminutive that it is extremely difficult to dine on."

I was all set to assert myself further, make a scene if necessary, and walk out. Rita had finished her glass of wine and her appetizer. She could now hold out until we found another place. After all, this was New York City, and we could dine at a different restaurant every night of the week and never go back to the same place. Continuing to speak to the maitre d' I maintained, "The table is too small and is ridiculously close to the service station. I cannot have silverware and plates rattling behind my head. If my lady dines comfortably and situates the table in front of her, the table is unsteady and rocks. I have no room to move, I am entirely pinned in, and cannot cross my legs. You really must move us."

I returned to Rita, who was listening to the entire conversation, and a nod by her corroborated my disposition to leave. She shifted her weight and because the table was unstable, knocked her glass of wine over. Suddenly a subliminal picture of bloody water on fire flashed in my brain, and for an instant, Rita turned mercenary and ugly. I let go of her hand, braced myself against the wall and took a deep breath. It was just a painful flash and I regained my composure.

The maitre d' moved quickly over to us.

"Sir, I didn't say no. Just give us a chance to set the corner table up."

His boss had obviously told him we were about to walk out and he wished to placate us. The waiters attacked the corner tabletop and set it up in a few moments. We slid into the cushy corner banquets and became comfortable immediately. Aside from the privacy I always like my back to the wall and face to the entrance. It is not only urban paranoia but also training from hanging out for years with my two detective friends.

Rita was grinning and having fun with the entire incident. Her speckled greenish eyes, her most outstanding feature, looked like shattered glass with a radiant light behind them.

"Mike," she said, "I've heard of musical chairs, but musical tables are a new game."

"That's what happens when a million people all try to eat at the same time and in the most enjoyable, affordable way."

"The evening's young," she said as she ran her soft fingers over my lips, "we can change again when we have some exquisitely sinful dessert."

"What's a sinful dessert? They will not let us do that here."

"No silly," she said, her cheeks blushing. "I mean a sugar shock worth the calories."

"Mike, tell me about your past. What were you like as a teenager and in your twenties?"

As if by cue the music changed and a group from the sixties, the Platters, softly and melodically, began to accompany my conversation with "Smoke gets in your eyes" followed by "Only you."

"I grew up in Brooklyn like a weed, roaming and exploring the neighborhood alone for adventure and amusement. I was a tall skinny high-energy kid who was reasonably bright and could not be handled by teachers. People said then and still say now that I use colorful language. But that's a cornucopia of bullshit. I didn't need sleep and I had to keep moving all the time, so I was always in trouble at school. When I was a kid I had an imaginary friend, he was an alcoholic, I called him dad. He was a wireless father- free after six. He wanted me to follow in his footsteps- quicksand."

"You are too funny. Let me interrupt you for a second. What kind of neighborhood did you grow up in?"

"Well, the community was defined by the beach and the Atlantic Ocean. The section that I grew up in, Manhattan Beach was the dividing line between rich and poor, so it was very dynamic. Areas were so tough that as kids when we flew kites we put razor blades on the tails to cut the strings of other fliers. Even the skies were competitive and aggressive and being able to run, fast and long, was an essential survival skill."

"And what about your parents?"

"My mother drove me crazy, gave me no privacy, especially with my girlfriends, although she had a great sense of humor. My father was never around, he was a treasury agent, and when he was home, he was a cold fish. I left home when I was sixteen and moved to Greenwich Village, with a friend, to become an artist and to be free."

"And... were you free?"

"No. Freedom requires money. I worked in construction and went to college at night. It was a struggle, but I was young and vigorous. I worked hard for a few years and then was wiped out."

"Wiped out?"

"Yes. It was easier and much cheaper to meet women if we had a party at our place. Since my roommate and I both worked days and went to school at night, we put the word out at each other's schools and people came to our parties. It worked so well that we had a gathering the first Friday of every month. It got to be a pattern, and we only invited back the guys who brought food or wine and the pretty ladies. One day I broke my foot in a construction accident and stayed in a hospital for a few days. My roommate, unbeknownst to me, decided to go away that weekend. It was the first Friday of the month. Someone went up the fire escape, through the window, and opened up the apartment. The party went on as usual without either of us being there. The party lasted all weekend and became an open house. When I got out of the hospital and entered the apartment, there was nothing in it except two junkies who moved in. Everything was gone. My bankbook, furniture, shoes, they even took the rug from the floor. I was on crutches with a four-day beard and went down to the Street because the apartment stunk. A bum offered me a cigarette."

"What did you do? How did you feel?" Rita said as she put her hand on mine. Strangely her reaction was more curious than compassionate.

"The same thing I do now, the best I can. The feeling was utterly devastating, like suddenly becoming a child again, at the loss and having to start all over, but at the same time clean and unencumbered, having no possessions. It was the personification of the Japanese Haiku; **My house burned down, but I can better see the moon.** And that was just the first time I was wiped out."

"It happened twice?" She said, looking at me with sympathy and yet incredulously.

"Not the same way. The second time was by fire."

"Tell me..."

"Some other time. It's your turn."

"All right but remember to tell me what happened. I went to private schools in the city. My father was a dermatologist and treated many skin cancers with radiation. This was before we knew about the consequences of radiation and he did not have adequate protection. He died of radiation poisoning and I was all alone. You know Mike…" She hesitated and a look of sadness washed over her face. "If you don't mind, it's just too painful now to talk about it and the evening is so good…"

"All right, I understand. Tell me about the girlfriend to whom you gave a lift downtown." I tested, trying to catch her unaware. She didn't miss a beat.

"Oh, she's just a new friend that's looking for a man. Although, in our conversation she did say something funny. She told me she knew a woman who went to her boss and said, "All the other women that work here, married or single, rich or poor, homely or cute, are suing you for sexual harassment. Yet, in all these years that you have employed me, you have never sexually harassed me. I'm suing you for discrimination."

We chuckled, and I felt very close to her as we ordered our main courses. I told Rita that sitting at the last table reminded me of the man who had too little room in his apartment. My Kamikaze knew I was setting her up to tell her a story. She loved my stories and my soul soared when her contagious laugh filled our space. She drifted closer next to me and put her hand under my arm. Looking at me, she rolled her eyes and looked straight up, as if to say, here we go again…

The story, about space and concentration, took a full ten minutes and ended in, "Rabbi, I have so much room now, how can I thank you?"

Rita laughed and asked, "So you really think that **your focus determines your reality**."

"Absolutely."

"And do you also think that we are a bunch of animals all trying to feed at the same time?"

"I didn't say that Rita, but that could be one interpretation. Although it's not as good as the first explanation."

Our entrées arrived and, despite the small portions, they were delicious. We talked of living space and the culture of the city and considered how lucky we were that we both owned cooperative apartments. On the other hand, we seriously but jokingly lamented that our apartments stopped us forever from moving in with each other. Between us we had five bathrooms, and who in America could give that up. Still, we both would have liked more area.

Rita's soufflé and espresso arrived, and I saw my chance to sandbag her. I was carrying her beautifully crafted silver ring, which her mother had given to her, that I retrieved from the subway vent where she dropped it on our first meeting. I knew that I wanted to give it to her tonight on our third date, but I did not have any idea about how to present it. I first imagined planting the ring in a box of popcorn and have Rita discover it in a dark movie theater. But I had to find another opportunity. I directed Rita's attention to an interesting group across the room and while she was momentarily distracted I placed the ring on her coffee plate behind her cup. We talked for a while, and as she stirred her espresso, as was her habit, she turned her plate. The ring appeared like magic.

"Look," she said, her face lighting up with surprise.

"Amazing, someone must have left it there by accident."

"How did you do it, magic? I'm so grateful. You're incredible."

She put the ring on her finger and looked at me with affection and a big grin. She was quiet and a little overwhelmed as she moved closer to me and tucked herself into my side."

"I'm getting to know you better," Rita said. "You're always trying to lead me down the garden path. In the beginning, I didn't understand that you would do anything to deceive me into a joke. Now that I'm more used to you, I can see how you delight in sandbagging me."

We discussed changing tables for dessert. I asked her, "If the road of excess could eventually lead to the table of wisdom."

She replied, "I believe that we will remember this evening for a long time." And she recited a poem.

"I wonder who is haunting

the little snug cafe,

That place, half restaurant and home,

since we have gone away;

The candled dimness, smoke, and talk,

and tables brown and bare-

But no one thinks of tablecloths when

love and tear are there."

"Wow, how apropos my Kamikaze, yours?"

"No, Charles Devine, he lived in the first part of this century."

Rita was ready to leave and I pulled the table out for her.

The owner of my gallery just strolled into the restaurant, and I waved hello.

"Mike, doesn't it seem an unusual coincidence that your gallery owner showed up here tonight?"

"No honey, there are only a few thousand people in New York and all the rest are done with mirrors."

As we were leaving, on his way out, Peter Jennings, the retired newscaster from ABC news came up to us. He had observed us and been amused at our manipulative table changing, and said jokingly, "Everyone needs a little help sometimes." Rita and I looked at each other, the three of us exchanged knowing glances, and we all smiled.

We parked her car and walked home slowly holding hands and enjoying the coolness of the evening. The Streets were unusually quiet, and the walk to Rita's apartment took too short a time. The two young doormen straightened up and nodded as we entered the large pristine lobby, and we walked through it and into the small wood-paneled elevator.

I reached my hand out and played lightly across Rita's breast. I felt her nipples perk up and she smiled. I pulled her close to me, and she put both her hands around my neck. I put my hand over her ass cheeks and felt her tight behind through her dress. We kissed and embraced and everything was natural and comfortable. We kissed again, and we became lost in each other's lips. She closed her eyes and all the tension in her body disappeared, replaced by a sweet longing and I slid my hands under her dress, and her skin was clean and exciting. My hands roamed under her panties and into her crotch all too fast but so instinctive and spontaneous. Our lips slid back and forth over each other's mouth, neck and face. I opened my fly and tried to position Lazarus nearer to Rita's crotch. Surprisingly he woke from the dead more rapidly than usual and penetrated her slightly, sliding back and forth over her wet sex. I was about to say something but Rita put her pointer finger to her lips signaling me not to say anything and gestured her eyes toward a speaker in the elevator.

We arrived at her floor, and I was carrying her with her legs wrapped around my waist. I walked straight into her apartment, kicking off my shoes, and leaving a trail of clothing. The living room sofa was straight ahead, and I was not going to take a detour to the bedroom. We lay down on the soft gray leather and removed each other's clothing. Rita's panties were so wet that if I threw them against the wall, they'd have stuck. She slid herself over me and slowly moved. My eyes closed and opened and we both were smiling. Rita's eyes were like an alien. Instead of dark pupils surrounded by some color, her eyes were all blue, green and brown specks. Like the brilliant marbles I played with as a child and held up to the sun to watch the pure colors dance, the light in her eyes shone through. Perhaps it was her burning intelligence and passion, but they were too alive and strangely brilliant. We flowed in and out of each other and the dream we shared. We played for an hour and Rita went off like a pack of firecrackers exploding at the same time I drove home in her. We lay in each other's arms, sleeping, dreaming and enjoying the closeness. We got up slowly after a while and showered together.

Since Rita was going to Atlanta early in the morning, I didn't sleep over. She promised to call me when she returned, and I headed home satisfied, and almost content that I had, at last, found a companion and lover.

A few days later, I was passing Rita's building on my way home from a sculptor patron's new penthouse apartment. I would usually call someone before I came over, but this was unplanned. Perhaps she was home, and I could surprise her. I entered the lobby and a uniformed doorman that I had not seen before held open the door.

"Could you ring 8A please, Ms. Rita."

"Are you expected, sir?"

"No. I just happened to be in the neighborhood."

"Well, Mrs. D'Amico is not home sir, but Mr. D'Amico is, shall I ring up?"

"No, I wanted to see both of them. Perhaps some other time, thank you."

"Good afternoon sir."

I walked around the corner. I was hurt, angry and vastly disappointed. But Rita hadn't lied to me, she just didn't inform me. Could there be a mistake? I went to a phone and dialed Rita's number.

"Hello." A man answered.

"Hello, Sir. Mr. D'Amico, this is quality control from the New York Times. Are you happy with the delivery service? Are you receiving the paper early enough and do you have any complaints or suggestions?"

"I don't think that there are any problems, but I travel a lot and I'm not the one to ask. Call back some other time and ask my wife."

"All right sir. Thank you for your consideration."

For certain I was not going to pursue a dead end, no matter how much I liked her. I should have known since it was too perfect. Now I know why my acumen was picking up so many conflicting clues and I was sure there was even more of which I was unaware. My prescience was skewed. How could I have been so naive and unsophisticated? I was out of the dating game for too long. I wasn't sure who I was angrier with,

Rita for taking me for a ride or myself for being so stupid. I wanted to speak to her and ask her how she could do what she did, but in the end, I knew what she would say wouldn't matter. She ripped my heart out, put it in a blender and pressed frappe. Well, **life is for learning,** and next time I'll ask.

I felt all alone, and my stomach was churning and eating my guts out. I went home determined not to be depressed and to concentrate on my trip, but my left eye started to tear. By the time I got home, I could not see. The tears in my eyes were continual as if cement dust had blown into them. I wasn't crying because I was sad, my eyes wer e overflowing with tears because of all the unfulfilled desires and lost opportunities I missed. What was that line my friend Gregory said, **"I'm never in denial."**

No matter what the situation, do not let your emotions overpower your intelligence.

Life does not get easier; you just get stronger.

Intimacy

Intimacy comes in many forms. Close ties with friends, relatives, community members, spiritually, and of course loved ones. But now days it is in increasingly short supply. In the past people spent their entire lives in the same town or neighborhood, where they knew everyone and people truly knew them. Today many people move every few years, have intense work schedules, and socializing take a back seat to doing more "important things." Face to face takes so much more time than emails or texting. The problem is that harmonious communication, loving and being loved, socializing, and physical contact, are not just luxuries but a necessity for health and survival. Intimacy lowers stress and calms the heart, lowers blood pressure, strengthens immune responses, and reduces the destructive effects of anxiety. So, learn to communicate your feeling, open up more emotionally, and while respecting others boundaries, look for opportunities to get in touch.

First the engagement ring, then the marriage ring, then suffering.

Honor

I have a friend of many years. When we get together we talk about, relationships, both with others and ours, Zen, and life. My friend is very smart but does not **take full responsibility for his actions or inactions***. Instead he uses his intellect to create excellent rationales for excuses. One evening I brought this to his attention, having confidence in the Zen adage:* **Love he who tells you your faults in private.** *Defensively he answered, "I don't think that's true, sometimes things just happen."*

"But that is just another justification, like saying it's fate or serendipity."

"No, junk happens that's out of your control. Like your computer loses information or you get hit by a car or lose a companion."

"But isn't that your fault because you didn't back up on a separate drive or have more awareness of what's around you, or have sensitivity or make a positive effort?"

"Hey, shit happens."

"That's just a rationalization for not taking accountability. If you acted, then it produced a reaction. Unless it is, or was, completely out of your control, you are responsible. I think that even if I gave you the secret of life you would find a way to avoid culpability or act." I teased.

"All right, tell me the secret of life." He challenged, as he looked up and rolled his eyes.

"The secret of life, and many other exceptional ideas about relationships are in my new book, AWayToLoveLaugh.Com. All you have to do is just click my site and buy it on Amazon."

"I think with all the help I have given you, with editing you're writing, you should just give me the book for free."

Nothing is more detrimental to your life than self-deception.

Four Tushie

I pilled the straps of my bathing suit a little tighter. I was swimming home, using my thighs instead of my knees, and developing skill using my new fins and equipment. Turn right, stroke, inhale and glide, turn left, stroke, exhale and slide. When I turn left, I see the side of the dune for a second; when I turn right, I see underwater and then the sky. When I move right, I see four squids, in formation gliding through the water, right in front of me. They are otherworldly looking with their smooth locomotion and intelligent eyes staring back at me. On one move, left, I saw four women were walking together through the surf on the beach. They are wearing tiny bikinis, no more than a triangle and dental floss. When I turn my head, like an afterimage, they line up perfectly with the squid. It is a strangely enjoyable illusion. After one right side of sliding, I saw Mike coming out of the water. He was carrying three big lipped couch and his gear. I immediately knew that Mike would talk to the women. But how? After a few more strokes, I saw the four women stop and just look at the sea. Two more strokes and Mike was walking with the four women, two of them carrying large conch shells. Mike also had a conch shell and his gear.

We may have plans, opportunities, expectations, and dreams but the reality is that we are all just produces of our hormones and DNA. We just want to feel alive, and love makes us feel good and fools us into believing that life goes in a straight line.

Lessons in life come from a multiplicity of sources, and we must learn that our every action produces a reaction.

A best friend woman I have known almost all my life, used a response I had, thirty years ago, to a remark she made, to rationalize a defensive reaction she took to correcting her English.

Before we were friends, we were lovers and went together for many years. We were both control freaks, totally nuts, assertive and very independent. Out on a date one evening, she told me that she was angry at the fact that I looked at other women when I was out on a date with her. I went ballistic.

"How fucking dare you try to control my eyes? **All you see and all you touch is all life and you are ever going to be.** Don't you ever try to control what I see, ever."

My reaction, to what she believed to be a reasonable comment, was so extreme, that thirty years later she not only remembered it but also used it as a rationale when I interrupted her train of thought and corrected her English. I was flabbergasted, amazed that an overreaction on my part, whether justified or not, would be remembered for so many years as a significant and even a transcending moment.

Elegant women and especially educated and intelligent women possess an inner solitude that carries depth charges.

Your focus determines your reality. Sometimes saying the same thing in a slightly different configuration or even just repeating it allow you to absorb its understanding.

The Samurai were respected for their fighting skills, their code, and their loyalty. Although these particulars are exemplary, this is not why the Samurai have been revered for centuries. The reason that they are remembered is because of their entire life style and the living examples' that they encompassed. They lived in a continual state of being involved, with honor, true to their word, focused in the now, persistently improving themselves, their relationships, skills, aesthetics, attention to detail, and striving not for perfection but excellence in all their endeavors.

So how do we emulate them, gain mental strength, and positively change? First identify points of failure and make small changes. This will help you reap disproportionate gains. Take full responsibility for your deeds or indecisions. At the same time, you must understand and internalize that **hope is not a strategy, dreams are for those asleep, this existence is not a dress rehearsal, and life is action.** Satoru

"Here I am! Now what are your other two wishes?"

"How many times do I have to flush before you go away? "

A Loving Profession

Love and Imagination

The school changing tone blasted over the loudspeaker system signaling fifteen hundred children it was time to change classes. Two minutes later the tone shrilled again, and the students emptied into the halls and scurried to walk a city block from one end of the poorly designed building to the other. The school could have been built in a circle or had some hallways and staircases to facilitate the interchange of students, but the school has been constructed for appearance and lacked planning for the human element. Another example of the poor design is the fact that the hallways have a dozen blind angle changes on each floor making them impossible to supervise adequately.

Around a corner, in the hall near my room, a fight broke out. Two boys were testing themselves and had worked their way toward an all-out clumsy battle. One boy, a chunkily built Hispanic, was bouncing around on his toes throwing short jabs in the style of a boxer. The other boy, a lanky Asian, was standing flatfooted and picking his punches carefully. Every time the squat Hispanic boy came close the lanky Asian lad hit him in the face. Students were crowded around the boys, splitting into two ethnic groups, urging them on to fight. A dangerous situation was developing rapidly.

Roy Lordal was walking toward me from the other end of the hall. We each grabbed one of the fighting students and walked them in opposite directions. A new teacher walked past us and held his hand up to one side of his face like horse blinders, so he will not be a witness to the incident. I took the child into my empty room and had him wash his face.

"Use some cold water on your face and then sit down and chill out. I'm locking the door behind me, and no one will bother you. Go to class after you catch your breath."

I walked out into the hall and met Roy again. The corridor was empty of students, and we could talk freely. We looked at each other and simultaneously said, "Are we schmucks?"

We both exposed ourselves to problems because we grabbed students while another teacher had averted his eyes from the entire scene.

"That's what we get for being old-fashioned mules. We have to imitate the new mice and remember it's become a job, not a profession," Roy said to me.

"You're right. We just do the right thing without thinking of the consequences. I hope we don't learn the hard way."

On Tuesday, the principal, a martinet named Bowman Shlong came to my classroom.

"I'd like to see you halfway outside the room."

"Alright."

On the way, out he commented to the class.

"What fantastic work you're doing, beautiful."

I thought to myself, "He must be in a good mood today, he's trying."

"Mike, I went to Roy Lordal's room today and saw a picture of this girl, one of our students."

"Yes, he showed it to me yesterday. An excellent photograph."

"You gave the girl a list of modeling agencies, and he photographed her so she could submit an 8 x 10."

"Yes, Bowman. We've been doing it for ten years. Some of the kids have paid for their college tuition modeling. They don't know how to get started. I pick perhaps one child a year, boy or girl. I have a sharp eye. Then Roy takes a photo. If we both agree that they're photogenic, he gives them a negative, and I provide them with a list of agencies. I make sure that they follow two instructions. One that their mother goes with them to every agency and shoot, and two, that they give absolutely no money to anyone except the ten percent standard modeling commission."

"You can't do this anymore. It might be misinterpreted. You know modeling is just about sex. If anything at all happens, it's two teachers getting a child into modeling. I can't cover for you or myself."

I knew better than to argue with Doctor Shlong. I thought of him as a bold denial of anything constructive. Besides, in this case, his point was well taken. Why expose myself to risk in a society gone mad and preoccupied with sex and bring someone down.

"You're right, Bowman. It's a pity to deprive some children cyberspace actually getting a job, but I will not do it again."

I went upstairs to see Roy. He looked at me, as I entered his room. He put his hands up in the air and talking to the ceiling said, "Is it any wonder why I get headaches? Do you know who told him I was taking pictures, my supervisor, Greenfield. Look at this."

Roy led me to a wall in his room where he had lined up ten photographs of the special education children in his class.

"It's alright to take photos of these kids because Greenfield wants these for the mural on his wall."

"Who pays for this, Roy?"

"Special Education budget. I don't lay any money out anymore since we are never reimbursed."

"Incredible. That's what we get for caring and doing something real and practical."

When I told the story to Jane Shapiro, a supervisor, she looked at me knowingly but with sympathy.

"Well Mike, you know that Bowman Shlong is into control and that he has the Midis touch in reverse, he turned this school of gold to crap."

"I know that Jane, and it's a shame and he and the system are correlated. But that's just a manifestation of Bowman's deeper problems. The key to why Bowman is so compulsively into control is because he lacks imagination. That's why he has destroyed all the initiative in the school because he cannot make dynamic plans without hope. Hope cannot be projected *without imagination. Situations and the future have to be conceptualized as different; instead, he just concentrates on attempting to perfect the present. And feeding into this compulsion is his math teacher training."*

"You know Bowman has been made paranoid by the district office. You know most of them are gay."

"What does that have to do with modeling? I have gay friends, and they're only as sexual or even less preoccupied with sex than my straight friends. I think it's because Bowman is just uptight, has a tiny penis and no girlfriend. But why knock myself out anymore to try to help students integrate into the real world when we have to work without supplies and our hands tied. It's just that a system, that incorporates this philosophy, makes me drained. How can an educational system teach our children unless it has imagination and love?

My love for teaching was matched by the excellent, dedicated teachers that came into the system with me many years ago, and that were going to change the world, one student at a time. We would never have believed that the system could morph into a political job market for minorities and incompetent administrators. It was time to give up my love affair with teaching and move on. Mel Hantz. Student Teacher Coordinator, Tenured Mentor, Motivational speaker, Head of Dept., Teacher of the year, NYC, UFT. BA. AA. MS. MFA.

Leroy's Polonaise

I loved teaching. I had the crazy idea that because I was anti-establishment by inclination, but integrated into the system by my degrees and license's, that I could change it for the better. The young and older teachers in the school had a calling and the insane common denominator that we were going to change the world, improving one student at a time. The energy and devotion that the pedagogues displayed were phenomenal. But that was all before, the asshole of the universe, a politically appointed martinet, became the school's principal. He has a magnified ego, a tiny penis, and the Midas touch in reverse, he turned gold to garbage. But I will tell you more about his catastrophic effects and his martinet personality later.

Like most of my colleagues in the school, I was dedicated, professional, educated, independent and happy. When you are doing something, you love, work becomes a pleasure. I am a sculptor and artist, and I was teaching a subject that most students loved and in which I was proficient. The cooperation among the staff was excellent, and we worked together and supported each other. This allowed the school to function with a golden educational glow. I even went to work early to make coffee for six colleges. In my preparation periods, I created aesthetic attractive bulletin boards and displays throughout the building. I invited and bought lunch for a few favorite and needy students. One of these students had a talent for art and was smart. Unfortunately, Leroy lived in a disadvantaged black environment and was taught to be prejudice all his life. Leroy was needy, defensive, strong, young, and did have a clue about how to conduct his life and have any semblance of success.

While riding my bicycle through the neighbor park on Saturday afternoon, I spied Leroy in the bushes with a girl. He waved to me and smiled. I continued to ride making a mental note to tell him to use protection. A few days later, he was in my spacious classroom eating lunch and drawing. We were alone for a change, and I thought it a good time to give him some advice about sexually transmitted diseases and birth control. As usual, I was playing some music. As I approached Leroy, he said, "How can you listen to that old white man, no words, junk?"

"Leroy, are you listening to the music with your eyes closed and your mind open or with a closed mind and open mouth?"

"That music is old, unsexy, and boring."

"Do you know who wrote this music and who is playing it? Perhaps if you had more information you could at least understand it and maybe accept it."

"It doesn't matter. There are no words and only one instrument and it vibrates funny."

"That's because it's a harpsichord, not a piano. What if I could give you some of the words, would you listen if it could change your life?"

"How could some words and music change my life?"

"You didn't answer my question."

"All right, I'll listen."

"The music is Vladimir Horowitz playing Chopin's Polonaise in A-flat major. It's classic and considered by many, almost a cliché, because it is played so much and is so overt. So, first I want you to just close your eyes and become familiar with the theme."

"Yeah, but it's still honky bullshit. And you're just a cracker who wants to impose old white man shit on me, putting down my black rap."

"Surprise, Leroy. The world is not just black and white; it is many shades of gray in between. And if you want to make it in the world, especially in New York, where twenty different nationalities, speaking many different languages are riding the same bus you are riding, you had better start to think for yourself and not be such a pushover for prejudice propaganda."

"I believe that you're just mad at me because you saw me with that girl in the park, and you're not getting any."

"Leroy, I am not angry at you. However, that girl was way under age, and

you can be put in jail for that. And I bet you did not even use a condom."

"You're just jealous. Even the language you use to talk to me is white man's rap."

"OK, Leroy. How about... Even frogs can fuck, and if you go to jail you will become some man's bitch, and you will be fucked in the ass by different niggers and be forced to suck both black and white cocks. And, if you resist, they will knock out your front teeth, so you can't bite. Then no one will help you, love you, or care about you."

"Shit, I never heard a teacher talk like that."

"Sometimes you have to modify your language to communicate. Did I get the message across to you?"

"I never thought about; even frogs can fuck."

"Do you want to hear some more music? I want you to listen to The Platters and The Ink Spots."

A Woman Who Reads

One morning a husband returns after several hours of fishing and decides to take a nap. Although not familiar with the lake, his wife decides to take their boat out. She motors out a short distance, anchors, and reads her book.

Along comes a Game Warden in his boat. He pulls up alongside the woman and says, "Good morning, Ma'am. What are you doing?"

"Reading a book," she replies, thinking, "Isn't that obvious?"

"You're in a Restricted Fishing Area," he informs her.

"I'm sorry, officer, but I'm not fishing. I'm reading."

"Yes, but you have all the equipment. For all, I know you could start at any moment. I'll have to take you in and write you up."

"If you do that, I'll have to charge you with Sexual assault," says the woman.

"But I haven't even touched you," says the game warden.

"That's true, but you have all the equipment. For all, I know you could start at any moment."

"Have a nice day ma'am," and he left.

MORAL: Never argue with a woman who reads. It's likely she can also think.

Touching

Doctor Louisa had a lot of trouble with her ankles. Because of this, she taught primarily from her desk. This did not necessarily make her a less effective teacher since she could project her loud, clear voice, her perfect pronunciation, and her organized specific instructions. Coupled with an extensive vocabulary and a warm, caring attitude, her stationary position was not a liability, especially in her subject area, which was English and reading. Unfortunately, her physical appearance was less than perfect. Doctor Louisa weighed close to three hundred pounds.

As teachers, tenured in a school, provided the administration is mature and humanistically oriented, we learn to utilize the most positive elements of the staff. There is no other way considering we must interact with these teachers for many years and perhaps for a lifetime career.

Many years ago, members of the staff realized how to utilize what in another profession would be a disadvantage. Many of our children had problems. Some were hyperactive, and some were angry and most needed more attention than we had time for. Almost all of the problem children, however, had one thing in common: they all needed some affection.

I'm not sure how Doctor Louisa came to assume this role in the school, but somehow she became the Camp Mother. When a child seemed to need a hug, they were sent to her. She would talk to the child for a while. If they reacted positively to her suggestion, she would hug them. Her ample girth and enormous breasts would engulf the child in warmth and caring. Some of the worst behavior problems in the school would let their anger dissipate into the soft body of Doctor Louisa, and they returned to class more relaxed. Sometimes a hostile child would even return from her treatment smiling. The Camp Mother position continued for twelve years.

When the new school, built by an architect that did ask for any feedback from the teachers, and the administrator, who was not screened properly, came together, a new policy that permeated the system was instituted. No touching allowed. The sensible act of merely consoling a child by putting your hand on their shoulder, let alone letting them cry on yours or hugging, became verboten. The contact might be misinterpreted. So, for the one-in-a-hundred student that might react negatively to some well-meaning or slight contact, the ninety-nine children were deprived and forced to live in a colder, non-touching environment. This is the direction of our new over-litigious society and our safety oriented culture.

We spend so much time working, often sitting hunched at a desk, and typing for hours. Our bodies need a chance to relax. Natural movement, whether outside or in the comfort of our homes, does wonders for us physically and mentally.

Life is a great teacher. When you don't learn a lesson, it will repeat it.

Forget what hurt you but never forget what it taught you.

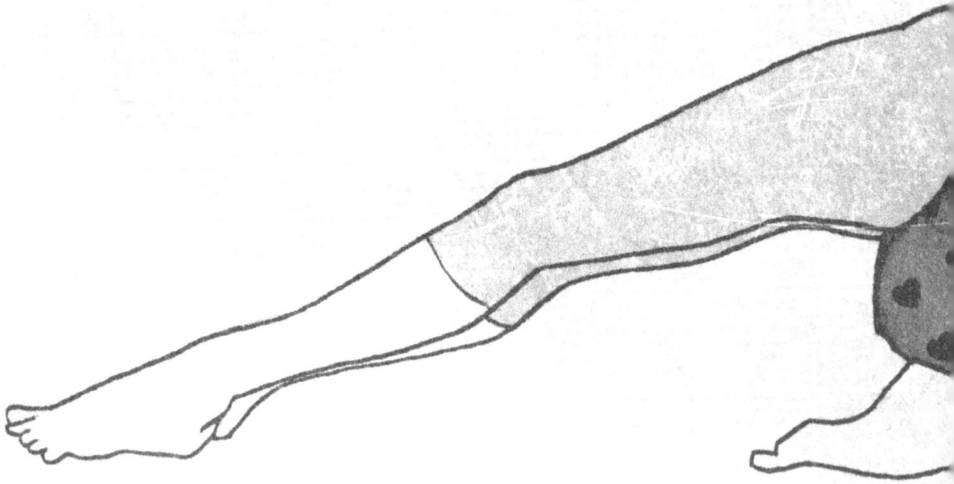

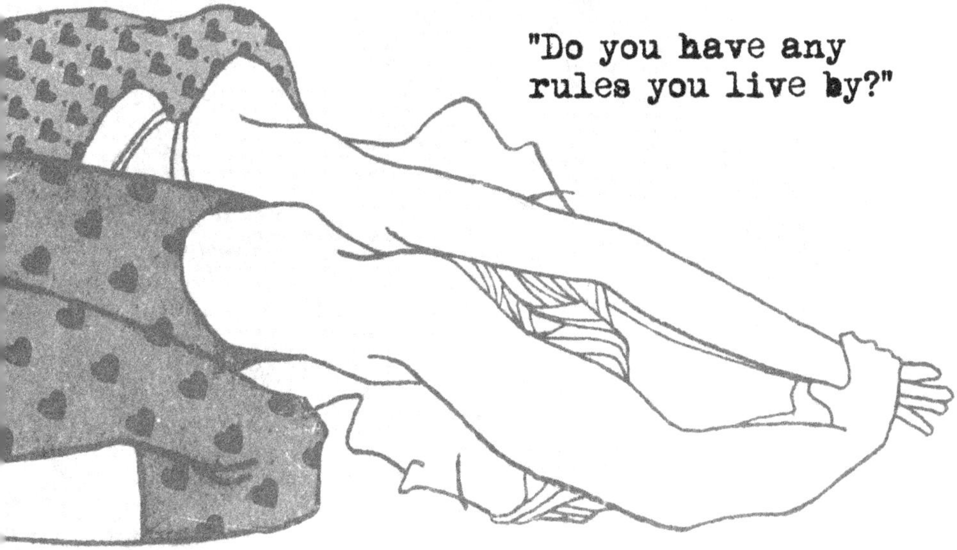

"Do you have any rules you live by?"

"See no evil, hear no evil, and date no evil."

The Vulture and The Peahen

It shows in her eyes that last month went by very dry and life is just do or die.

I was at a party and was introduced to a bright-eyed, soft and yet tough, woman lawyer with a genial but slightly pugnacious air. I was not attracted to anyone for a while, but this woman made the hair on the back of my neck stand up. I was living with a lady half my age at the time, who was getting lazier by the week. I was reluctant but ultimately lost at the prospect of feeling again.

The woman I was living with grew away from me and was moving toward an independent life. We both knew that it would only be a short time until our relationship changed significantly and she moved out. An old man would be a fool to believe that a young woman would stay with him, as he became an old geezer. I was born at night, but not last night.

I invited the intensely verbal lawyer out to lunch with the hope of establishing some foundation for interaction in the future, and to tell her the truth about my situation privately. I also wanted to experience her again and consider if the intense feelings I felt were just an evening's fluctuations or a significant positive emotion.

I was a little confused emotionally because I wanted to hold and comfort her, something I felt that she needed. At the same time, I could not read her feeling toward men and me in general. It was even more confusing because she radiated competence, yet behind her eyes was a deep sadness.

When I called her, I got the impression that she would always be too busy. She was overworked and under-loved. She had been scared in the past and had little faith in "married" men. She thought I was disingenuous, but she was trained as a lawyer and thought linearly. Because she thought linearly and was so independent, she lived alone in an emotional desert.

How could I explain to her that I was unprepared when I met her? For **the future always comes before you're ready to give up the present.** It was little use telling her that things were going to change. She did not believe me. It was the same romantic misfortune again.

Was I destined to repeat the same mistake? For weeks, after meeting this woman, I dreamt that I was and came back as a buzzard. I circled above, seeing the fresh earth and desert below, never allowed to rest upon the solid ground. My emotions were encapsulated in the eggs of my chicks, and a peahen was barely keeping them warm. Was I being punished for some past transgression in a previous life that I did not remember? **In this life, as a Zen Buddhist, I can accept and discern the positive in almost every situation. As a vulture, I can get around, fly over the earth, no one will bother me, and I can eat anything.**

A few months later, as scheduled, Mercedes, the woman I was with moved out. We broke up. Swallowing my pride and ego, I sent the brilliant lawyer a copy of this whole story in the hope that she would call me, and that we could meet again. I mailed the letter on a Thursday, knowing that she would receive it on a Monday. I was excited by the prospect of interacting with her again. At the gym, on Monday afternoon, I cut my work out a little short because I was thinking so much about talking to my sad lawyer again.

I could not get her out of my mind so raced home to her voice or message. The answering machine recorded three messages, but none were from her. I must have guessed wrong, but I thought that my introduction, a four-page story about us, would be unique enough so that she would call. Perhaps she was already with someone else or simply did not want to have anything to do with me. I was sad and disappointed. As often was my way, I put all my proverbial emotional eggs in one basket, and nothing hatched.

Perhaps I should call some of the women that I was only peripherally interested in and get back into the harmonious communication for which I strive. After all, I was certainly out of practice. I called three women whose numbers I gained from various occasions. One I knew for several years and only wanted as a friend, but it still would get me back into a dating scenario. I made one date for the following week and slightly assuaged my deflated ego.

The phone rang, while I was working on my desk. It was Ashley, the beautiful lawyer, with her hypnotic voice. She had received the letter early in the day but put it aside because she was too busy and wanted to read it privately. The letter flattered her. I was delighted.

"I'm so happy you called. I was beginning to wonder."

"I wanted to call you from the office, but it's always so busy. What did you mean by linearly? Do you believe I think so narrowly?"

"No. I didn't mean to imply narrowness, just a particular follow the numbers, this must be in place before the next phase occurs."

We talked for a while, an intricate arabesque of expectations and intentions, and she gave me her home number. She was open and accepting of me, and I languished in the potential. We made a date to talk the next day, and I hung up feeling elated and relieved. The next day we talked for a half hour, and she revealed to me why her marriage broke up. I knew from her sadness, which made my heart go out to her without really knowing why, that she had been burnt by her marriage. I did not know, however, that she had been tortured. Her ex-husband lied to her about everything that was important to her and lacked integrity. But, how could Ashley, who had such a right level of perception, have fallen for this man or believed him?

An hour later, I was on my way out and into the city. The walk sign across the street blinked on, and I looked at the oncoming traffic. I was still thinking about Ashley and the pain she must have gone through. A blue car was making a quick right turn careened around the corner heading straight for me. I ran ahead to get out of its way barely avoiding the car.

"You asshole," I yelled at the driver.

"I wasn't going to kill you. There is no reason to talk like that."

"What would you have done if you hit me? Said you are sorry? You are driving too fast, and you did not have control of the car, and you can't handle the horsepower. So, you are an asshole."

"You have some vocabulary."

"Yes I do, it's extensive and very precise."

This man almost hit me with his car. If I were not quick enough to jump out of the way, I would have been injured. Now he was arguing with me for calling him a name. Ten years ago, I would have planted a karate kick to the side of his car and dented it. Then, if the guy dared to open his door to get out, I would have kick slammed the door across his legs. But, today I was hesitant. Could I have mellowed or was I getting old? Perhaps I was only weary of fighting with incompetent people who suffered from anal-cranial inversion.

I spoke to Ashley the next day and mentioned the car that almost killed me. She never asked about the details. She also seemed unaware that empathically, I felt her pain. Was she completely self-possessed or hadn't she anyone to talk to about herself, or someone who cared? Or perhaps she was just trying to tell me about herself and assumed that I would tell her about me.

Somehow Ashley slowed me down. My tendency to jump in emotionally with both feet was tempered by her caution and lack of trust. Then again, I thought about her a lot more than she had thought about me. After all, the week after she met me, she probably forgot about me, never thinking I would call again. Whereas, I started to write the story, knowing that I would again attempt to interact with her.

I must still be impulsive because I want instant closeness. Perhaps I miss the intimacy of a relationship, the compensations, privacy, and quiet, are not enough. I also want a woman that needs a man. So many women today have predisposed themselves for a life without a male companion, or such a particular type of individual that when they meet an available, compatible man they screen him so comprehensively, that unless he can cut through their prerequisites, ghosts, and baggage, he just becomes someone to use as a transitional diversion or someone who might slightly improve their life. Amazingly, from men, I hear the same less complicated reason as to why they are not in a relationship. "It's just not worth it."

I started to think of Ashley as ice cream, or maybe ice queen, but definitely as dessert. She was sweet, beautiful to look at, complex and possessed good taste. The only problem that I did not yet know the answer to, was, is the dessert good enough to be worth consuming all those calories?

The story of my interaction with Ashley should have ended here. For three weeks, I tried to make a date to see her, and all that occurred was some long phone conversations. Although I could listen to her forever, because I loved her intelligent phraseology and her seductive voice, I was not used to being such a low priority. However, since she appeared to be such a fine and special lady, I continued to pursue.

When at last she seemingly reluctantly made a date with me and gave me her address, number 444, a few pieces of the puzzle aligned themselves. I went back to the novel, Dead Man Float; I'd been working on and scrolled up to the chapter named 444. I had no doubt that the story was written coinciding with Ashley moving into her new apartment at 444 East 77th Street. Was my prescience playing tricks with my mind and life?

FOUR FORTY-FOUR

There was not enough fresh air, and the room was too hot. My left ear was against the pillow, and I could feel the throbbing pulse of a vein in my neck. I half opened my eyes and stared at the clock. The red display was four forty-four. In my semi-awaked state, the numbers resembled three devil's pitchforks. Like the eyes of a snake, the colon after the first number blinked menacingly every second.

I was troubled about waking up so many nights at the same time, and my sleep interrupted by a reoccurring dream. I knew from previous experience with my prescience that the 444 was going to correlate with something negative, a particular location, and a woman. In the dream, which was full of anxiety, frustration, explosions and destruction, I needed this woman to put her arms around me so that I could rescue her, and she could warn me. She was reluctant because I was a stranger. Ironically, at the same time, a friend was betraying her. Her openness and trust and my speed were essential, but I could make no headway convincing her. Perhaps the dream was symbolic of my frustration, but knowing my proclivity for predictions, I saw the vision as a future event. My mind would not turn off and I started to worry about everything; my declining strength, the lack of space not being able to throw out books and things that I have saved for years.

I got out of bed and walked to the kitchen. The apartment was full of eerie tiny diodes and lights. All the light switches had minuscule white bulbs inside them, and every appliance,

speaker, stereo component, computer, external drive, Wi-Fi box, modem, router, transformers, signal boxes, answering machines, phones, and all the audiovisual equipment possessed a luminous clock or several colored diodes. Four rooms had small, green, night-lights, permanently on, that disappeared in the daylight. The entire apartment possessed the potential to come alive with light and sound if any of the tiny lights were disturbed.

I drank some cold seltzer and turned the cap tightly, so the gas would not escape. I had to switch hands because my left thumb was sprained. I always felt apprehensive and vulnerable, when something on my body was injured. Perhaps that was why I had this floating anxiety?

I walked into the living room and looked out the window. No lights were on across the street or in the two high-rise houses a block away. I wandered around aimlessly waiting for the emotional pain I was feeling to subside. Too many little pains and parts of my body were breaking down. All the injuries I succumbed to, and all the accidents in sports, the army, and work, were now adding up to one big hurt- the death of a thousand cuts. Perhaps I was trying to deal with the cumulative pain. Perhaps it was the realization of the beginning of the end, getting old, and the end of my immortality.

I went into the den and sat at my desk. Leaning back into the luxuriously soft leather of my office chair, I put my bare feet on top of the expansive maple desk. The luxurious texture and comfort of the chair made me feel better.

What troubles did I have that were unsolvable? I thought about the worst-case scenarios that could develop. I could handle most of them, so why worry now? I should wait until there is a serious difficulty that I cannot resolve before I lay awake at night trying to find solutions to troubles that do not yet exist or that are not solvable at this point.

The quilt felt warm as I slid under it and covered my cold feet. I mused, learn from yesterday... live for today in the now... look to tomorrow... rest in the now tonight.

I read the story and reviewed what had happened so far between Ashley and me. It explained some of my feelings of wanting to comfort her but begged other questions. For sure, she didn't trust me because of her past experiences or was not attracted to me, so I could never rescue her from her sad future. I was probably too late anyway, considering her indecisiveness and procrastination in allowing me to enter her life. She did not seem to need saving from anything or anyone, but I was so emotionally attracted to her. Another loose end was, who was the friend that would betray her and what did that have to do with saving her? As if it were possible to save anyone.

Pygmalion and Galatea are the names in the story of the sculpture whose work became real after the sculptor put everything he had into creating, changing, and saving his work of art. Saving someone was how I felt emotionally, but intellectually... no more Galatea's for this sculptor.

Time has a peripatetic way of playing with my life and emotions. So many times, I have been able to know events in the future, but rarely have I been able to change the outcomes. Should I show Ashley the ending to the story and risk her turning away from me forever? Perhaps she might give me the correlation's necessary for closure? At least now I think I understand both dreams.

Ashley was a peahen. She was beautiful in every way and possessed everything except spirituality. I knew her future, but her lack of spirituality would be a formidable obstacle to our mutual happiness. She did not know when to compromise, which is essential when entering a new relationship. Not without reason, Ashley was an emotional chicken juxtaposition against a flying risk taker. With Ashley, I was driving in the wrong direction on a one-way street. She was the personification of the expression, "What care I how good she be, if she not be good to me."

She was a woman whose future I could read, but she was emotionally inaccessible. She said, "We have very different lifestyles." I answered her, "Yeah, you drink white wine and I drink sake. That certainly makes us incompatible." The thoughts and images that she projected would only make my life and nights harder. I had time and circumvented the step of how to become a millionaire by just living like one. She, however, wanted to live like one but instead simply spent her life working.

Even though I knew her troubled future, the problems that she was going to endure, fool that I was, I was still willing to interact with her because I looked into her essence and it revealed a remarkable mind and soul. It was much more her loss than mine, although we probably did not have the same expectations. She would never know.

There is always an obstacle
in the way to love, but that
is what contributes to the
intensity.

My Friend Ann Emailed Me

Hi Mike, I had dinner last night with S & H friends of mine for many years. They remembered you from various occasions and asked for your e-mail address. They have a lady friend who they think would be of interest. Best, Ann.

Hi, Ann: Send us Mike's contact information and let him know we are passing it along to Annie M. a formerly married, (possibly divorced,) artist and a set designer. S & H

Hi, Thank you, Ann. I hope everything is good with you. Please give S & H my regards and email address. Let's have a drink together. Cheers, Mike

Hi Mike: Thought you might be interested in meeting a friend of ours Annie. She is an artist, (just had a show open in Chelsea last month,) and designer. Besides, she is attractive, witty, and would be a delightful companion for a drink, coffee, etc. Hope all is well with you. H & S

Hi Annie, Friends have a tendency to say nice things about us and raise our expectations. But, since I am a little unconventional, I thought I would send you a personal ad I'm thinking of going on-line with. It has a tagline that I believe will attract the woman I want. It also tells of my interests and is honest and hopefully enticing. Do you live in Manhattan? Cheers, Mike

Personal ad.

Hi, I'm looking for a tallish, slim, attractive woman, 35-45, in good health, non-smoker, nurturing, who is oral and into necrophilia.

She must have a sense of humor and be spiritual. I am six feet tall, blue eyes, some gray hair, and in fair shape. I sleep in the nude. I only make love in the morning and drink good red wine every night.

I live with my cousin Quasimodo and his wife Esmeralda. We are bell ringers. I am looking for the last woman I am going to be with.

I enclose a picture of me taken just a few hours ago. If you're interested in getting together, please send me a photo of you. Serious resonance only, please.

P.S. I'm getting contact lenses soon.

Cheers, Mike

Dear Mike, I do live in Manhattan - Upper West. Here is an ad that I placed and oddly got very little response:

A menopausal woman in the midst of ugly divorce seeks soul mate or just a one-night stand. Successful, intelligent, well read, considered threatening by some. Drinks and takes antidepressants- in splendid shape. Has child! Can't travel to exotic places at the drop if a hat! Hates golf. Hates boating and hates those sports shirts with no sleeves. Also, hates anyone who uses the term LOL, which rules out just about every-one on dating services.

Loves painting, writing, friends, food, art, and nature. Is pagan. Funny that you live with the Modos - I have known them for years. Charming people though a little on the deaf side. If any of this interests you, must be very peculiar - which is a start... Anne

Hi Annie,

How refreshing, someone who can communicate. I assume you are a painter, can I see your work? Most people try to give a good first impression. I believe in putting my worse step forward without a facade. Then, if you accept the worse, there is no place to go but positively forward. So, here are few of the highlights: I am a workaholic, but I want to be a lazy bum. All I really want to do is learn to play chess and drink fine red wine.

I used to know everything, but now I'm drain bamaged. I am a student of Zen Buddhism. I am a health and clean nut. I write about my friends. I am thirteen hundred years old. I am an elitist and liberal Nazi. Much more to come. Isn't Annie usually spelled, Anny? How old is your child? Do you have a 9-5 job? What do you drink? Soon, Mike

Dear Mike, Thanks for passing the first test. You responded.10 points for Gryffindor! It seems we have a few things in common.

Also, a workaholic - in my youth driven by burning ambition and the desire to both please my parents and leave them far behind. After living on my own for years I should have been in college, (I ran off to Hollywood and worked in the movie studios as a draftsman and model maker.) I returned east and went to Vassar drama school for graduate school to study design.

I was 21. I graduated at 24 and began working as a designer and never stopped. You can see images on my website, which are very nice - but they don't really show what I do - concept, storytelling, transformations, movement, light, and timing - the sculpting of space.

As a designer, I am an old Grand Dame. I am in all the books of the last 25 years. Young aspiring grad students look at me -drooling and eager and think, "How come she has such an impressive career - I want it, I want it!" I wave my leathery spotted arm and croak, "darlings, in my day, we didn't need actors - we had scenery!"

As a painter - I am much younger- an "emerging" artist with all the hopeful ambition that it accompanies. Mostly - when it is going well - I just enjoy it. It is like an intense meditation that also utilizes everything that I have ever looked at and all that is before me.

But I think I am getting a little pretentious here so; I love to drink wine - exquisite red - very cold and dry white and rock gut retsina. I am highly social, but also need great swaths of time to be left alone. My son is 6 and is a miracle. He is the smartest funniest and most beautiful and empathetic person I have ever known, and I love him beyond anything.

I also have great love for humanity, but loath the person standing next to me on the Starbucks' line asking for some ridiculous drink while talking on the cell-phone and holding on to her double stroller. I am somewhat tired of living in New York, but I am stuck there till Chris goes to college. I have a gorgeous old stone house from 1780 upstate, which is surrounded by woods - which I can escape to, (I am here now,) and hope that I don't lose it in the divorce, as it keeps me sane. The sun is out and I have to go back to the city this afternoon, so I must paint.

Your sets are excellent. I appreciate your competence. I have to see your paintings in person to get an accurate view. I'm afraid if I tell you all about me, I will have no stories to tell you over drinks. But, here are some more highlights.

I was born in Brooklyn, left home when I was sixteen to live in the Village. Married in my twenties for seven years, (we were both too young.) Didn't have any money. Worked days and went to school at night for twenty-seven years. Became very smart, peaked early, went into education, systematically lost intellect and vocabulary every year.

Now I know nothing, so I have written a book giving advice on how to live. You might keep your stone house, if you have a good lawyer. Talk more soon. Mike

Dear Mike, Thank you about the sets. I am (was) excellent at that for a while but now feel like a dinosaur, as I design with a pencil - know only a little Photo-Shop and no Cad drawing at all. The paintings evolve - and that is all I can say about them. I am always surprised at what they turn out to be, as I feel that I am not really the one painting - the result is that I don't take it at all personally, if people hate them - sometimes I find them ugly myself, but that is all part of moving forward... which brings me to the absorbing subject. I think we would have a lot to talk about - I am very interested in Zen philosophy and would love to learn more. I credit Zen thinking with allowing me finally to successfully have a child. Now more than ever - I am thrashing around trying to "solve" my life - and I need to be reminded that the path of least resistance - the Way - is the way -so don't worry about "no stories."

I also was born in Brooklyn, and I also moved out at 16. In fact - I gave my parents a kitten, the Christmas, that I announced I had rented an apartment with a friend on East 88th Street - (a frightening dump with a male prostitute living right across the hall from us - his befuddled clients used to come to our door and looked very dismayed when a beautiful young girl answered the door - we would politely point to his door). My parents loved the kitten and said good riddance to me. I almost got married in Las Vegas- driving across country at 18 with a man on my way to live with him in California. Thank god - my parents talked me out of it.

I used to be super smart too. And always the youngest person in the room. Now, I am the oldest mom in my son's grade class and can't remember to tell my doctor that I am experiencing memory loss.

You sound sagacious. When I get a moment, I will read A Way to Live-Zen. My days are filled with nonsense. Later?

Annie, I know how you feel about designing with a pencil. I was trained at the Cooper Union to do paste-ups and mechanicals. The kids today don't even know what that is, let alone to use rubber cement.

I LOVE RUBBER CEMENT. MY FATHER TAUGHT ME HOW TO USE IT WHEN I WAS THREE.

I used to be a Luddite then jumped into the new computer age. But what is LOL?

LAUGH OUT LOUD. People write it after they think they have said something funny - it is very annoying.

The book was just given to my excellent agent. The blog, just two months old is the book. If you want to read it, just start at the blog first post. I understand you're trying to solve your life; I am always trying to "finish" mine. Interesting that we both gave up home early risking security for independence.

I had to get away from them (my parents). It turned out to be a really interesting experience, but it was hard and scary. I was glad to get back to school after three years of adult life.

Mike, your website, knotscupture.com, is amazing. I love the knots! Very ancient - Delphic. I have been to the Omphalos - have you? I designed a play once, based on the life of Cellini, so I had to bone up on the lost wax technique. It is funny - you do work to last for the ages - and mine lasts for five performances. I would love to see the work in person - it looks very touchable. Where is your foundry? And do you live there? I can't imagine a coop board allowing iron mongering but who knows... I am looking for apartments today. Which is even harder than finding love - though hope spring's eternal. Later. A

Hi, Annie, Change seems to be accelerating. Now it takes me a whole day just to go to the gym. All my foundries in the city, as well as the plating companies and iron men, have closed. I cast in Arizona, New Jersey, and LIC. How did you know I live in a coop? Glad you like my site and sculpture. Why are you looking for apartments? Where? Love... You are an optimist. I can't even find a good foot massage. Talk more next week. Cheers, M

Work problem is so sad, about the foundries. I used to have a work only studio on the top floor of a big building on Washington Street. Every morning I would walk down along 14th Street and through the hanging headless cows. The butchers would hold the carcasses aside to let me pass through. They were so gallant in their blood-soaked white coats and yellow rubber boots. Now they too are all gone. Ha! I have a foot massage MACHINE, but I don't use it much. I go to the local Chinese Opium Den for reflexology. It usually is pretty good. So, another thing we have in common - love of foot massages. My feet are a mess - ever since I gave birth to my son, the three toes on my right foot have gone numb - and the odd thing is I remember feeling the contractions IN THEM. Doctors laugh at me when I complain about this. If you had a Chinese doctor, he not only would believe you but also cure you.

I am looking for an apartment on the Upper West Side - and I think I might end up in Harlem. As you know - having space in the city has always been a problem and those of us who need a studio - not a little corner to put a desk and a computer- have always had to be adventurous about where they live. I have a huge apartment now, but I will probably have to sell it and split the proceeds in the DIVORCE.

Can't you give him the stone house and keep the apartment? What a pain to have to move. Sorry.

I don't want to fight for it - there are other things to fight for- and I need the money as well. So - I am looking at stuff to see what I can afford - that has two bedrooms, a living room and that extra room to work in. I am also stuck on the Upper West as my son goes to a school on West 96th Street. The hundreds by the river look very nice, and there are some larger apartments though so far I have only seen things with a view of a brick wall - which will make me suicidal. How did your work go this weekend? Annie

Work always goes fine but I must reevaluate my goals. The excellent gallery Vorpal, (read storage and sales,) I was in for twenty years closed. I am so spoiled and used to having space and selling. But everything in my life is changing, and I'm changing everything in my life. Cheers, Mike

Dear Mike, I have been looking for an acupuncturist for my foot problem - could you recommend someone?

My soon to be ex, has no interest in the stone house - and I love it to bits. A New York apartment is a soulless thing - the house is a living breathing home for birds, snakes, and mice, etc. and it comforts me. There is no controversy - plus regarding monetary value - it would not make enough of a difference to warrant giving it up. The cleaner break - the Tou way is to sell and move out of here.

Talk about life changing ... I feel like I have lived at least ten lives already - not counting the ones that came before this one! I guess, when push comes to shove, I am pretty resilient. And, as a designer, I do like the psychological ramifications of a new space - a new plan - clean white new walls. Something good always comes of it.

I found a place yesterday that I really liked. It is in a new neighborhood too, West 110th Street. Do you know up there? It has a very nice feeling - more like old New York. The price is higher than I would like - but from my bed, I could see a large swathe of the river with boats going by. And there is a bedroom for my little boy and a library/ studio for me. I will try to put a down payment together and make an offer. So many artists are in the same boat - galleries closing right and left. Who would have thought that everything would get so crummy as we got older? Well - at least when we were young it was exciting, and there were so many possibilities - everything was better than expected.

I feel so sorry for young people today. I went to a grand design show at SVA the other night - and I don't even know what to say to these kids anymore. At least we had our day! Say - you still haven't told me what neighborhood you live in. Are you going to divulge that? Annie

Annie,

Sure, why not? I used to work in the foundry at SVA. I cast Styrofoam every week for years but then they just became another place that closed down when the smell of casting bothered the neighbors.

> By car take FDR drive south downtown. You pass under the Williamsburg Bridge. One exit past the Houston Street exit is the Grand Street exit. Make a right turn & get off the Grand Street exit and drive down Grand Street. Count six (6) lights. Look for parking. There is a CVS pharmacy on my corner.
>
> BY TRAIN B, D, Q Grand Street stop.
>
> (Be sure to see the fantastic fish and tree mosaics on the walls.)
>
> Stay on the north side; walk in the direction that you exit (East) for about ten minutes. (12 short blocks.) Walk east until you pass a large church on your left, (Saint Mary.)
>
> Scenic route. #6 Spring Street stop. Take a cab or twenty-minute walk. Walk three long blocks south, downtown, to Grand Street. Make a left on Grand. Walk east through little Italy and Chinatown past the Lower East Side shopping district.

M, Wow. How exotic. Do you have a huge loft?

No, I have a small apartment with a slit of a terrace but excellent views and light.

You are on the other side of the world from me. Do you think this will come between us?

Absolutely.

I am upstate with my son this weekend — and working at The Met all of next. Hoping this difficult phase of my life will smooth out soon. I am not at my best — but this virtual chat has helped so thanks for that.

That's my role-a cyber space fantasy.

Later. Cheers, Mike

I believe that my sarcastic answer or joke about absolutely not traveling to "the other side of the world" to see Annie turned her off to communicating or maybe it was that saying my role was a cyberspace fantasy was taken in the wrong way. Or maybe she chickened out or just changed her mind. I waited in vain for Annie to email me back and ask "why?" I wanted to sandbag her and convey how incapacitated I was without crying. I was going to tell her why traveling, even though it was only an hour or two away, was out of the question for a while. I was going to email her the story and the letter to tell Annie about the two accidental experiences that I had in rapid secession that made traveling to her impossible. The letters and the story said it all in the way of explanation but she never emailed me again.

Moment of Truth

Lands' End Electric Equipment & Supply Corp.
Grand Street NYC10013-3735

Dear Sir,

Some time ago I bought several cases of bulbs. The CXL bulbs, 75PAR-20FL indoor/outdoor HALOGEN flood, 2,000-hour life, (See receipts enclosed,) made in China are all defective. All the ones I have used have exploded.

One bulb exploded as I passed under it, spraying glass and startling me. In my haste to protect myself from the shower of glass, I walked into the corner of my sofa fracturing my toe. This injury will take at least six weeks to heal before I can walk normally. The doctor that treated me is Steve Abraham. D.P.M. Foot specialist 425 Grand Street, NYC10002 (212) 475-5540.

Another bulb exploded in a carpeted room showering tiny slivers of glass onto the carpet. Aggressive vacuuming still is unable to remove the tiny sharp glass shards from the carpets. Since I do not wear shoes in my home, glass on the floor and in the carpets, is a major problem.

The exploding bulbs are directly responsible for these incidents and my injury. The CXL Chinese company has no address or contact reference on their box or cartons. Please send to me the contacts for the company, the importer, or the distributor so I can bring this matter to their attention and request compensation for the damages. I believe your importer is Topaz Electric, but this company asserts that they only use American made bulbs. Also, these incandescent exploding bulbs may be responsible for some of the many fires that the Chinatown area experiences and should be investigated and taken off the market.

Thank you.
Mike Lance

Moment of Truth

I was on my way to pickup two cutting discs for sculpting at the hardware store and then go shopping for groceries. It was a clear sunny day and the air was cool, perfect for walking. I always try to stride the less crowded Streets to avoid people who walk slowly or sideways. Also so many people who use cell phones are unaware of their surroundings that you have to dodge them less they bump into you. And now, since the advent of tiny speakers, it's imposable to tell the crazies since so many souls appear to be talking to themselves.

I turned off the main avenue and down a dead Street ringed with parking lots. Ahead of me were three people slowly walking and talking.

Two men flanked a woman in tight jeans and high boots. The taller man on the left wore a camouflage jacket and black jeans. The shorter man had a red bandana around his head and very loose fitting pants and jacket. They blocked the sidewalk and their cigarette smoke stunk and I resolved to go around them by stepping into the gutter. As I approached them from behind, the red bandana man turned around and said to me, "Are you looking at her ass?" I thought of answering him, "Am I supposed to walk with my eyes closed?" But I ignored him and moved to pass them in the gutter. The taller man looked at me menacingly and moved toward me to cut me off from passing. If my knees were in better shape, I would have turned and put some distance between us, but I can no longer run.

These guys were stoned ultra macho and out to impress the girl by beating up another man. I looked around for help but the Street was empty. I was going to catch a pounding and maybe worse. The bigger guy ran toward me with his arms out to catch me. The shorter one began to take off his jacket. As the big guy ran at me, I moved to the left and ducked under his right side at the same time, grabbing his arm and putting it in back of my neck. Stepping in back of him and putting my right arm across his chest and using his momentum, I leaned forward and threw him over my back. He landed hard on the concrete as the shorter man repeatedly hit me in the back from behind. I turned and kicked his locked knee, bringing my foot all the way down to his calf. His knee splintered and his eyes opened wide with pain and disbelief. The other man was up, blood all over his camouflaged jacket, and ferociously swinging his fists. Professionally he moved to the left as if he was fighting a right-handed man. I faked a right and set him up. I caught him with a good left straight from the shoulder, felt his jaw fracture, heard the tear of my arm muscle, and watched him go down.

The entire fight took less than five minutes. In that short time I went from competent to vulnerable to disabled. A wave of nausea and frustration permeated me. How stupid can I be? Why didn't I use my brain to extradite myself from the situation? I thought of our solders in Iraq. This must be what it feels like to take a bullet in the arm. No, a bullet has to be much worse. I looked back only once to see the woman leaning over the men, who were lying on the ground, and the big guy spitting teeth.

My arm popped when I hit him and I instantly realized that I hurt myself badly. I could not lift my good left arm at all. I walked away, went home and called the doctor for an emergency appointment. Two hours later, I was told that I ripped the muscle off the bone and that after the operation it would take six months and lots of therapy to repair the arm.

A week after the operation, with my good left arm in a sling, I was replacing a bulb that had burnt out. In each room, one of the light fixtures is wired to an automatic on/off switch that turns the lights on at dusk. These light usually burn out first since they are used the most. Later on that evening, as I passed under the living room light, as it went on, it exploded. To avoid the flying glass, I walked into the corner of the sofa and fractured my toe. It would be six weeks until I could walk normally and put a shoe on my foot.

What you wear affects how you behave.

If you can't change it, let it go.

Mistakes and Failures

As a human being, one has been endowed with just enough intelligence to be able to see clearly how utterly inadequate that intelligence is when confronted with what exists. I sometimes say, when I meet a sharp younger person, "If I knew what I know now, at your age, by now I'd be king.

All of us have the desire to know more and have made so many mistakes. Taking ownership of failure builds the foundation for success. Use the experience to go forward having learned what not to do again. Do not be disheartened by occasional blunders or failures. Turn the next similar situation around by not repeating the error. Do not dwell one moment on your past miscalculations. So why not learn from my faux pas and the errors of others. Or, you can live a few lifetimes and make all the mistakes yourself. Can you afford it?

All flowers need manure.

Open your eyes and see in the Now, simplify, understand, journey, search, meditate, read, plan, and begin.

Some people are so independent that they are alone.

If you let a little set back stop you from action or if defensively you don't take the chance at communicating, or at least obtaining an explanation that discontinues the communication, then you have not allowed yourself the opportunity for discovery.

Women need us. You can't take batteries home to meet your mother.

Life is either a daring adventure or nothing. There is little room in the middle ground. Security does not exist in nature, nor do the children of men as a whole experience it. Avoiding danger is no safer in the long run than exposure - Helen Keller

Rejection like old age is a part of life, both suck. The alternatives, no action, and death are a lot worse. Unfortunately, we hear rejection louder than praise. But, we have to live with refusal and accept the negative aspects; we must accommodate and move on. If you are actively seeking a new love, you must be somewhat aggressive. You will be bashed and dismissed: so what? The idea is to end in triumph and obtain your goal.

Some thoughtful strategies might be to tell yourself and believe; the person didn't know me anyway, they didn't want to take the risk, there is no accounting for taste, no one really knows how good I am, no one knows what I have to give. But, most of all, it only takes just one person to accept and love you. You can lessen the pain by just trying again. If they say no, just say to yourself, next!

Great love and great achievements involve great risk.

Hate is easy. Love takes courage.

Modern pornography carpet bombed the darker images of sex and brought every tiny sexual aspect into the bright spotlight. Imagine the Victorian reaction of a full penis virginal modern pornographic sex scene the size of a movie theater scene. Our entire concept of sex is continually evolving but is it getting better?

If you have to choose between two evils always pick the one you have never tried, and never regret. If it's good, it's wonderful. If it's bad, it's experience.

A young couple moves into a new neighborhood. The next morning, while they are eating breakfast, the young woman sees her neighbor hanging the wash outside.

"That laundry is not very clean," she said. "She doesn't know how to wash correctly. Perhaps she needs better laundry soap."

Her husband looked on but remained silent.

Every time her neighbor would hang her wash to dry, the young woman would make the same comments. About one month later, the woman was surprised to see a nice clean wash on the line and said to her husband:

"Look, she has learned how to wash correctly. I wonder who taught her this."

The husband said, "I got up early this morning and cleaned our windows."

And so, it is with life. **What we see when watching others depends on the purity of the window through which we look.**

New bars are opening up where you contact each other through a computer and live television screens. Is this the future of singles bars for the joystick generation? A generation that has fantastically fast reflexes developed by playing video games and minds that have never been challenged for original thoughts.

Be careful of the computer age and the Internet information age. It is becoming easier to download information a second or third time then to memorize it. We no longer have to remember anything. Just Google it, and the machine and phone remember for us. We are spending our lives in front of a screen mixing, mashing, downloading, uploading and feeding the network. This magnified, collaborative interaction, complexly ebbed, into our environment and lives, is morphing into our identity and diminishing our verbal interacting abilities.

ALERT: Scammers have become rampant and more sophisticated about your Emails. Do not click the link of anyone you are not completely sure of, no companies, free coupons, unsolicited free info, from anyone, even what looks like a highly credible source. Your phone has also become scammer "phishing" heaven. Do not give any personal information to anyone for any reason whatsoever. I'm sorry about the profiling, but, when someone with an Indian accent calls me, I just hang up.

Reciprocity should come easily and often. For some however, even if you positively changed their lives significantly for years, by your interaction, support, creativity, work, and actions, it is not enough. Perhaps you should develop some new friendships?

Traditionally sex has always been a secretive personally private activity. It is a powerful force to unite people. If you share your intimate secrets with friends, it dilutes the intimacy of your relationship and your individuality. Sharing your secrets brings you closer to you friends and communicating secrets helps to establish human and especially working relationship. If, however, you are too open, too bragging or too indiscrete you are condemned as having neither honor nor backbone, and you are a silly non-respected gossip. Friendships nowadays are being ratcheted up to the point where they are sabotaging our romantic relationships. Be careful whom you confide in. **Keep your own council.**

"Hi cutie, how about you and I hitting the hotspots?"

"Sorry, I don't date
outside my species."

Golden Locks

Love is out to get me.

Mary and I just met in a coffee shop in the West Village while we were both buying fresh ground coffee. We both put our fingers into the sack that held the great roasted beans called Blue Mountain and extracted a few to chew. The coffee costs fifty dollars a pound, so we looked around carefully before absconding with a few treats.

"I never met anyone before who chewed beans," I said to Mary.

"Oh, they are so delicious. I used to chew them all the time."

"I can tell by your sun-bleached hair that you're not from around and you don't spend much time in New York."

"No, I'm from Hawaii, but I'm going to be moving to New York soon."

We had just finished our purchases and were leaving the store.

"Are you walking east?"

"Yes."

It was cool out, and we were both wearing light jackets, but I could still tell that Mary was slim built with a great shape. She looked to be in her late thirties, but the tan and her tall gait gave her a more youthful appearance. She seemed friendly. Since she was new to the city, I surmised that she might be amenable to a new friend and maybe romance.

"Where are you staying now?"

"My sister lives upstate. So, I'm going to stay with her. Then I'm going to Europe for a while, and then I'll move to the city."

"Terrific. I'll take you out to dinner when you are set up in town."

"That's great. How sweet of you."

"Here's my card. Call me when you get back."

We said goodbye, and I felt as if I had planted a seed.

A few months later, Mary called.

"Mike, I have a new job, and I'm subletting an apartment. Here is my number. Call me if you get a chance."

I called her a few days later and invited her out to dinner. She insisted that she, "come to me," because her apartment was not set for entertaining. When she arrived at my place, I took her purse and put it on the side. She was wearing a casual black outfit that showed off her shape. She was even more attractive than when I first saw her. I asked her what type of wine she preferred, and she said, "red." I said, "How about a hug to break the ice?" We hugged each other, and she subtly brought her hips forward to make contact. My prescience was at about one-third power, but it was enough. She had no respect for me. She didn't have a clue where I was or how she could interact with me. For a forty-five-year-old woman, her perceptions were limited. She had no reference for me, and her demeanor was defensive and augmentative, in an intellectual way, but with a stubborn streak. She was going to play the game and see what I had to offer.

We drank a lot of wine and then went out to dinner. She loosened up a little, and I was not sure if it was the wine or time spent together. I took her hand once more and got the impression that she had a boyfriend. Why was she dating me? Perhaps she wanted to leave him or thought that she could acquire new friends through me. She was not very warm or responsive. The excuse she used in her mind was that we had just met. It would be months before she responded to me or let her defenses down. I didn't really have the time, but I thought that perhaps if an evening opened up, I would take her out again and correlate my perceptions. It was too bad for me, and I felt disappointed.

Right or wrong you have to challenge your perceptions to grow and hone their accuracy continually.

"My foolishness is all that I regret.

I wanted you. You wanted anyone you could get.

Losing you might be the best thing yet."

(Losing You by Jimmy Martin)

Women and men do not seem to realize that they are in competition with all the other people in town. Most of all, they do not realize that they must compete with all the people younger than they are who have been indoctrinated and learned much of their behavior from television. On television, all the action is aggressive. The shows would be boring if they were only about two people talking unless the personalities were dynamic, powerful, or unique. So, the younger people keep it moving by allowing for quicker action and more physical contact. They also seem to talk and listen at the same time, at a New York speed. But, most of all, they will call, ask you out, and screen you sexually by playing and interacting aggressively.

Older women, who have been raised with a demurer demeanor don't have a chance. Inevitably they wonder why men prefer the younger women. It's because they were home waiting to be asked out, while the younger women were on the phone applying the principals of action rather than a passive, lady-like antiquated patience.

Pandora was given a box by Prometheus that contained all the world's woes. Although she was instructed to leave it closed, she opened it and released... well, you know the rest. What has often overlooked is the fact that hope was also released.

Kissing

Kissing is almost more personal than sex for both sexes. It's very intimate, emotional and personal. Sex can be more trivial when the sex organs, horniness, and loneliness come together.

A kiss on the lips is perhaps the ultimate intimacy. Put your cheeks together and run your tongue across his or her lips from the side. Yes, it's not a full, open, passionate smack. But, it is a subtle, strange, exciting beginning. You can always go full on, lips together, tongue in, smack. But, it might be more effective; less stressful, humorous, and more pleasurable to start really slow.

"Honey, how would you, as a woman, tell a person how to kiss?

A kiss is feeling his or her soul. Have your cheeks touch each other and feel slowly his cheeks, nose, and lips. Scrutinize and synchronize with his breath, feel his warmth, and smell. Appreciate the beauty of being together, and not just pursuing your sexual desires. Run your tongue across his or her ear from the side. Don't be too fast or hard. Tease his or her eyes and lips. It is subtle, intimate, sensual, respectful and delicious. We all have different appreciations about intimacy. Men always have to stick things, and it is very unZenlike but very American. Hope I inspire you a tiny little bit.

How long can you live without a kiss?

"I know how to
please a woman."

"Then, why are you still bothering me?"

The Voice

Burning castles

Hold out for everything you get nothing.

A mutual friend gave me Diana Marie's number after asking her if she wanted to meet a nice single guy. When I spoke to her on the phone, at her workplace, she sounded busy but beautiful. Her voice had qualities that were both annoying and elegant, depending on if she was relaxed or not. The higher tones that would emanate from her when she was nervous or perhaps excited were reminiscent of Midwestern twangs and falsetto male singers from the sixty's rock and roll records. The lower ranges were like a velvet fog like the tragic singer Whitney Houston at her best, a smooth and profound permeating tone that seduced your ears and relaxed your guard.

We played on the phone for two weeks, leaving each other messages, teasing, and joking. She seemed flexible and bright, and I had my heart set on meeting her. I already told her I was bald and slightly hunched over; she said she was only five foot one and pudgy. We both lied wanting to sandbag each other.

It took two weeks for us to finally go out on a date. That lapse in time factor should have given me a clue, as to what her future schedule would be. But, after we spent several hours together not much mattered except seeing her again.

She was just the right height for me, about five foot six, slim built, with a big butt. But, most of all, since I was dating several women and doing what I euphemistically called, "A run of the crazies," she was real, uninhibited with a natural reserve, and lovely. She also was unaffected, extroverted, preoccupied with self-improvement, warm and made the most delightful funny faces and expressions. For what more could I ask?

This was our first date, so when she used an off-color term I pretended shock and dismay. She inquired as to my overreaction. I told her the story about Miriam, the lawyer.

"A close friend fixed me up with his lawyer friend. We spoke on the phone a few times, and she seemed business-like and smart. My friend told me that she loved to joke and had a great sense of humor. I relaxed and joked with her as if I had known her a while. We arranged to meet and go out. The day before the meeting, she broke the date claiming I was crude and disgusting. It turns out that she didn't like a story I told her because I used the word 'pee.'"

"Perhaps, you should have said 'urinate.'" "Perhaps, I should have said 'tinkle.'" But, any adult who cannot tolerate someone saying 'pee' is a little too uptight. After all, they even say pee on national television. Apparently, she was looking for an excuse to avoid any intimacy and like many people she had grown so used to being alone and independent that they don't want to break the habit. **Change is probably the most difficult thing anyone deals with.** Everyone attempts to alter their new friends to conform to their style of living and their preferences. So, any new meetings are thwarted with the danger of having to **modify your behavior and still maintain your individuality.**"

Diana Marie listened to what I said and studied me. She seemed to like me. I could hear her brain processing the conversations. It was a delightful warm summer evening. She was wearing a light dress, and I wanted to take her home and rip it off with my teeth. The dress was so thin that I was able to see her panties and bra through it. Unfortunately, they didn't match, so I knew that she had no intention of sleeping with me that night. I was able to pull back and relax.

We visited several different restaurants before deciding on one. I liked the fast gait with which she walked. Over dinner, she told me that she was very interested in having a relationship with me. She opened up, told me her life history and a few very personal things. We joked, teased, enjoyed the closeness, and the excellent dinner and wine.

I called her many times the following week and left messages on her machine at work and her home. She never answered or called back. Perhaps she didn't like me using the word 'pee.'

Humor and Hyperbole.

The name that the Secret Service called Richard Nixon was different from the name that they called him among themselves, Pencil Dick. I was thinking about this cryptic name when I entered my building. Stationed at the entranceway there is a security guard named Tommy. He is six feet four and probably weighs two hundred and sixty pounds. He knows me and asked for some information about taking classes at night. Upon finishing the conversation, I continued to enter the building and said, "All right Tiny." Near by a neighbor was also entering the building. She was newly arrived from Germany and said to me, with a puzzled expression on her face, "Vos is loose mit dear Tiny?" Another guard was nearby and guffawed. I explained it was a joke, but she did not understand.

Over time Tommy adopted Tiny as a nickname. A few weeks later a woman was having a problem getting out of her apartment because the door was stuck. She called downstairs to the guards' post and asked for help. Tiny answered, "Tiny speaking, can I help you?" The women said, "Can you please come up and help me open my door?" Five minutes later there was a big commotion. The woman had called the guard office and the police. She told them that there was an intruder in the building, impersonating a guard, and knocking on her door. When the police arrived, they helped the women open her door and detained Tiny even though he was in uniform. The police asked the women why she called. She answered, "I called the guard downstairs and he said his name was Tiny. Then this man showed up." The officers were all smiling as they took the elevator down.

Zen, laughing, and humor, are essential ingredients of life. Perhaps laughing was invented to encourage social interaction. We laugh more when we are with others. We want to be with people who are happy and make us smile. When was the last time you had an evening of laughter with others? Shutdown the computer, TV, and IPhone for a while and make the effort to find some new social contacts and reaffirm older ones. Laughter is good for the heart, relieves stress, and reaffirms our humanity.

"Don't let it get you down. It's only castles burning." Neil Young

Anything worth doing is worth overdoing.

Work like you don't need the money.

Love like you've never been hurt.

Dance like nobody's watching.

Sing like nobody's listening.

Live like it's Heaven on Earth.

Enjoy every moment, and live life fully in the now. This is Zen.

The etymology of enthusiasm is, to have god within.

It would be comforting to have a special faith, and to believe in resurrection, afterlife, or reincarnation. But after thousands of years of humanities believing in these fairy tales, no evidence or proofs have ever surfaced. Reincarnation is the most appealing to me of the many choices. But if I analyze the millenniums that wisdom should have accumulated in reincarnated individuals, there should be more talented and smart people on the earth, including more statesmen. Instead we have orangutans running for office, politicians that only think of power and personal enrichment, an unholy alliance between government, business, and media, all benefiting by billions of dollars from this partnership. How are we to have faith, have enthusiasm about trying to improve the world, and ourselves, faced with the realities of our lives? It ain't easy, but we still have to try.

Perhaps, to be more objectively analytical, considering **action and time are life's most important concepts,** we should concentrate our beliefs and faiths in taking advantage of what we have and do it in a timely fashion.

In this life, all we see and touch, is all we will ever have. This is not a dress rehearsal, soak it up and do it now.

Don't look for the answer. This is it.

One of the greatest gifts is to discover early in life what you are meant to do or be good at doing. It may not be as exciting as working at developing many different skills, but specializing and becoming an expert in something can turn your early passion into competence, enjoyment, excellence and increased earning power.

Remember; to spend some time with your loved ones, because they are not going to be around forever, to give a warm hug to the one next to you, because that is the only treasure you can give with your heart and it doesn't cost a cent, to say, 'I love you' to your partner, but most of all mean it. A kiss and an embrace will mend hurt when it comes from deep inside of you, and cherish the moment. Give time to love, give time to speak.

You must not be a casualty of someone else's dream.

At some point in your life, if you are not happy with your relationships, you have to decide whether to continue your attitude and old ways, have many regrets, or make the changes necessary to achieve your goals. Bear in mind that if you have a lot of excuses not to alter your existence that they are probably well planned lies.

"The heart is the shock absorber of the soul."

Alexandra

Empty Holiday

I met Alexandra three times, on three different occasions and parties, before I asked for her number. She was leaving for her native Cyprus, and I was going to be in the Caribbean for the summer. I called her when we both returned in September. Alex was too young for me. I thought that she was a bit older when I met her because she had such excellent carriage and poise and she spoke with a beautiful clipped English accent.

But, on our first date, I found out she was even younger, a baby. Still, she was interestingly bright, perceptive, and very articulate. She was also beautiful, had a great shape and was mature in a European way that in her case was to have more scope. So, what was she missing? Age?

Perhaps it was just a forbidden fruit. To go with a woman so young, was much more than iconoclastic; it was nuts. She had nothing in the way of possessions or wealth. She could do little to make my life better or easier. How could she relate or understand a man who was more than twice her age? Still, she was mature and evidentially I'm totally whacked.

I decided to let her into my life very slowly and see what happened. At least, she had not been too frightened or marked by men and life. Was she open for a little romance? Well, she was good company, and she didn't get cold. She liked the same food as I did. She was wise beyond her years and never had anyone who could build her up, or know her, as I could.

I would try to interact with her without going overboard and evaluate where she was. What the hell, I've given up most of the time my life to be with beautiful young women, why change now? But, it's hard to write about her. She is too positive, and the good stuff is not amusing or entertaining.

I invited her over for dinner often, and since she was a vegetarian, salad and good wine. A woman her age, with her smarts and looks, could have everything. Of course, not having the foreknowledge to know that forces would have her struggle for a decade, to achieve a modicum of success was something she did not know. If she knew how valuable she was, life would be much easier for her. Unfortunately, we all have to go through the ritual of independence and struggle.

If Alexandra were with a man like me, she would never have to struggle again; live a significantly better and easier life, be stimulated and satisfied intellectually, emotionally and physically, and one-day have more assets than she could gain in several lifetimes of work. But, until all of us have gone through the struggle, of trying to succeed, we have no appreciation of how long it takes and how difficult success is to achieve. So, why should she trade her youth for security and a better life when she thinks that she will make it on her own and perhaps even more interestingly? She might be totally right.

After several weeks and many good sexual nights together, I decided to do something I had never done before. I would divulge my peripheral prescience to her, tell her some very personal things about herself, some events that would govern her future life, and what I had in mind for us. I knew that if she ever hooked up with me, let down the emotional shield that she erected, we would be fantastic together. It might overwhelm her with truth; it might scare her emotionally, but I had nothing to lose.

I have an unusual prescience since I was a child although the gift didn't develop fully until I was well into my thirties. I inherited the trait from my mother who was a witch with an acute sense of humor. She'd take delight in confusing the minds of my friends and disconcerting them the first time she was introduced by immediately talking about their deepest insecurities. What no one realized was that the precognitive ability was conveyed by touch. As soon as mom put her hand on your arm or held your hand, she knew everything.

I also needed contact to read someone, but I inherited the added covenant that the more skin I was in touch with, the deeper I could delve into someone's emotional future. This was both a blessing and a curse when I was involved physically with a woman. Sleeping together sometimes overloaded or short-circuited my emotional and mental response. I never knew how it would affect me sexually and the range fluctuated from indifference to Superman.

To make matters infinity more complex, the skill was not directly under my control. Months could pass without my having any unusual insights. Then without warning, I'd suddenly be able to glean fountains of information from superficial meetings. I would never know if I was going to be "on" or "not" and to what intensity. Often, when I most wanted to screen someone or rapidly work a gathering or party, the gift was dormant. At other times, I'd be blind-sided by the overwhelming information that a peck on the cheek or a handshake would reveal.

The gift was somehow akin to eidetic imagery, also referred to as a photographic memory. I believe that the terms intermingled in my case. I do not take a picture when I make an effort to memorize something. Instead, I use my gift of organizing principles and vocabulary to aid my memory. The images that I see are never under my control so the memories I get from them are blurred, usually very rapid in sequence, although sometimes I can use my mind's eye to visualize what objects will look like and create my mental pictures.

Sometimes, days or weeks pass without a premonition. At other times, I would be plugged in continually until so wired I had to jump up and down to relieve the overflow of input. At these intervals, the only thing that seemed to allow the assault of stimulation to dissipate was working out at the gym, especially swimming, as the water physically calmed my emotions.

My friends did not know the extent of my perception least I be turned into a parlor trick or burned as a warlock. The very few times, in the past, I shared just the slight extent of my gift resulted in my friends experiencing adverse reactions, from apprehension to disbelief, to thinking I was tricking them, to believing I was a wicked character.

My intuition and prescience were fluctuating nowadays and becoming more erratic. Somehow, I was becoming more of a peripheral visionary. I was able to glimpse the future, never transparently, always opaque, always way off to the side. Images flashed past me askance containing vast amounts of information. If I had not had hints of the precognition all my life, I would have thought that I was going crazy or that God or the devil was talking to me. I knew from the years of experience what I was seeing. Sometimes, it was like being high or drunk with the images blindsiding me with their force. It was as if the world was in black and white; without any warning, whatsoever, I would be transported into a Technicolor Fellini movie. Just long enough to see the ornate and incongruous scene, but not long enough to become a part of it. My unusual foreknowledge was changing and evolving, revealing mixed images that drained my energies and I did not know what direction the change was going to take.

Months passed, and Alex, and I saw each other many times. She took classes on Mondays so that became our fresh salad day where we would talk and relax with good wine and music. She was not very happy and revealed that she had a floating anxiety that she could not shake from her mind. Alex had gone home to Cyprus for a few weeks and called me when she came back. It was unusual for me to be locked into a double approach-avoidance conflict, but I liked her. The conflict was that she was too young, had nothing but years of work ahead of her, and probably could not make my life any easier. But, she was fresh, desirable, beautiful and smart. She could also open up some possibilities that I already closed, such as having children.

I always invited her over for drinks and dinner out. When I greeted Alex at the door, she gave me a big hug and kisses. Her attitude toward me had changed significantly, and her emotional predisposition was altered. Her mind was full of so many contradictory images and rampant emotionality that I had trouble screening out single thoughts.

She calmed down after a while and told me about her travels and her new job. As she talked, I stroked her arm and fed the images that she conveyed to me. Since she knew that I had a unique ability, although she could not be aware of its extent, she enjoyed the experience of "having her palm read."

"Can you see anything?" she inquired.

"Yes, I can. There is so much that I'm having trouble sorting it out. But, let me give you a taste. During the past few months, you have been getting a lot of bad advice. Although the advice itself was not necessarily poor, it was not very pertinent to you. The people that gave you the advice were only telling you what they would do and the information didn't pertain to your needs or future."

"Can you tell me how I can become happier in the future?"

"Happiness and misery depend as much on temperament as on fortune, so try to cultivate a better outlook and disposition, and your chances for happiness in life and love are greatly enhanced."

Your screening devices should reflect from whom you take the advice. For example, kissing is almost more personal than sex. It's very intimate, emotional and personal. So, you have to be very careful whom you kiss and from whom you take advice.

For example, your contemporaries cannot give you advice about money since they don't have any- they could only tell you what they can do, not what you should do. **When someone advises you about money, you have to evaluate if they are rich and what lifestyle they conduct.** The same is true with advice about love and careers. You have been taking advice about love from people who were and are afraid to take a chance. **Love requires risks, and great love and great achievement involve great risk.**"

To break the seriousness of the conversation, I added, "And, Never Moon a Werewolf or Lecture a Dust Storm. Always stir clockwise, and think counterclockwise."

"Wow, that's a lot to take in. Do you have any predictions?"

"Only one that comes through very strongly. You are good with short-range tactics of life, but not too well versed in strategy. Now you're coming to a fork in the road, (the french say: when you see a fork, take it,) where if you use a gambit as a tactic your entire life will improve.

The gambit, however, requires a long-range strategy, which you are not too good at. The most important point is that **hope is not a strategy for living or a substitute for action.**"

"Do you have advice on what I should do?"

"No. Because I don't know what the crossroad is and it's your decision."

"You know you scared me a little bit the last time we were together, and you said that in about January something would happen that would bring my sister and me closer together."

"Well, I hope it's something positive, but I don't know."

I looked at Alex more closely than I ever had, as she talked about her new job in the hospital. She looked fatigued and worn. The city and the job, her long hours were taking their toll on her. She was naturally beautiful and possessed an attractive, sophisticated face. When I saw her from different angles, she looked like several different people at once.

"You know Alex," I said to her quite seriously, "You are my double approach-avoidance conflict."

"How?"

"Well, I like you a lot, but I know that you have the potential to drive me mad. My worse fear is that we will get together, become tight, and then you will start to smoke again."

"I don't know why you want to get together with me. What can I offer someone like you?"

"That's easy; potential. You can open doors that I thought were closed. Perhaps having children. I might be just an old man who has never grown up and in love with physical beauty but, I've always been iconoclastic and nonconventional and given it all up for a beautiful face and a keen mind."

"Iconoclastic?"

"From the root icon. One who smashes idols. Could I have a hug before we dine?"

She stood up, and I walked over to embrace her. Her touch was strange, and she drew her hips backward. She did not want me at all tonight, though she was very receptive to me emotionally. Still, she was dating some young man who was a dead end for her. She was just going along with me to see where it might lead.

"We can see each other again on Monday if you like," she said as I kissed her neck and held her protruding ass cheeks, "I have two days off."

"I would love to, but my schedule is totally jammed for the next week. I'll call you to set something up."

We had dinner together several more times. She always stayed overnight and the love making was good but never spontaneous or quite enough for her. Although she surprised me one night by saying, "Pull me into you harder and drown me in your love."

Alex liked good wine and was knowledgeable on a multiplicity of topics. We held each other for hours one evening. Even though I felt close to her, I could feel her vulnerability and her self-destructive streak asserting itself.

I picked up images of the past few men that she was with, all who treated her poorly, or very badly, or played negatively with her head. Her past relationships were reflected by her defensive attitude toward me, and she could not conceive of a relationship with a man so much older than her.

But most of all her self-destructive streak, of which I was very aware, but I could rechannel, manifested itself by not allowing herself to be cared for. If she was treated well, she didn't know how to act and would be forced to change perhaps even dropping some defenses. These changes were too much for her to take and it would always be easier for her to run away.

Alex was a love junky and believed that the prince would find her and they would live happily together forever. The next man would be her last man, one that she could make a total commitment to and one with which she could grow old. I could not be that prince or the one to tell her that the white knight's horse would not fit into the elevator and that forever was only three weeks. Her ideal lover was one that she "could fuck all night and still take home to her parents the next day." Apparently, she could never take an old man home to her parents, so it was over.

My prescience became apparently clear when I saw that time had taught her some valuable lessons and that she started to realize just how arduous life could be and how difficult it was to get ahead. She had played with the idea of reconsidering our relationship and interacting with me to feel things out again. But, it would be too late. I would be involved with another woman, and I would not want to jeopardize a relationship with someone who was giving and proven for someone who was transient and reticent.

So, it was over before it had begun. I knew that Alex had an initial interest to be with me since we were so compatible physically, but that soon waned. The give-a-way was when she had to have a cigarette. From that point on, she was just using me, but I thought it might be interesting to play it out. Eventually, there came the point that I had to end it.

I was tempted to get down on one knee and propose to her to watch her go screaming into the night. But, instead, I proposed to her, almost as a nonsequita, while she had a mouthful of salad, and she almost went catatonic. I used this ploy before on younger women who wanted to play the game. It always had them retreating and running away while saving their egos.

Cuse me, but you can't open the door for the devil. Once you do, he will walk right in.

Romance still counts. But the world is not a romantic place anymore. Women lack trust, enthusiasm and romance. Men want economic partners and unencumbered sex. In 1974 the earth's population was four billion people. We now have hit seven billion and are crowding out the earth. Don't worry, you will find someone, and after a while you will be totally consumed, working hard, and discontent like the rest of us. There is no easy answer. Live with it.

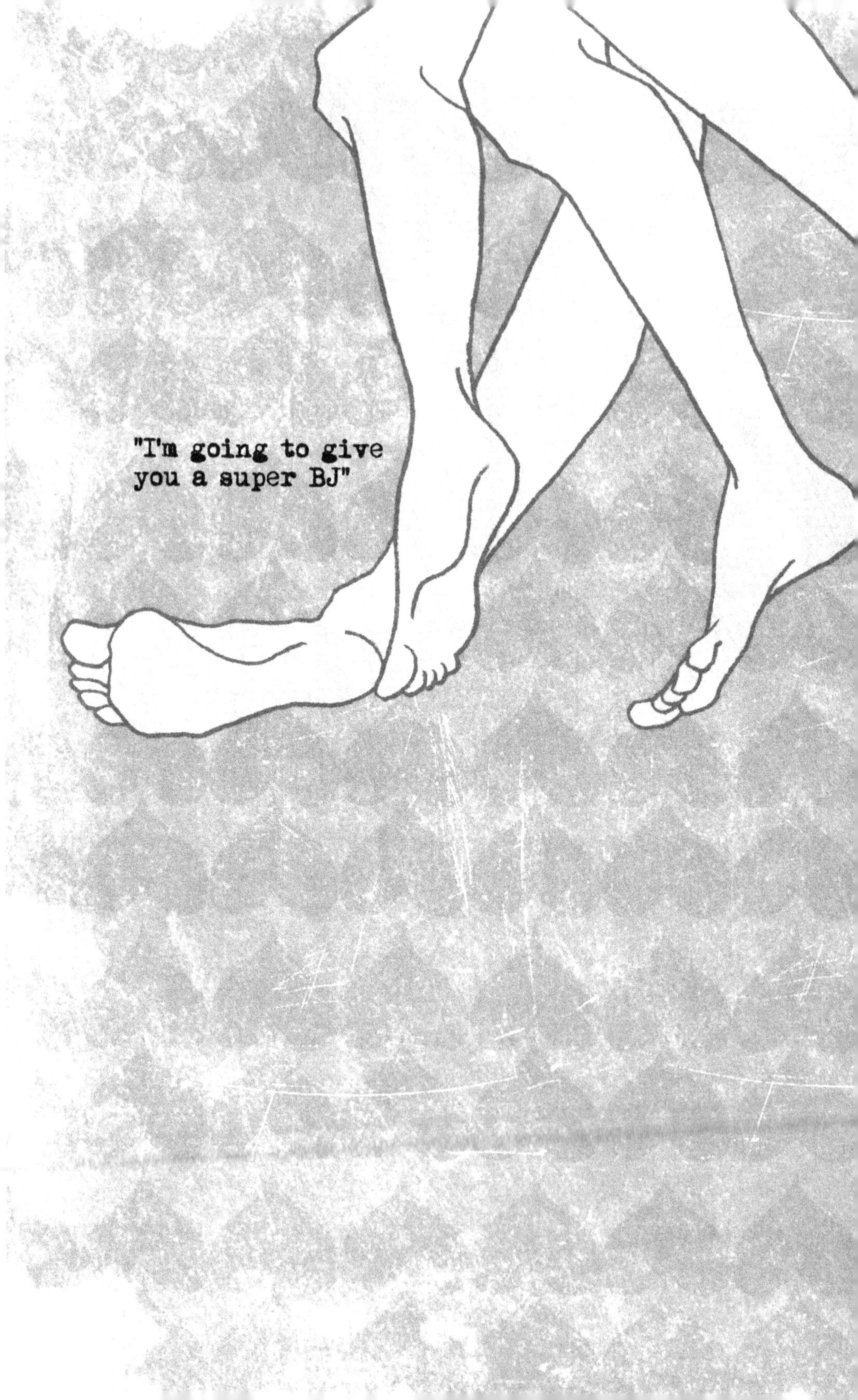
"I'm going to give you a super BJ"

"I'm going to make
you eat those words."

Death Of A Sugar Daddy

Gimme, gimme, gimme gimme, getme get me get me get me buyme buy me buy me. That's the price of love.

Take what you can and give nothing back.

This week, I went out to dinner with three different women, Ann, Carla, and Catherine. Every so often, after weeks of being busy, I turn optimistic about finding a new honey. My logic stems from many experiences. I ask for example, what are the odds of two gay lion tamers, about the same age, finding each other? Then I think that if Siegfried and Roy can find each other, it makes almost any other relationship a breeze.

All three women were well off financial, had been married and divorced, and were in their early fifties. I picked up Ann, gave her a little present to break the ice, and took her to dinner at a friend's home. The friend was a chef and prepared a wonderful meal. Knowing that the meal would be superb, I bought three bottles of fine wine. We took a cab home and kissed on the cheek goodbye.

I took Carla out for the second time and gave her a small present to start the evening out right. We took a car service to the restaurant and a taxi home, even though the place was close. She made reservations in a crowded restaurant. I had told her that I liked a lot of room and her reply was that next time I would handle the reservations. Inadvertently, over dinner, I held her hand, and she gently pulled it away. Over the course of the evening, we asked each other many questions, and although Carla was open and honest, it was easy to discern that many of her questions were about my finances.

"You know Carla when you talk about me being a downtown person," and I thought to myself, she didn't say downtown man, "and you being an uptown woman, it reminds me of a true story behind the lost paragraph in GENESIS, Adam and Eve."

"Really? I don't know that one, it's a little before my time."

"Well, I'll tell it to you in brief form, if you like."

"I'd love to hear it."

"Love? That's the most romantic thing you said all evening."

"Please, we're eating."

"I'm sorry," I said, noting that she hadn't called me by my name once all evening."

I dove right into telling the story. And Adam said to God, "Although I thank you for creating me, I am empty and lonely and have no one of my kind to talk with and help me." And God answered Adam and spoke.

"I shall make you a helpmate, a companion who will always be at your side. She will always agree with every decision you make. She will bear your children and never ask you to get up in the middle of the night to take care of them. She will not nag you and will always be the first to admit she was wrong when you've had a disagreement. She will never have a headache and will freely give you love and passion whenever you need it. She will comfort you and take care of all your sexual desires. But most of all, she will make your life easier and continually make you happy. She will give to you and never complain, and she will massage you when you are sore or in need, feed you when you are hungry, always be positive and nurturing."

"Wonderful," said Adam, "that will be fantastic. But, tell me God, a woman like this sounds like an amazing deal, what will this cost me?"

And God replied, "An arm and a leg."

Adam thought for a moment and asked, "What could I get for a rib?"

Carla was quiet for the rest of the evening and made no pretense to split or pay the bill. I was uncomfortable in the overcrowded restaurant and was happy when the meal ended. Carla and I were both leaving town, and we agreed that whoever was back first would call the other.

The date made me think that "Bending the world to accommodate our personal frailties does not help us overcome them" Jenny Jarvie, and what do we do when we realize that we're not as special as we thought we were? Yes, we are unique, just like everyone else.

It was our first date. Catherine had met me at the restaurant twenty minutes late, and of course, she made no effort to pay the bill. After dining, we went to a very private place for dessert. The cappuccino check was a mere ten dollars. She ignored the bill as any PAP (Park Avenue Princess) would.

Ann sent me a cute little thank you note. She thanked me for a lovely evening and said she hoped we would get together soon. Although I liked Ann very much and appreciated her intellect enormously, I was not particularly attracted to her sexually. But, she had the potential of a real friendship. I would try to cultivate her friendship and tell her that's what I wanted. I do not let many people into my life, but she was an excellent person. Would she be interested in a friendship? Would she drop me, if there were no hope of a sexual relationship? I didn't know. Even though she was overweight and out of shape, she was a very sensual woman with a Botticelli bottom that I would love to draw. A few days later, she invited me out for dinner with a few friends to celebrate Chinese New Year. We talked on the phone several times, and the conversations were light, and she was very open. I was optimistic.

Carla had gone to Palm Springs. As a screening device, I asked her to call me when she came back. On a whim, I called her just as she returned and we spoke for a while. She seemed obsessed with the idea that she was an uptown girl and I was a downtown man, some New Yorkers affectation.

"Let me ask you something Carla when we were together, you were naturally screening me, as I was you. Were you screening to accept or reject?"

"You know I don't know. I'll have to think about it."

It was strange that Carla was so open and honest and yet seemed so provincial in her outlook. I held her hand for a few moments and picked up a wealth of incongruities in her personality. For one, she had a talent for ruling guys out. She had no interest in anyone unless it concerned her or could improve her lifestyle, which was built around playing golf. She was not concerned so much with the man as the accouterments that he could provide. But sadly, I detected something most unfortunate. My mind had attempted to run through the myriads of tunnels of her insides to try to sense her sexuality and had been stopped where a black cancer was about to eat her alive.

It was sad that she would die alone without a man's love, although many older wimpy type men flirted and raised their egos by interacting with her. But what real man would want an asexual, high maintenance, passionless, self-possessed woman fixated on only the accouterments of a relationship and who didn't like rock and roll?

I certainly would not call her again. She stayed on my mind for a while; she was pretty, honest, and smart in specific areas. Sometimes, I try to visualize what nicknames a woman, and I would call each other if we became involved. I would have to call Carla Princess, and she would call me Daddy. Indeed, that insight turns out to be the key to Carla. Her dead husband, who was much older than her, had babied her, she was his little girl, and she never recovered from his rapid and untimely demise. She was still looking to be daddies' little girl, for a father to take care of her and everything, and further improve her privileged live style. She was a perfect example of **coffin screwing. When someone who's dead and buried is still fucking with your head.** I'd see her one more time to finalize my prescience if she called... a hundred to one shot.

Having dinner one evening with my good friends Stephen and Maggie, Maggie asked if I was dating anyone special.

"I did date a very special lady named Carla. If you could imagine the three most spoiled women you have ever known, this woman is probably the personification of all the princesses you have ever known combined."

"Where does she live and how did you meet her?" Maggie asked.

"She lives in the seventies off Fifth Avenue, and I met her through her friends whom I met at a party. But, I only gave her friends two critériory."

"Which were?" said Stephen.

"One that she was not a midget and the other that she was nurturing. She was a nice height, but she was as nurturing as a black widow."

"Did she pick up a check?"

"Yeah, right. But I'm picking up the check tonight, my treat."

"I was going to pay for the tea," Stephen retorted. "It sounds like she suffered from hipatitus."

"You mean, hepatitis."

"No, she was not sick, she just thought she was terminally cool."

"Thank you for dinner, Mike," Maggie said, "So, are you going to see Carla again?"

"You know you are one of the few people that know about my prescience. I held Carla's hand for a few moments over dinner, trying to get a sense of her, and was almost blindsided by the image of Cancer that was rotting quietly in her insides."

"Did you tell her?" Maggie asked.

"How could you tell someone that? And on the second date."

Steve said, "Take her out again. When the check comes, say, 'All right, the person who has cancer pays for dinner,' then hand her the check."

"That's a good one Steve. I think I'll put that in my next book and recount how diabolic you are and what a curmudgeon you are becoming."

"Do you ever hint to anyone about your powers? Since you have to touch to have your sense activated, is it like neurogenic telepathy? Answer the second question first." He asked, playing with the pace of the conversation to tease me.

"No. That's like phylogenic manipulation, you read and then manipulate someone's thoughts. I'm not even close to that. All I can do is sometimes see images. And I always keep the prescience hidden. People fear what they do not understand."

Catherine called and left a message on my machine. As smart as she was, she never said thank you for the evening. Perhaps she considered it business. Ann made a date with me to celebrate Chinese New Year, the year of the Red Chicken, with her and some friends. I always looked forward to being with her, an intellectual delight, and always fun and great conversation. Ann had the most wonderful friends, smart, well informed and totally diversified. We would meet in Chinatown that evening, and I was in a great mood looking forward to seeing her again.

The Human Body

It takes your food seven seconds to get from your mouth to your stomach.

One human hair can support 3kg (6.6 lbs.).

The average man's penis is three times the length of his thumb from the second joint.

Human thighbones are stronger than concrete.

A woman's heart beats faster than a man's.

There are about one trillion bacteria on each of your feet.

Women blink twice as often as men.

The average person's skin weighs twice as much as the brain.

Your body uses 300 muscles to balance itself when you are standing still.

If saliva cannot dissolve something, you cannot taste it.

Women reading this will be finished now.

Men are still busy checking their thumbs.

Unfortunately, a dead love never dies.

Many people hold on to their past much too long.

If a loved one has died they should be mourned and remembered but the living must move on. If you live in the past, and especially if you blame someone else for things that have gone wrong, then you can never change for the better and your interpersonal relationships will suffer. The entire realm of mean, hurtful and extreme actions committed against you cannot be allowed to accumulate. If you allow the building up of all the cretinous trivia then you will carry an unbelievable burden, physiologically and physically. You will be bent over by the load of carrying the past. Let it go.

The memories of the loves loss, and the lovers of the past, are like coins in the devil's purse: when you open it you find only dead leaves. (paraphrased from Sartre's Nausea.)

Venus is the only planet that rotates clockwise. Since Venus is normally associated with women, what does this tell you? Those women are going in the 'right' direction.

She was right, but she was left.

Is it any wonder that women complain that a good man is hard to find? Did it ever occur to a female after being helped on with their coat to help the man on with his? Isn't it just common courtesy after a man pays for dinner for the woman to pick up the significantly smaller check for dessert or a movie or the cab fare? How can women want or believe they are equal until they develop dating manners and stop acting like princesses? Don't they think men like to be treated as well as they do? I am always amazed and somewhat disgusted at most women's attempts to create the illusion that they are going to pay for dinner. A man automatically picks up the check or with another man splits it. Now, when a woman says to me, "I'll get it next time" I like to answer, "No, you pay this time and I'll treat next time." Don't bullshit me. Women hardly ever pick up the check. **Every action is a well-rehearsed subterfuge and bluff aimed toward assuming equality without it costing anything.** When a woman feints picking up a check, I let her, just to see what she will do. Nine times out of ten my credit card seems to get used.

I would never think of calling these women again. Now I will wait and see if they call me and invite me out. If not, good riddance to another princess who believed what her mother told her when she said,

"You are the most beautiful girl in the world. Someday a prince will come along who will treat you like royalty, a shining knight who will wait on you hand and foot and make your life beautiful. He will be a gentleman, sweet and understanding and give you everything you ever wanted, you can have everything, and your sex is a gold mine."

Daughters and some men are raised to be taught that the possibilities of their gender are limitless. How can anyone possibly compete against infinite possibilities?

What should a woman do to show a man that she is interested in him and perhaps a relationship? The answer is ANYTHING. If women are not passive or convey any action that the person can interpret as, "I don't think this is going to be the last date, so I will try to plant some seeds for future experiences." Then the decisive action produces and conveys some hope for the future. What about just saying that you had a good time, find him attractive, and want to see him again? How about surprising the man and picking up the first check? Would that make him more receptive to asking her out again? You bet your tushie it would.

Younger women who were raised by television, especially in their formative years, have gotten used to action. TV. Is boring initially as a vicarious medium with talking heads and cliché plots. To break up the monotony and make it entertaining, something has to happen. People under forty are used to seeing action and have subliminally attached being right to acting, moving and action. They do not hesitate to call and have several different plots or plans of action when they suggest getting together.

A love affair is like the ozone layer; you only miss it when it's gone.

"Whatever you give a woman, she will make greater. If you give her sperm, she'll give you a baby. If you give her a house, she'll give you a home. If you give her groceries, she'll give you a meal. If you give her a smile, she'll give you her heart. She multiplies and enlarges what is given to her. So, if you give her any crap, be ready to receive a ton of it back."

"Whisper my favorite words:
"I'll buy it for you.""

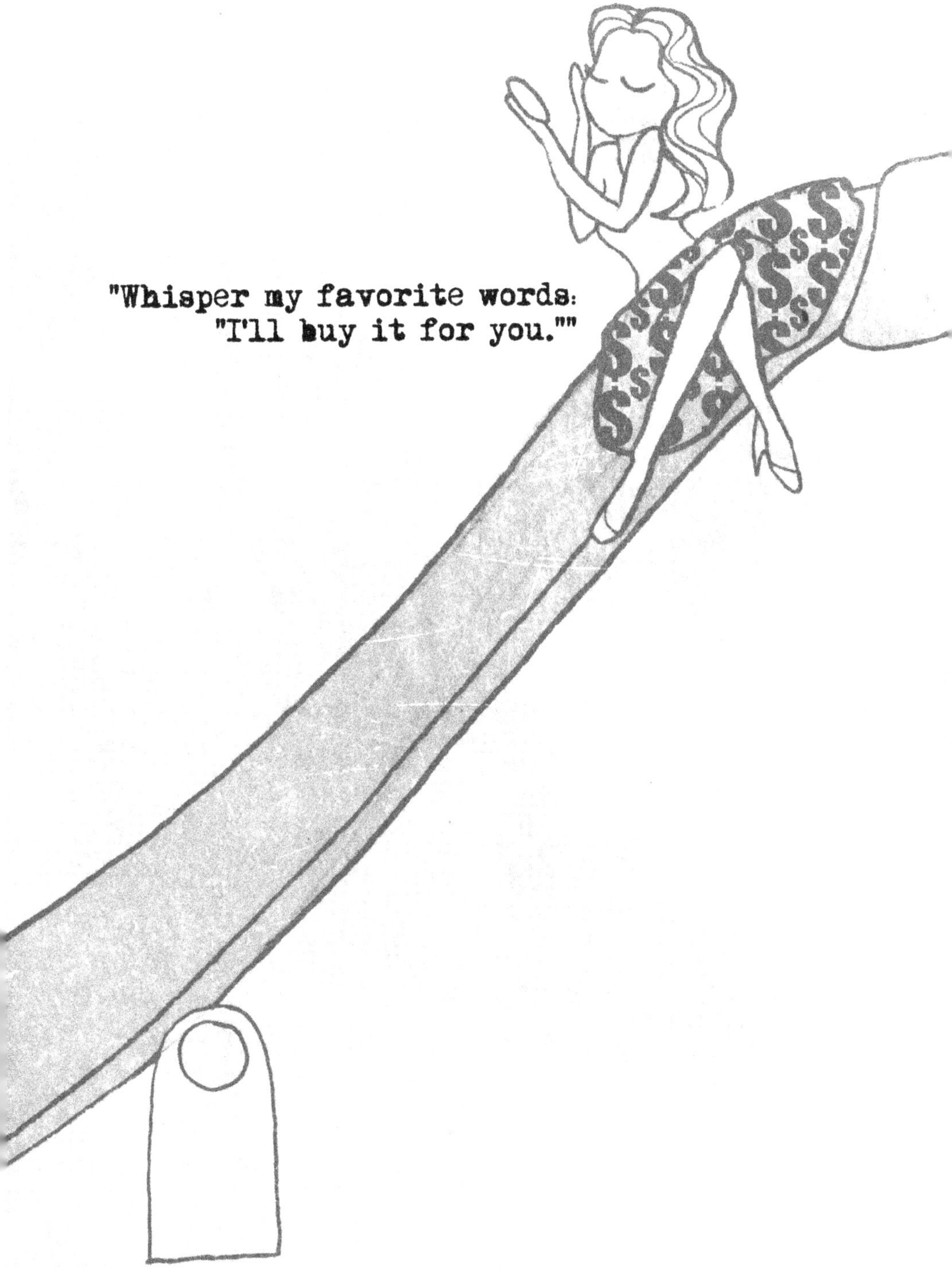

Serendipity

Needs and Wants

At last, I finished the built in oak cabinets on which I was working. Now, I could invite people over to my home again since looking into the gaping hole in the walls was not only unaesthetic but also the shaft ran from the bedroom through the bathroom wall affording little privacy in both bathrooms. To celebrate, because I had to go out to mail a few letters anyway, I decided to take a walk and have some breakfast out. I walked across town to Broadway to the Spanish restaurant that sold hot coffee con Leche, an espresso with a hot milk concoction that was similar, if not superior, to a cappuccino. I ordered an onion omelet and black beans and sat down. I was so happy that I finished the cabinets after several weeks of work. It wasn't that the work was hard, but the custom fitting in a wall that was not square, the overnight gluing of all the different sized cabinets. Plus, the overnight drying of the several coats of marine varnish took many weeks.

It was supposed to snow tonight. I asked the woman, who was eating chicken and yellow rice next to me if she heard the latest weather forecast. When she turned to answer me, I was looking at a pretty blonde face with a bright smile. She was easy to talk with, and she was so attractive that, for a moment I lost my concentration.

"What's your accent? Don't tell me, it sounds like the Midwest, like Dearborn Michigan."

"No, your way off, it's Georgia."

"Oh, wait a minute, you're pronouncing your tees and have no drawl."

"I've spent a lot of time in New York."

"Yes, so long that you talk much too fast for a southerner. I bet when you go back, they all say you sound like a Yankee."

She laughed and nodded her head. We talked for a while about jobs and the difference between the North and South. Since I was never going to see her again, I couldn't help asking:

"Considering how beautiful you are, how could you not be married or have a boyfriend?"

"Well, I just broke off with him."

"How come? I'm a perfect stranger. You can tell me."

"Well, it's too personal."

"I always simplified relationships down to three things. **In any relationships, there is only sex, in-laws (or friends) and money. If you have two out of three, you can make it work.** And perhaps a sense of humor."

"Well, I got along with my in-laws." She quickly answered.

I was impressed with her quick sense of humor and straightforward manner. It was evident how smart she was, and I had a feeling that she was perceptive as well. I meet so many beautiful women, who leave me cold, but with this one, for a change, there was some chemistry, and I looked over her tight body. I wanted to eat her up right away, but I couldn't tell from her body language if she was attracted or interested in me.

"I understand. I just broke off with the woman I was with. She was too young for me and didn't know what she wanted. You're over thirty, aren't you?"

She blushed slightly, a sign of good mental health, and nodded.

"You said your studio was nearby, are you an artist?"

"Yes, my gallery is just around the corner from where you work."

"I'd love to see your work sometimes."

"Give me your card, and I'll call you. Perhaps we can have some of this delicious coffee together."

"I'm only allowing myself one cup a day."

"Me too. Maybe, we can have that cup together?"

"I'm Sherry Holmes," she said and extended her hand. Mon Chéri I said to myself as I shook hands with her and knew that I would like to see her again. Damn it! The poor ones with nothing are always so attractive and accessible. Am I going to fall for a beautiful face again? I thought I was transforming into a wiser more cautious man. It will be interesting to see her reaction when she finds out that I'm a nice down to earth guy. She left the restaurant smiling. I watched her walk away. She had a perky walk and wore three-inch heels on her boots. She had an interesting mix of sophistication and openness that I was eager to explore, but most of all I wanted to lick her all over. What a nice way to start the day. Sometimes, I'd walk down the street almost hunting to converse with a smart woman and not see a good-looking face, and now just serendipitously I sit next to a lovely.

I finished breakfast, moved toward home, and passed a gallery with an enormous charcoal drawing on the wall. A week or so ago, I ran into Bob Blackburn, a consummate printmaker who I'd known for many years, coming out of this gallery. We said hello and talked briefly. I opened the door and looked at the drawing. A beautiful Japanese woman approached me and was about to tell me that the gallery was closed for installation.

"Did Bob Blackburn get home okay that day? He seemed to be a bit unsteady."

"Oh, I remember you. Yes, he is going to sell the first edition of prints that he has made in seven years at our paper gallery."

"Fantastic, Bob's such a great person and printmaker. He has devoted his life to printing. I have often used his facilities to make my prints, but now I need a bigger press."

"You know we just installed a sixty-ton press in the rear room. Why don't you take my card and we can talk about you printing here?"

"What an excellent idea. Does it distract from your directorship being so short?" I said jokingly testing her sense of humor. She didn't smile but said. "It's an asset because the office upstairs has a low ceiling."

She tossed her head of long black hair over her shoulder and handed me her card. "And you're the..." "Come around when the gallery is less busy, and we'll talk."

"Definitely."

I was on a roll with two beautiful women in the space of twenty minutes. Although I knew from the director's handshake that, this woman would be married in a year. I thought of all the women that play hard to get and the princesses.

Like water, everyone seeks his or her own level.

Have the wisdom to know what your hurried heart needs and not what your unsympathetic brain wants.

Sometimes following what the heart wants is not a good solution; sometimes we have to be reasonable.

We must distinguish the difference between our needs and wants.

When the power of love is stronger than the love of power, the world will know peace.

I Love To Write

Written Communication or Size matters.

Assert yourself if you believe in something, and pick a side. But you had better be accurate. *I have a friend who is an excellent, talented, smart, designer. When it comes to written communication, business cards, books, etc., she insists that the design and aesthetics are more important than the size of the fonts. I disagree and often tell her that communication is best served by making the font size bigger so that the reader has immediate clarification. Rapid and clear communication is the most important factor when using the written word. If you cannot get your information or message across then, it does not matter how crisp your design. Another factor in written communication today is demographics. The increase in aging populations means that there are older people, with less acute vision, which need to be reached.*

An example I gave to her was when I needed some photographs of my sculptures. Coincidentally, I met a lovely Japanese photographer who gave me her beautifully designed card. When I got home, I took out her card and was going to call her. Even with my glasses on I could hardly read the information. The script resembled wiry ants crawling across the card. I threw the card away and went to my business file to find someone else. You can be stubborn. You can hold to your beliefs and preconceived ideas. But, you had better be correct, or you will suffer the consequences of inflexibility and loss.

Are you capable of extrapolating this idea to other aspects of your life?

Quiet Harmony

I am on a tiny island in the Caribbean. I do not listen to music or watch television. The biggest event in the evening is dinner. At night, I reconnect with the sky, seeing thousands of stars because there are no lights. On the terrace, I meditate, with a 180-degree spectacle, miles of still ocean, an endless dark sky, and a pink-sanded beach. The view coupled with the isolation is spiritual, and I have reverence for the clouds, the sea, and the sun. The only two sounds are the rhythmic waves breaking on the shore and the song of the birds. The birds have an immense medley of wobbles, squeak, whistles, beeps and tunes. I am transfixed by the sounds of the birds and just listen to its songs. In the background, the waves are a steady Zen heartbeat. The cool breeze blows silently off the ocean, and I breathe the fresh air deeply. It is calm and quiet. Peace.

Try to develop a more aesthetic and extensive vocabulary. It will help you succeed more in relationships and life.

Rose

The Queen of Crisis

She was a banquet of opportunity.

I went to see what my old neighborhood looked like after not seeing Manhattan Beach in twenty years. I heard from an acquaintance that there were espresso cafes and other shops near the boardwalk and I wanted to see the changes. The eight miles of beach along the Atlantic inlet are divided into bays starting from Brighten Beach to Seagate. Bay one, in Brighton Beach, was the ideal place for me to start since I had been so familiar with the area.

I walked out onto the beach and toward the fence, where I recognized Lenny, a man that was referred to as the mayor of Bay one. We played checkers together decades ago. It was strange to see him in the same place that I had left him years ago.

We shook hands and were soon joined by others that I had not seen in many years. The conversations weren't particularly stimulating, so while listening my eyes roamed over the beach. A very Russian-looking man arrogantly walked down the beach to the water flanked by two women as mute and beautiful as two cheetahs on a leash. In the distance, I watched a woman walking out onto the beach that possessed a body straight out of Mad comic books. That is, she was the personification of a caricature of what the "sexy ideal" women would look like. She had beautifully shaped breasts that perked up from an excellent figure. She wore her sweet ass jeans and had a rear end that stuck out so far it defied gravity, long flowing hair, and a lovely face- with full juicy lips. She walked straight over to Lenny, standing next to me, and started a conversation.

I stared at her because she was absolutely beautiful, utterly desirable, and extraordinarily sexy. Unfortunately, when she began to speak, it was as if Venus was picking her nose. The mismatch with her looks was overwhelming. Rose had a pronounced Brooklyn accent. Could a woman change from a goddess to bimbo in just a few sentences? Considering what I was looking for, the answer for me was an unequivocal "yes." But her curves, which were a feast for my eyes, pulled this naked ape forward into some primeval reproductive union and her wet sexual spell.

We said a few words to each other and as an excuse to touch her hand I commented on her bracelet. I asked if I could see it, and she held out her hand. I took her hand in mine, and my prescience kicked into high gear. Rock on. The music suddenly switched from beach flowing mellow to hot honky-tonk rock and roll piano. The beat was heavy and redundant, and the bass vibrated my thighs. She was curious and saw me as someone from Manhattan that would take her to dine in a fancy restaurant. The fact that we would spend the night together was already a fait accompli, and she was already thinking of ways to entice me.

"Any chance you're going to the city tonight?" I asked her.

"Yes I am, perhaps we could keep each other company on the journey."

She was used to being social, having men hitting on her, and choosing whom she wanted to be with. Because she was always beautiful, she had developed many sophisticated traits and been treated all her life. She had developed a charm and wit that, although it was beyond her intellect, allowed her to appear as funny and gregarious.

After spending only an hour with her, the Brooklyn accent was twisting my brain. Still, her body grabbed my visual interest, and the future tactile sensations were enough to maintain my interest. Since our sexual evening was assured, I could not decide whether to go for a fast, good Asian restaurant or a slower more titillating fine dining joint. I left it up to her. Not wanting to appear as a gold digger, she opted for a Chinese restaurant. I decided on a more sumptuous evening and selected the Gotham. As the maitre d' seated us at an excellent "put on display" type table, it was obvious that Rose possessed a beautiful woman's style and grace. She smiled so much that I thought she didn't have a central nervous system. Dinner was uneventful, and we both wanted to have dessert at my place.

After dinner, we walked slowly home being entertained by the strange sky. We sat on my terrace for a while, drinking red wine, amused by the peculiar firmament. The sky was full of odd shaped clouds, puffs, dots, swirls, feathers and chunks as if someone was doing watercolors and stirring the paper with different brushes. We showered together and soaped each other's backs. We climbed onto my big bed and began touching each other.

"Let's play a game," she said.

"Any game you want except tie me up."

"I want you to be entirely passive and then when I tell you, absolutely aggressive."

"Sounds like a good game."

"Turn over onto your stomach and don't move or touch me."

Rose started to explore every orifice and crack on my body. She was exceptionally oral, and her tongue was long and pointy. She cleaned my ears, chewed on the back of my neck and worked her way down to my ass cheeks. She spent a long slowly licking the back of my balls and sticking her tongue in my ass. I was hard, and it was getting harder to be passive.

I said, "Rose, let's play the other half of the game."

"No, not yet. Turn over." I acquiesced.

I thought that she was just going to gobble me up, but instead, she tongued me like a lollypop and never put me in her mouth. She slapped my dick back and forth with her lips and hair until she was satisfied with her teasing, and she was heating up faster than a cup of Ramon.

"Are you ready for me?" She inquired with a broad smile.

She turned over on her back and spread her legs wide. I was going to yodel in the valley, but she stopped me.

"Fuck me. Fuck me now." I obeyed.

She was warm and wet, and I positioned myself a little higher to rub her G-spot. I tried to slow it down, but her rhythm kept building quicker. She wrapped her legs around me and came with a deep moan. I quickened my thrusts into her and was about to let go when she said, "Wait, wait, I want you to come in my mouth."

I slowed down and rested my body on hers, rolling around to feel her full hard breasts and her ass. I rolled over onto my back and relaxed.

"Give me a few moments," I said.

She would have none of it and put my dick in her mouth up to my balls. She didn't move her head up and down but instead ran her tongue up and down along the underside of my penis, massaging the large sensitive vein. When she licked her finger, and put it up my ass, I could not hold back any longer.

"I have to come. I'm coming."

Rose moved her lips quickly up and down on the head, one hand pumping the sperm into her mouth and the other fingering my anus as if she was fucking me. She swallowed my come as if it were a gourmet treat and did not stop until I was empty and asked, "OK, please let me rest."

I turned on my side, as she slid into my arms and we held each other very tightly. We were stuck together with every part of our bodies touching.

I said, "Could you move a little closer please?"

She laughed, and I thought that we could just fall asleep. About twenty minutes later, just as my entire body was about to let go and sleep, she slid down and began giving me a slow blowjob.

"Rose, I'm sorry. I'm not that viral. After what you have done with me, I think I came from my toes, and I will have nothing left for at least a week."

"It's all right you don't have to perform. Sometimes I like when it's soft. Just go to sleep." I listened because I was completely spent.

It was a real dream. I was totally relaxed and dreaming I was sleeping and yet I was being pleasured. I half awoke because some sensitivity was returning to my dick. Her slow, steady licking, teasing, and sucking had given me a chubby.

"Rose, you are so good, but you cannot get a marshmallow through a keyhole."

"Go back to sleep and dream of my lovely ass."

I slept for a while. Perhaps a half hour, but awoke with my dick in Rose's mouth and her fingers gently stuck in my anus.

"You're hard now, so get behind me and stick it in."

Her ass cheeks were right to bounce off, and I grabbed her hips and trust into her without a care. I was half asleep but wonderfully alive, and I pounded her ass with what I thought was too much force. One good turn deserves another, and I put my thumb up her ass and wiggled. I felt her cunt lips tighten and throb. She came off like a pack of firecrackers, and her hand reached back and tickled my balls as I came again. We collapsed together and slept for a while but then she started talking and didn't stop until it got light.

The lovemaking was so good that I thought that over time I could get used to her Brooklyn accent. But as I thought about the evening, I realized that Rose was a real foxy foolish; sexy but not too bright and totally encumbered. I also suspected that she had runway lights on her mattress. She raped my ears with her litany of complaints, troubles, and stories. It became overtly apparent that she would always create more unsolvable problems for herself. When she revealed that she harbored two cats and four dogs, I suggested that these animals were stopping her from leading a healthy life. She answered; "These dogs have taught me more about life than anyone." She reinforced the certainty that she was a dead end with which I did not have the time or energy to play games.

Light travels much faster than sound. This is why some people appear bright until you hear them speak.

Crystal Lear

Her name was Crystal Lear. We had a twenty-minute conversation that was strange because I felt and thought that she was hiding something. Her middle name turned out to be Chandra. I met her for drinks, called her several times, took her out to dinner, and called her again. She didn't have much enthusiasm and seemed to treat the evening as a business. Her body was in great shape, but her face had a striking resemblance to a Pekinese. Not that she was a dog, because she was cute, but in a funny face way. She could have simply said, "I had a good time with you this evening, let's do it again, call me." That's all the little encouragement I would need. But no, she was too independent. In retrospect, what she wanted was someone to treat her in a style that she'd like to be accustomed to and at all cost, she wanted to be the boss. The opposite of love and enthusiasm is not hate but indifference. Too bad, I liked her sharp mind and saw a lot of potential at least for a friendship. It took me a while to realize that she was the only woman I had ever met who had no central heating. But, as my grandfather taught me, never drive down the wrong way on a one-way street.

Before you knock yourself out in pursuit of a new honey, understand that some people just like to have their egos built up, be entertained, like to be treated for dinner, but ultimately are happier alone.

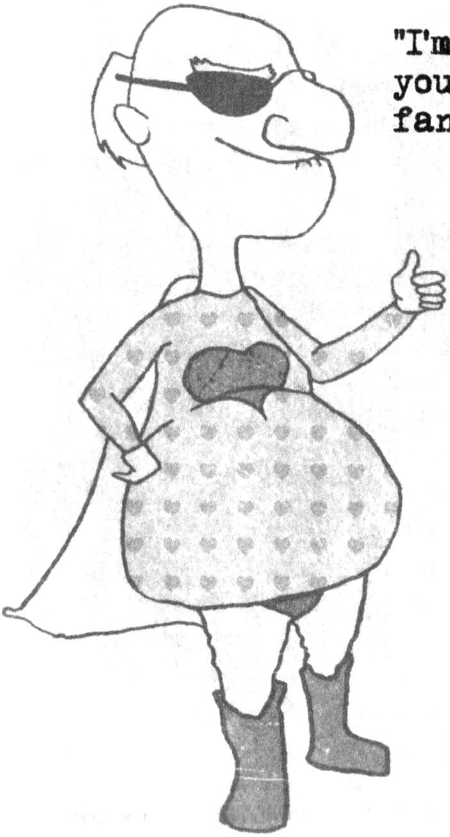

"I'm here to fulfill your every sexual fantasy."

"You mean you've got both a donkey and a Great Dane?"

Sandy Smith

A cyberspace fantasy.

Kiss me once and kiss me twice, it's been a long, long time.

You'll never know how many dreams I dreamed about you, or just how empty they all seemed without you. Kiss me once and kiss me twice, it's been a long, long time.

When I first saw, her working out at the gym, her back was toward me. When she turned around, I was surprised. She had a sweet wasp face and a black ladies steodapegee behind. I approached with caution. Her dark eyes had no discernible iris, instead big black baby dolls eyes with sparks shooting from them like beautiful hothouse flowers. Evolution had accelerated this women's kiss-me-eyes making them emotionally bonding and instantly prominent. Hollywood white teeth and a six-pack stomach completed the picture. I knew that I would talk with her. Looking at her rear end, I said, "Wow, backfield in motion. I'm going to have to give you a penalty." "What?" she said, "you're going to penalize me?" Ten minutes later, her enthusiasm and quick mind reached out and grabbed me. We got together and started to email each other.

Mike, You're terrific. No, you are! It was wonderful talking to you today, and not just the other stuff, although you were soooo right. It was nice sitting on you on the couch and talking to you. I can't wait to do it again. I am hanging out with my roommate now. We are staying in tonight though because of the rain. I hope you have a great night and can't wait to see you tomorrow. So sorry, it is crazy with all this packing crap. I'm out of my place, but I left a few things on accident, so I am about to go back and get them. I will call you tonight. Miss you.

Hi Sandy, wish we had communicated more. My housekeeper could have come to clean while you packed. Can you come over on Friday? Dinner with some friends in the evening? Are you OK? Cheers M

Hello, Mike, I hope all is well. I tried to call you back a couple of times, but I always received a busy tone. The school is very hectic; I'm taking 18 credits again; however, I made all A's last semester, so I am very happy. Tell me what is going on with you. I miss talking to you.

Everywhere I go, there are earphones in my ears. The only way I can study without getting distracted is by forcing myself to stay in the bathtub until I have all the material memorized. I once was in the bathtub for four hours (of course, when the water turned cold, I re-ran the hot water to be comfortable!). I frequently talk in my sleep, I don't sleep too often because I don't want to turn into Rip Van Winkle, I eat hamburgers plain, I don't put the lid on the toothpaste, I love watching people argue in different languages, guessing what they're saying. I hate automatic flushing toilets, I never hear my alarm go off, I hate artificial lighting; I wake up every hour to flip my pillow so that it will be cold, I HATE shots, and I also hate dogs. I have a major phobia of frogs, shushes give me a brain freeze, I don't have common sense, I am obsessed with working out. I have a bathroom journal where people can empty their thoughts while emptying their bladders, I always speed, I hate shaving my legs, and I only drink Gatorade and Orange Juice, and I LOVE to eat. I get really bothered by crooked posters on the wall, my DVD's are in alphabetical order, my clothes are color-coordinated, I like everything on shelves at a 90-degree angle, I have a habit of picking my scabs at least twice a day which will eventually make me where I can be on the proactive commercial, I'm thirty minutes early everywhere I go, I have restless feet syndrome. I wish all seats were toilets because I think bathrooms are really comfortable. There's an ill's bit of information to base your opinion of me off of.

Hi Sandy,

Good letter my little cyber ghost and real communication for a change.

Did you come to New York for New Years? What happened to your phone and email address? I played a lot of different sports all my life. I was superb in all kinds of handball and paddleball and scuba. I used to run for miles and do radical skiing and climbing.

Unfortunately, what the books do not tell you is that the injuries are cumulative and stay with you always. So now, I only have swimming, yoga, weights and learning chess. The last accident, falling off the mountain, really slowed me down. Yes, I am very attracted to you and hope to get together with you. It would have been good for us if we had spent more time together at any point to having some more good memories. Two of my books are finished, but my agent is a procrastinator. In the meantime, I am changing all the electronics in my New York apartment to digital. Then I'm rerecording all my tapes and getting rid of old tape decks and my old computers. It's a pity you did not tell me that you liked old records because I just gave away my Garrard turntable and my entire record collection. Stay in shape. Do you have a new email address?

I was genuinely concerned for your welfare and safety. I could not figure out what happened. So, I said, no rationalized, that you were too good to be true. And that you changed your mind about what you wanted. Don't ever think that you are stranded or in trouble. If you can contact me, I will always bail you out. We have a date for Sun, but can we get together tomorrow late afternoon? I'm open to spending time having fun in the city or anything you like. Don't think you have to stay in NJ. Give them their privacy and stay with me.

Mike, just got the Internet hooked up on this computer. I didn't know my roommates' wireless password, so this is the first time I have been on since I have been in this place. My cell phone screen is busted (and being that it is a touch screen; it won't let me answer or call out). I bet my mom is freaking out. I had four emails from her demanding the number of the person I was living with because she thought something happened. But, my new phone will be here sometime today. I also don't know how to get to the city from here yet, and my roommate is at work, and I can't call her. When she gets home, I will find out what I need to do. I miss you so much. I am so sorry we haven't been able to talk. We will see soon! After all, we have a two-hour season finale of Desperate Housewives on Sunday.

What happened? Are you all right? You have not contacted me for days. I once met a woman with shining eyes; we spent a brief magic moment. She would become stronger with me but then she was gone.

Oh, NO NO! Don't think you are getting rid of me that easily! I have been in a bit of a crisis with my Friend (the girl I am living with). Her dad had a Stroke, so hospital visits have been every day. He just came out of ICU and back home today. Therefore, I haven't been able to go into my Internship, or into the city at all for that matter. I've been thinking of you, though. I miss you. We have to hang out soon. I believe that we need an everyday process of somehow meeting up.

Hi, SS,

Everything works on this end including the phone. You can make all your calls from here. Why are you allowing yourself to be stranded in NJ? I would love to anticipate being with you tonight. But, I have no idea what's happening. Fingers crossed. M

Sandy's lack of communication forced introspection. Life is action, not words. It is also communication. So, instead of getting lost in the fantasy of us being together because truly she is a fantasy coming true, I will try to get back to being grounded in reality. The dream is such a turn on. But in reality, although I kept all possibilities open, I had enough brains to know we were playing. You have to be part of the times in which you live. This was the new way to flirt. Words are beautiful but. Come to me. I changed my mind and never sent this message.

"Words are beautiful, but life is action. I called you many times, I had such great plans for us, but I can't plan without your communication. I realize now that I am not a priority and that you are just a cyber dream. Still, the fantasy was so real and so good."

Mike, you must not have listened to me when I told you that I would be in the Hampton until' Monday, silly! I just got home, and I did not have cell phone service or a Laptop out there, so don't yell at me! I miss you and want to see you too. We just got back to the City a few minutes ago. I will call tomorrow. Miss You. I do think about you often. We will get together when I come back. Miss you lots. I listen to you very carefully.

Waited for your call. I'm out doing some errands, studio, etc. I have to set up my week. Will I see you tonight? Gym, dining? Can't make plans without communication. Leave a message or email me. Taking a class at Apple Soho, Home by 7:30. Dinner with you? Did the dog eat your phone?

If Sandy wants to play, and this is the game, then I will engage the tease and see if I can compete in one of the millennium's new sports. So, I composed the emails so that I could use them for this book.

Hi SS,

Now you know how crazy I am to expect you to dive into a real relationship. I must have scared the heck out of you, even though you are a very special woman. I was silly. Sorry, I will not bother or yell at you anymore. I assume you are going to Florida? Give me a ring one day, and I'll take you out for a steak dinner. You see I am a facilitator and excellent planner. I already solved all your problems and worries. I believe you, but thousands would not. It's been three weeks since I held you. I would have given you everything, but you could not find a pay phone.

There is too little communication and too many disappointments. What care I how good she be if she not be good to me? No more words.

I wrote a new western song called Sandy.

"Oh Sandy, Oh Sandy,

What Can I do?

I've got tears in my ears because I've been lying on my back while crying my heart out over you."

Baby! I called twice today. I called at 2:14 and 3:42! It didn't go to voicemail or anything but check your ID! When could you hang out with me? I worked most of the day today. I am working night shift this weekend. So, what about Friday?

SS,

I like you so much. You are the girl of my dreams. But my prescience and your actions tell me you have another boyfriend. With me, you will be tan between your toes. Do you have air conditioning? The next few days are in the 90s.

A relationship must be cultivated. If you want to be with me, you have to give it much more effort. Little communication equals no planning, equals no future. I'll think of you.

Mike, I was thinking of you the other day. I was thinking what a shame it would be if we didn't keep in touch when I have never hit it off with someone quite like I did with you. I am currently in Florida. My sister is moving to Israel and is leaving on the 5th, so I am here hanging out with her. However, I bought a ticket back to NY the 8th. I would be so very excited to see you again.

You called me just in time. If you could get a job in NYC, what would it be? What would be your wish for an ideal job? I would love to communicate with you. I wanted to invite you for a weekend or week at my beach shack. If we have a future, you have to make some effort. I'm leaving for the month of November. I'll be back in December. Do you think you can compose an email in that time?

Hey, Mike! I just got done with exams. I would love to go to your beach shack. I have tried to call your phone. Have not heard back. Hope everything is going well for you. I am planning to come to New York all of my Christmas' break and through January. I really want to spend time with you.

Hey, Mike! How are you? I hope you have a great trip. I just got done with all of my "exam 3" tests. I have a week break- then time to study for finals. What are your plans for Christmas? Are you going to be in New York? What were/are your life goals?

I have many things I want to accomplish. I get confused and stressed because I am a perfectionist and want everything laid out the way I'd like. Ha-ha. You should know that from my OCD. I love the fitness industry. I would like to be involved in some aspect of the fitness life (commercials, promotional events, or even to the line of a personal trainer). With my major being finance, I could go into the financial sector, but it isn't my passion. Most likely, I would be doing it only for money. I enjoyed being on that television show and I would love to somehow land a few more gigs. I miss talking to you.

Hi,

I'm back. Everything that could go wrong did. But it was a third world country, and they are always broken. My answering machine is on when I leave the country. I have to be out of town in Dec. Otherwise, we can be together but I have to make plans around you. When are you coming in and when are you leaving? Looking forward to beating you at chess and seeing your face.

Hey Mike,

Hi my cyber dream girl,

It is so so good to hear from you! I was thinking of you yesterday because I was in the gym watching a girl do squats incorrectly, and I thought to myself, "What would Mike do in this situation?"

Nothing.

How in the world are you?

Overextended and extremely busy.

I'm sorry I haven't been available on email or phone or anything. The reason is that where I am living these past two months; I have no Internet at all except on my phone. I seriously don't know how people live without the Internet; I'm going crazy. I have it on my phone, but it is so hard to type on it that I don't use it much, but I did figure out how to type a word doc. On my phone and Bluetooth, it to my phone.

Where are you living now?

I have so many fun and crazy stories to share with you, and I will be home in less than a month. I cannot wait! We can finally get into that routine we have talked about for years!

That will have to wait until Oct.

How has everything been going with you? Any women replace me yet?

You are irreplaceable, but I have two new women. One is a head nurse in the Caribbean -but she is too encumbered to give me what I want. The other is a young grad student who unfortunately and stubbornly believes that efficiency is a reality. I think that she will probably go back to Japan after the next semester when she graduates.

I have bought some new heels to play chess, in hopes of distracting you; I WILL win this next match!

I don't think so.

Any new books in the making?

A Way to Live Zen just went out to my agent. Finished at last.

If so, be sure to hand-write them so I can type it in the nude soon.

Best offer today.

School here is so much harder than back home. I know we will have a fantastic time together! We can help each other improving as people so much.

Good-life is for learning.

I don't remember the last time we talked, but I went to Africa, and it was incredible. When I first got there, I realized I forgot my camera, so I went into a shop to buy a disposable one, and I asked if they had a bathroom and they told me yes. So, I went downstairs, and it was a little hole in the floor with no toilet paper; unfortunately, I was in desperate need of toilet paper because I was bleeding, so I went back up to get a tampon, and they asked if I needed toilet paper. Relieved, I said yes, and he handed me a damp bath towel... I am assuming other people had just peed and wiped with it or something.

Just like my place in the Caribbean.

So, strange. But it was a really neat and eye-opening trip. We did a 3-day Morocco tour and spent the night in the Sahara Desert. I brought a broom with me and got pictures "sweeping." I am about to go to the beach and try to get tan for you, so I can sit on your face, but please write me back when you get a chance! Love and miss you!

I will be in Florida hunting for my penthouse. I want to buy a place before December. I need a place very near the ocean so we can swim every day. I also need a large terrace with a BBQ. I need a reserved parking space for our new BMW. Can you look around for me? Don't get burnt too quickly. Welcome home. Soon... maybe.

One thing I find both commendable and impressive about you is your steadfastness. It almost gives me hope that one day we will really get together. Until then I must think of you as a cyber dream, a dream girl that lives in my computer and telephone. My life goals used to be - To be the first man to be stoned on the Moon and to be a beach bum. But someone beat me to the moon, and I've lived the beach bum. Time to move on. Mike

My calendar is closing down. You never sent me the dates you are going to be in town. I'll try like hell to block out some time but... My new girl-friend, (Photo enclosed), is very jealous. She is not as pretty as you but she is an angel and she emails me every day and communicates.

Hi, Perfect, did you read the emails I send to you? Also, tentatively definite, Sat afternoon to Sun afternoon? You have to let me know now so I can modify my plans, which also concern other people. I don't remember college being so stressful. Don't disappoint me. It leaves scars.

Ha-ha :) Exams again. FINALS time. Blah. Stresses me out so badly. I am most likely coming up on the 28th, but will only be able to stay with you until the 4th because school begins the 5th. Will write you more tonight. Your real girlfriend attached and as you can see I have a six-pack.

I am off to the lake house and Nova Scotia and the Bay of Fundy Tuesday night. I had to make plans since I did not hear from you. I wanted to surprise you and take you to see the rushing tides. It would have been romantic and beautiful but... Perhaps it is only a funny game to you? We have 24 hours together if you want when you come in. Maybe we can at least touch base and each other. Perhaps we should wait until you move back to New York next year? You don't answer your Emails and your phone mailbox is full. No wonder I believe that you are just a cyber ghost.

This lovely young woman is driving me crazy. Which admittedly is more like a short walk than a long drive. It's over, I know it, but I don't want to let go. Control is such an illusion. **Nothing and no one controls anything, let alone a relationship.** Communication is always at best one-way and erratic. The game is over, and it does not matter who won. The lesson for me is that I am playing someone else's game. But the touch, the feel of this hard-young beautiful body is like a rejuvenator. But being realistic and mature, I realize it is a young woman playing, and I am too. I must take my good friend Richard's advice when we were talking about how difficult it would be to lose a limb or a digit. He would be devastated by the loss of a leg. I would be ravaged by the loss of my eyes. But then he said the most insightful yet funny line he ever said. "Yes, but you would get laid so much more." I guess I'm still a sucker for a pretty face and lovely young body. But I can't help playing the game one more time with an all-in bluff.

Sandy,

I cannot pursue you any longer. There is too little communication. If you ever want something real, if you ever want to be with a man and build, if you can give me time and priority, call me. But, that entails you and me together. Walks, wine, sunsets, parties, dinner, staying over, long mornings, getting together consistently. This is called a relationship. No more short afternoon delights and daytime quickies. No more baby games or excuses. What it comes down to is, I don't want to die with the music left in my heart.

One of the illusions of life is that the endless opportunities you will have will change your existence for the better. The reality is that only a very few opportunities will contribute to altering your actuality and give you time, space, love, and everything else you want.

If you want a significantly enhanced life with me, the door is still open for a very short while. If not, you will remember that you had the option and that you passed. But **everybody learns the hard way.**

I wanted you. You wanted, anyone you could get. So, losing you, might be the best thing yet.

Almost love, M

I never saw her again.

An excuse is just a well-planned lie.

Trust but verify.

Listen carefully to what your new honey says. Analyze the statements to understand if they are based on beliefs or evidence. Ideas based on innuendo, cultural proclivities, and hunches are doomed to fail and cause multiple problems in compatibility.

"Are you crazy?"

"Why do people keep asking me that? If I was crazy would I know?"

Loss

That's it. No more women who can communicate and aren't responsive. The first thing I'll do is to change my answering machine message. This should also eliminate the people dialing wrong numbers and the idiots who keep leaving communications for the post office. I changed the message to... "Hi, at the beep leave your name and number. Please be kind enough to leave a brief explanation and justification of the ontological spiritualism necessity of modern man's existential dilemma, and I will get back to you. Ciao."

Unless, at sometimes, sweat has streamed down your back, you cannot see the boat sail before the wind.

The wine god was Dionysus. Was he often drunk on Love?

The five most essential words for a healthy, vital relationship are "I apologize" and "You are right."

Women are like apples on trees.

When you first meet someone, you have to fight to be totally open and receptive, especially if the other person is complex and has a different life than yours. On some occasions, we have probably met a person that we could be happy and compatible with but we closed down the opportunity before it began. I'm reminded of the lyrics in a Rolling Stones song. "Think of all the years you have spent looking for... You may be right. I may be crazy. But I just might be a lunatic you're looking for. Take me as I am you might enjoy some madness for a while."

You don't want to waste your time and effort on ambivalent and lukewarm.

Can we circumvent fate? Does the inevitable admit a loophole?

Zen masters used to reinforce their lessons with blows. If this seems cruel, consider the lessons life teaches and the heavy blows with which they are hammered home.

Music is a bridge between earth and heaven. Music can also set the tempo for intertwined sex and make it last longer creating a more intense, complex, joint activity.

Although you might say the same thing about loss or grief, opportunities that can give you quantum lifts in your life are rare. Sometimes something runs by you that you should be able to apply life's experience to and recognize. But instead of taking action you watch it go by and think it will reappear or turn out to your advantage. Usually, something happens and it does not come to a culmination. You look back at all the signals that you should have paid attention to. But, in life and love, like luck, it passed you by, and you didn't notice it, or procrastinated until it was too late. Make your decisions faster and implement them more efficiently.

You may think that you have time. You have one free pass, that was it.

There is sadness lurking at the edges of every adult life. Fate is the mere reverberation of other people's power. Our regrets can occasionally overwhelm us for the life not led. But, even if we are all going to die it doesn't mean we have to camp out in cemeteries.

If You Woke up Breathing, Congratulations! You have another chance!

The 70 million baby boomers soon to come of age would be dubbed the me generation for indulging in obsessive self-interest decay. In his 1979 book, Culture of Narcissism, Christopher Lasch said, "Americans wanted to transcend their self-absorption, but had become trapped by the language of individualism into seeing no point in trying to reconnect with others, that's exactly what we must do, say today's communitarians, not just for the health of our democracy but for ourselves."

Medical studies confirm that individuals are sicker and die sooner in direct proportion to the degree that they are isolated from others.

If you cannot find love and the truth right where you are and in this book, where else do you expect to find it? As one lamp serves to dispel a thousand years of darkness, so one flash of wisdom destroys ten thousand years of ignorance.

We worry unnecessarily most of the time about things that have not happened and perhaps never will. This is especially true in many relationships. Was the kiss good enough? Was I too passive sexually? If I lost my job would he or she leave me? Wait until it happens to see if the event or action will produce change. That way you save a lot of worry and might be pleasantly surprised. And what should you really worry about and be afraid of? The follow statistics are based on annual averages and estimates. These are some threats many of us fear and their riskier counterparts.

Burglaries 2.2 million. Identity thefts 8.3 million.

Shark attacks 28. Dog bites 4.5Million.

Deaths by allergic reactions 100.

Death by unintentional poisoning 28,000.

Women who die from breast cancer 40,000.

Women who die from cardiovascular disease 440,000.

Fatal airline accidents 340. Fatal car crashes 34,040.

Americans audited by IRS 1.4 million.

US deaths 2.4 million.

Savor your life. Chew every mouthful thirty times. If you rush you will miss something remarkable.

Keep your perspective, but try to laugh at the worst that can happen, then you can better cope with the consequences.

Love and meditation is not about cutting yourself off from the world, but opening yourself up to it.

Love yields to circumstance. Don't look for the answers, this is it.

The women were not the most attractive, but they did not have to be. Because of their availability and responsiveness, they were much more desirable then any of the made up, finger nailed polished, long haired, long legged women, who teased, and chastised men for their sexually Darwinian aggressiveness. Or, as one crass man said, "It's hard to fuck somebody on a pedestal."

Neural pathways in the brain and body have a tendency to set. This is why most people find it so difficult to change.

Come into my tender trap, please.

Remember; to spend some time with your loved ones, because they are not going to be around forever, to give a warm hug to the one next to you, because that is the only treasure you can give with your heart and it doesn't cost a cent, to say, 'I love you' to your partner, but most of all mean it. A kiss and an embrace will mend hurt when it comes from deep inside of you, and cherish the moment. Give time to love, give time to speak.

Attitude

Stephen Covey repeats, in The Seven Habits of Highly Effective People, a compelling story of a captain of a battleship that has just been informed by a lookout that light has been spied dead ahead through the fog in the distance. The captain orders a signal sent by flashing light.

"We are on a collision course, advise you alter course 30 degrees to port."

The signal is straight away returned, "Advisable for you to change course 30 degrees starboard." The captain ordered his communications officer to send back, "I'm a captain. You had better change course 30 degrees' port immediately."

"I'm a seaman second class" came the reply. "You had better change course 30 degrees starboard."

Now extremely irked the Captain spit out, "I'm a battleship. Change course 30 degrees' port now."

Back came the flashing light. "I'm a lighthouse."

Just because the past, or a relationship, or a love affair, did not turn out the way you wanted it to, does not mean that your future affairs cannot be better than you ever imagined. Try again. You have the power, all the time, to say that this is not how the story will end. Change is difficult, growth can be stressful, but nothing is as painful as staying in the same place, or with the same person, especially if you do not want to be there. Discipline is living in the now and taking control by forcing yourself to do something different and in spite of what you feel. Listen more, you will learn more about how to set new goals.

Sunrise

The sun came up, and the rooster crowed. The farmer went out of his house, fed the chickens and gathered the eggs. The rooster strutted around the yard and chased some chickens. The sun came up, and the rooster crowed. The farmer went out of his house fed the chickens and gathered the eggs. The rooster strutted around the yard and chased some chickens. The sun came up, and the rooster crowed. The farmer came out of his house fed the chickens and gathered the eggs and cut off the cocks' head.

Just because the sun comes up, we cannot assume the day will be the same. ***If we repeat the same actions, we will usually get the same results.*** *One day we may get our heads chopped off. Repetition and redundancy are not growth. If we want to grow and prosper, we must refine and make changes in our day-to-day lives.*

Social Media

Transformations in communication, and the haiku like shortening of written interaction have deteriorated our abilities to express ourselves in complex ways and nurture connections. *A prime example is the embellishing of the communication by sending cartoons, symbols, pictographs and pictures, instead of communicating with words. Virtual communication is deteriorating human relationships. Instead of mingling or opting to meet with friends we text, we miss someone's else's reactions, expression's, body language, and tones. Emails and smartphone conversations depersonalize encounters because they do not allow in person sustained eye contact. This primate exchange, unique to humans because of the high contrast between the iris and the white part of the eye, releases oxytocin, a hormone associated with social bonding. Even when the encounter is in person, a technological phenomenon intercedes and they appear to be driven by the one all-encompassing goal, the selfie.*

Love of Country

"Jesus Mike, you're so fucking negative at times, and antigovernment, and anti-authority..."

"That because my generation grew up with Vietnam, the JFK assassination, were the dreams of a generation were buried that day, and the atomic bomb. And they were all human-made events. Imagine as a child having drills and hiding under wooden desks to escape the ten thousand degrees' nuclear fireball. That engenders trust in a government."

A military film titled The Big Picture was produced for the armed forces and the American people. It was to instruct soldiers before they participated in atomic maneuvers. The military Chaplin in the film calms and tells anxious soldiers what to expect. "No need to be worried the army has taken all possible precautions. First, you will see a bright light, then a shock wave follows. Then you look up and see the fireball ascending to the heavens with all the colors of the rainbow as it turns into a beautiful sight to behold the mushroom cloud." The soldiers after witnessing the atomic explosion from as close as 3,000 yards from ground zero return to camp bleeding from their eyes, ears, nose, and mouth.

When I was stationed in Alaska, in The Yukon Command Headquarters & Headquarters Company, as a specialist, I observed many incidents and situations that I questioned. Although we obviously need superior armed forces, some military actions, especially when putting Americans in unnecessary jeopardy are unacceptable.

Today's millenniums just have hurricanes and tsunamis, all natural phenomenon. Hey kids, ain't ya heard the news? We are causing all this grief because we are changing the earth's climate, and it is already too late. Our rising water world covers 70 percent of our planet; we have only begun to explore it in the last few decades while decimating it when extract-

ing its resources and polluting it at the same time. And it supplies most of the oxygen we need to breathe.

"Love seeps in over time, just like hate. I'd gotten so used to the decency of our President that I had come to think of decency as a right rather than a privilege. I was wrong about that." Ann Patchett, Time Jan. 2017

Direction is more important than speed.

The past is your lesson. The present is a gift. The future is your motivation.

Attraction

Women evolutionarily have a keener sense of smell than men. They biologically can screen men's odors for MHC molecules, a complex of genes involved in disease resistance, filling a genetic gap, thereby having more diverse protective genes in their children when they search for a mate. The more differentiated the MHC is in the man, the more they are attracted. **So, women love with their nose and ears, while men just love with their eyes.** *Women are also more attracted to men with deep voices. Men's preference is breathiness.*

Symmetrical appearance is preferable and most attractive for both sexes, as are faces that are similar, positive, happy, and are associated with good physical characteristic and health.

Love Notes

It is not your admiration that I adore.

But why am I music to your ears?

Young, wild-haired child, dreams too vivid to ignore.

With wisdom, only age allows,

As a child, I wrote a poem.

Futile love for an older, wiser man teasing, taunting.

But with you, I will never lose my innocence,

You are armor against the mundane.

Often you are curiously, beautifully younger than I.

With all your beauty, intelligence and venom too it's amazing you're still single. Have I lost you?

Honey, you can't have everything. Where would you put it? I love you madly, and I will be delighted to give to you all that you need. But, I cannot give to you all that you want. In life, you must be prepared to give something up for you to obtain goals, wants needs and achievements. You usually will have to give up time and energy to earn money. Give up space and funds to achieve aesthetics. Relinquish some ego, privacy, and a lot of time to obtain love and intimacy. I will support you in any endeavor you desire toward your path of self-actualization.

But, what are you willing to give up to obtain what you need? Those who hold out for everything off time wind up with nothing. So be careful, and choose you're prioritizing carefully.

Dating websites

Satoru, I have broken off with my last sweetheart and am searching the Internet for a new love. But I am in conflict with my Zen proclivity and the disappointment of my digital search. I read your last blog and laughed as I applied your Zen advice. My problem was completely alleviated. Can you help me with this new dilemma?

The dating websites should be declared a large, permeating, buyer-beware zone. The most obvious problem is that they do not vet potentials for truthfulness, so the biggest impediment in all online dating is dishonesty. However, if you accept this fact, then screen very carefully, you might find a winner among the many players. But you must move on from a screen-dependent life and rethink your relationship to technology and our new always connected culture and its many forms of digital exhaustion.

Communication in the present time is instant, constant and overwhelming. The television remains on for the company, the radio plays, the sound system emanates books out loud, our cell phones are around our necks, we are e-mailed, voice mailed, junk mailed and spend hours in front of vicarious mediums like movies, games, and computers. There is so much going on and being said that to maintain your sanity no one listens, after all, what is there left to say?

If you are much more comfortable with e-mail and instant messaging than person-to-person contact, then your social skills need to be honed and reintroduced to face-to-face interaction. One question might be how is the Internet going to help you develop a more agreeable or pleasing personality? With the caveat that for business the information highway is the catalyst of connections and the incongruity that sex has always powered the Internet gold rush. When ***you spend time on the Internet, you do not hear a human voice; you have no real interaction, and you never get a hug.***

For years' television and weed were a great zone out form of relaxation and a way to escape involvement. Now **the digital age has given us an interactive diversion that sucks us into believing that we are connected and refining our relationships and lists.**

Conversation, physical interaction, visual stimulation, sensory experience, and meaningful bonding connections have taken a back seat to our computers, pads, and cell phones. Not to denigrate the wonderful accomplishments of communication and facilitations that the digital age has given to us. But, interpersonal relationships, eye-to-eye contact and acquiring a new honey, are about being in a state of communication, living physically, and in the now.

That said, considering the ubiquitous of the Internet, time constraints, being part of the age you live in, and the abundant choices of and on the dating sites, you have to give it at least a try. Of course, it can also open the floodgates regarding choice. When you at last think that you have picked a winner, in a short time, you might feel that you are taking a sandwich to a banquet. Or going to an all you can eat buffet only to have all the great chefs in the world dumping their food creations on your plate. The plethora of romantic possibilities and practical options negates the likelihood of you making a decision, committing or actually dating.

So here is a partial list of some of the sites available today. Remember the law that governs all acquisitions, **"Let the buyer beware."**

Apps for online dating

For the hook up generation and multitaskers obsessed with digital distractions. Although dating apps launched just nine years ago have revolutionized the way romance happens.

420 Dating (For pot smokers)

Bumble (Type A women make the first move)

Clover (Uber for dating)

Coffee Meets Bagel (Noon meeting)

Cupidtino (For Apple fans.)

Happen (based on location)

Hinge (Sifts Facebook)

How about we (Poses fun dates)

Howaboutwe.com (matches based on similar activities.)

Match.com (Adjust contacts & preferences)

Meet Mindful (health and fitness singles bond over things restoring.)

EHarmony (uses algorithms to extrapolates behavior patterns.)

OK, Cupid, Hinge, Afrormance, plentyoffish, fitness-singles.com.

OKCupid (free, users rate the matches. Based on unusual answers to quirky ques.)

Sea captain Date (for Sailors and fans.)

Stache Passions (For mustache lovers.)

Tinder (interesting UK app download. Users scan photos and profiles to Like or dismiss)

UK Shag a Gamer (horny geeks find no-strings nookie)

Vampersonals (For vampire enthusiasts.)

In my inquiries, I found that some women use the sites just to be taken out to dinner.

Some men use the sites just to get laid. (What's new?)

Remember I told you, so ***forewarned is forearmed.***

If you get something for free, you are the product.

A date is when two people actually meet and not just type words at each other over a cold screen.

Reciprocity and Symbiosis are good manners.

When someone makes a gesture toward you in making life easier for you or helping you in some way, pay him or her back. If they invite you for dinner whether or not you have the dinner with them, call them the next day to thank them. Never accept an invitation to dinner and show up empty handed. If you cannot think of an appropriate present, a scented candle or music is always appreciated, or you must bring a bottle of wine or flowers. If you go to a party, eat the food, drink the wine, met new people, next time you go out and invite them for dinner pick up the check and send them a thank you card. Payback and reciprocate. ***Everyone likes to be appreciated.***

Show your appreciation and be a good friend. Even making or not making a simple phone call can be a significant contribution or distraction from a relationship or friendship. **Friendship must be cultivated.** *If a stranger does a good deed for you, pass it on.*

Women are like apples on trees.

When just a few paragraphs ago you read this, what did you think? What was your reaction? What was your emotional response?

Women are like apples on trees. The best ones are at the top of the tree. Most men don't want to reach for the good ones because they are afraid of falling and getting hurt. Instead, they sometimes take the apples from the grounds that aren't as good, but easy. The apples at the top think something is wrong with them, when in reality, they're amazing. They just have to wait for the right man to come along, the one who is brave enough to climb all the way to the top of the tree. Share this with women who are good apples, even those who have already been picked.

Now, men, men are like a fine wine. They begin as grapes, and it's up to women to stomp the crap out of them until they turn into something acceptable to have dinner with.

A friend of mine sent me this apple comparison story that she got off the Internet. After reading the "Wisdom," I realized that my friend, who was a woman, has an entirely different perspective on the story. As a man, I have never found that the best women were located in any particular place, area, or group and that the women who were easy were much more appealing because of their accessibility. Also, because the women were reachable, all the low hanging fruit gets plucked early. Although I have pursued some women who were at the top, generally, I have found that not only were they not amazing but pursuing them was a dead end, their self-image was skewed, and they were full of illusions.

If I want to analyze further, Women are like apples; I might say, "Yes because they are juicy and delicious. Or the ones on top look the best, but you never know until you bite them. Or the ones that have just fallen are usually full of sugar and juicier since that are so full that that cannot hold themselves up. Or who wants to risk all that time and effort to climb and find the supposedly best apple when, considering that man seeks to fulfill his desires by the least exertion, that an apple on the lowest branch can be just as sweet."

In a conversation with my friend, who sent the story to me, I brought up that women are like apples simile. I pointed out that she accepted as the fact that the comparison was accurate and she was reluctant to discuss the variations. The opinions we do not discuss can never be refuted. Since different ideas are sometimes threatening and ego deflating, we are usually reluctant to discuss them. I have found, however, that discussions of negative aspects are one of the keys to effective communication in a relationship.

All alone or all one

Sometimes I wonder just what in the hell I'm doing with my life. Attempting to write and live an aesthetic life of a sculptor. Creating beauty in a world that has little understanding or interest, except for a few elite and a few arts educated people. Secretly living life according to the rules of design and art, variation, dominance, repetition, texture, etc. It is my passion, and I have little choice. It's as bad as trying to make a living as a musician- but at least the music is good, and they get laid a lot.

If the price you have to pay for not being alone is never to be alone, then the expense for not being alone is too high. Alone and lonely or never alone and bored is a tough call. What does it all add up to anyway? Love is a theoretical concept at best; sex the total driving force of most lives. Or, is it just not wanting to sleep alone? To be driven by that primeval instinctive force after having a shitty day to go home to someone, make real love at night, and feel that you can go on for another day.

I always thought that for me, just another naked ape, that subliminally going back eons of time, she sleeping next to me made me feel secure, even though I was so much stronger than her and could protect her. She would wake me up in time to counteract the danger facing us in the cave or on the savanna and know the relationship was symbiotic. We 'd support each other against the world. Or perhaps we were both crazy, and we'd stay together because it was a complimentary neurosis. On the other hand, even with a good relationship, even if you both like each other and share having children, we live so much longer now, it always seems to end. But ultimately, aren't we all alone.

There ain't no slack in my act, jack. I was really something in my day, but that day is long gone.

Overwritten

She was without question the most beautiful woman he had ever seen in his entire life. He gulped down the last of his martini, and without hesitation, walked to where she sat at the end of the opulent bar.

"You must forgive my rudeness," he said "but when I beheld you sitting here, all wrapped up in exquisite white fur, the lights dancing in your hair like stars, I had to speak with you. I've never gazed upon such beauty as yours before. I want to lay Manhattan at your feet, buy you jewels, exotic perfumes, and a thousand other wondrous things. If you bid me welcome, we will fly this very night to Paris, then on to Rome, India, and finally to Egypt for a trip down the Nile."

The young lady was utterly taken with this rugged, handsome, stranger who stood tall before her, with tan skin, hair prematurely graying at the temples and wearing a dark, Italian, perfectly cut suit. She was almost speechless and could only manage a breathless, "Yes yes."

"The go prepare yourself my Juliet, my Venus, my Helen of Troy. When you are ready, call me at this number, and I will come for you".

"Is this your private number at your townhouse or your country estate?" she sighed.

"Well," he said "Actually it's the delicatessen downstairs, but they'll call me.

grá
aimer
каханне
liefde
愛
amare

Divorce

Life IS for Learning

There appears to be a common denominator for the divorced women I met. First, they have a sense of failure for the first few years after the separation. The ones that successfully moved on have redefined themselves as single women looking for another relationship that can be mutually supportive and beneficial. The unsuccessful women still define themselves through their marriage. They say, "I am a divorced woman with two grown children." Most of the time they are untrusting, because they once made an ultimate complete commitment and after giving everything, the best years of their lives, their youth and time, they were rejected, usually for another woman. The rage that they have is internalized, and they cannot help being passive aggressive.

One of the most interesting manifestations is that the divorced women now want "a real man" as compared to most of the men with whom they have been exposed or interacted. The dichotomy is that they also want control and assert their need to control the relationship as well. What they really want is someone to dovetail with their time and profession, entertain them, and fit in perfectly with what their mother told them they should have connected to thirty years ago. Unfortunately, times have changed, and they do not realize that they are in competition not only with all the women their age but all younger women. The younger women understand that Dreams are for those that sleep and life is action. The younger women are much more aggressive, proactive, and seem to handle rejection much better. The older women do not handle rejection well at all and do not try. They still need to build their self-image up by being pursued, something most men, considering the single ratio is thirty females to one male, are loath to do.

Relationship Rationales

Bob and Mike grew up together and became partners. One day Mike caught Bob opening their safe and taking out money. "Bob, how can you do this to me? I supported you in all your endeavors. I got you your coop apartment before I got mine, because you had to move out of your crazy girlfriends' place, and you made thousands when you sold it. I loaned you money to start your business that you never paid back. I gave you good advice throughout your career. How can you have so little regard for me?"

"Yes, all that is true. But what have you done for me lately?"

The new and accumulating research suggests something heartening: People who are single are doing much better than we realized. Marriage is unlikely to bring lasting improvements to their health or well-being, and could even result in decrements.

Socrates

Keep this in mind the next time you are about to repeat a rumor or spread gossip.

In ancient Greece (469 - 399 BC), Socrates was widely lauded for his wisdom. One day an acquaintance ran up to him excitedly and said, "Socrates, do you know what I just heard about Diogenes?"

"Wait a moment," Socrates replied, "Before you tell me I'd like you to pass a little test. It's called the Triple Filter Test."

"Triple filter?" asked the acquaintance.

"That's right," Socrates continued, "Before you talk to me about Diogenes let's take a moment to filter what you're going to say. The first filter is Truth. Have you made sure that what you are about to tell me is true?"

"No," the man said, "Actually I just heard about it."

"All right," said Socrates, "So you don't really know if it's true or not. Now let's try the second filter, "The filter of Goodness." Is what you are about to tell me about Diogenes something good?"

"No, on the contrary..."

"So," Socrates continued, "You want to tell me something about Diogenes that may be bad, even though you're not certain it's true?"

The man shrugged, a little embarrassed. Socrates continued, "You may still pass the test, though, because there is a third filter, "The filter of Usefulness." Is what you want to tell me about Diogenes going to be useful to me?"

"No, not really."

"Well," concluded Socrates, "If what you want to tell me is neither true nor good nor even useful, why tell it to me or anyone at all?"

The man was bewildered and ashamed.

This is an example of why Socrates was a great philosopher and held in such high esteem. It also explains why Socrates never found out that Diogenes was having sex with his wife.

Zen, life, and relationships are too important to be taken gravely. Life is a cosmic theater where we should endeavor to play our essential roles significantly while not taking them too seriously. The powerful play goes on, and you want to develop a verse, edit, and rewrite your own story. Your reach should exceed your grasp, so keep your feet in the mud but aim for the stars. If you only grab the moon accept it cheerfully.

The Gift

I was living in my beach shack retreat on the Island. I strolled back from my daily swim along the shore of the deserted beach. I was annoyed that the water was milky with little visibility. It is always a joy to swim in gin clear water and observe the life in the sea. When the ocean is evident I swim for two hours, a mile out, weaving through the outlying reefs. But, when it is this opaque, it is too dangerous, so I stay a few hundred feet off the shore. Still, I mused, it was a good forty-minute workout. Because I cut my swim short, I took a break and sat down on the chairs, on the beach, in front of my beach shack. The isolation was splendid, and I had the whole three-mile beach and the vast ocean to myself.

Having time to stop and meditate on the seemingly unlimited vista of the sea in front of me, I put my fins on the table next to me and made some tiny adjustments to my mask. I took off my knife and checked the release. I don't usually swim with my big dive knife but a six-foot hammerhead shark surprised and scared me a few days ago, and the blade gave me some security. But experiences of a lifetime of diving and swimming taught me that large dive knife was like a toothpick against a giant.

Gazing on the panorama, a mile down the shore, a person was walking toward me. I looked at my dive watch curious to see how long they would take to pass me. After they passed, I would walk up the dune to my beach shack to shower. As the person came closer, I saw that it was a woman. I was amazed at the fortune of the view because the woman was young and attractive. As she passed in front of me, I yelled out, "crowded today." She could not hear me over the thudding of the waves and ran toward me. Her legs were strong, but the rest of her body jiggled as she moved. She possessed very strong legs that held up a big tushie, my kind of woman.

I said, "crowded today" and her smile transformed her face. We small talked for a while, and she relaxed. She evidently had been thinking and resolving some problems, as she slowly walked along the beach, and now she opened up to a stranger. She revealed that she could not bear children because of an early in her life hysterectomy and her husband wanted a family. He wanted to have a child with his ex-girlfriend, and they would raise it. She said, "Why doesn't he go back to her." It was a dead end for her, and she was breaking up with him now.

I listened as she unloaded her burden. Her eyes smiled but her words clothed hurt emotions. We talked more about jobs, relationships, and the wonderful private beach. She asked what I did, and I told her of my books. She said how much she liked to write. I suggested that perhaps if she wrote her feelings down, it would help to finalize her thoughts. We talked a lot about expressing emotions with the written word and how difficult it was to edit your own writing. I gave her my email and invited her for a drink the next day. An hour before we were to meet she emailed me that she did not feel well and sent me this note.

Sitting at her favorite coffee shop on The Island, she listened to the sounds of the world. Three days before, she and her husband strolled along the three-mile pink sand beach, with destiny leading them down different paths. Her fire and zest for experiences, people, and places opened her soul to all that she had to give, while his desires were to create roots in the small mountain town he called home. The clash of dreams and desires, along with future aspirations had closed this chapter of this ill-fated love story.

As she waved goodbye to her husband from the government dock, as the water taxi sped across the bay, she wiped the tears and said "Thank You" amidst a long sigh. Thank you for the time together, thank you for the experiences, thank you for the growth, and especially the acknowledgment that closing this chapter was best for both. Choking with emotion, she went to her new favorite escape, a Caribbean Coffee Retreat. There is something about the atmosphere in this coffee shop that invites conversation, opens up her senses, and creates space for the words to pour through the strokes of her keyboard.

She had been here before, heartbroken, hurt, and open to the possibility of what is to come. It was not the first and would certainly not be the last time that love had failed. It is part of the process of life. Growth only comes with choices that have taught us what we did not want, or what was wrong. Learning from this experience, she was more vibrant and radiant that ever before. The difference in her heartbreak now, was that she knew there was more to discover. Choosing smiles over frowns would heal her wounds and allow her to share her knowledge with those that needed it.

Her talents and gifts were shaped by her experiences. There is a gift in each day, in fact probably several. The gift of staying on this remote island an extra week to heal, the gift of conversation with the people of the Isle, and the gift of opening her heart to the world. Her gift would be shared through words. For so many years she had needed the gift of the words "I Love You" from someone else. What she realized, she always had that inside of her, and opening her heart, meant spreading her love and passion to all of those with whom she came in contact.

The healed scars on her heart had given her a new perspective. The choices and experiences had propelled her to this exact moment. As she turned the page to a new chapter, the coming words would be different.

We ran into each other at the coffee shop a few days later. She was working on her laptop and making calls. She was all business and the light up welcome smile was gone as well as the friendly demeanor. Had she revealed too much to me in our conversation and was now taciturn? Did she regret the letter that she sent to me? Not wanting to intrude, and because the pleasant expression was gone from her face, I sat for a while at a separate table having breakfast as she worked. I didn't want to impose on her space, but as I got up to leave she was off the phone and looking around I said to her, "I'm sorry you are so busy. It would have been nice to talk."

"Yes, me too."

"If you expand your letter into a short story I'll put it in the book that I'm editing now."

"All right."

She was preoccupied, distant, and indifferent. I said goodbye and ka ka mun.

Love has nothing to do with looks, but everything to do with time, trust, and interest.

Happiness and misery depend as much on temperament as they do on the fortune so try cultivating a better outlook and disposition. Your chances for happiness in life and love will be greatly enhanced.

Change your physical routines and move more toward action. Acting happy creates a better mood. Look in the mirror and laugh out loud. When was the last time you laughed with a big stupid grin on your face? Feel the stiff muscles give. But on some music and dance, move, scream, yell, and shout out loud and remember that other people are home or at work sitting and typing.

Maria Shriver, in her book "Ten Things I wish I'd known before I went out into the real world," wrote, "One thing that can kill a marriage or relationship is the Prince Charming Delusion. That's expecting your partner to do it all for you: make you happy, fix you, fulfill you, complete you, define you, and make your life meaningful for you. Giant mistake."

The better you look, the more you see.

The happiest people don't necessarily have the best of everything; they just make the best of everything they have. Life isn't about how to survive the storm but how to dance in the rain.

Ordinary, everyday love, is selfish, darkly rooted in desires and replete with satisfactions. In the general context, when everyone speaks of love, this is primarily what he or she are describing. Often individuals treat the person they love like a lemon or chewing gum. They squeeze out of the other person everything they can, and then they throw him or her away. Most people do not differentiate between their needs and wants, a common monumental failing. People have particular needs, physical and emotional. They find someone to fulfill those needs, and they call it love. And when they feel or think that the person no longer satisfies those needs, they say, "The dream and reality that once was our love is changed and gone." That is what you hear in so many favorite songs: Listen to, What About You by Dr. Hook or There Goes My Baby by the Drifters, or Sweet Annie by the Zac Brown Band or A Sunday Kind of Love by the Del Vikings. There it is: "I need you." It is based on selfishness-desires and satisfaction. And what happens when I don't need you anymore? "Good-bye, baby!" No wonder there is such a high divorce rate!

Life is a big ocean and love is a tiny boat, but it can float.

If you have a partner or two people who agree all the time, then one of them is unnecessary.

I told my first wife, when she said she wanted a divorce, sign here, take everything. She did. It was the right decision and I moved on clean. Do not dwell on the loss, time passes and so does the pain. Next!

Smart

You meet one of the smartest people in the world.
What do you ask them?

What question would allow you to fill the blank space that has the potential to fulfill you?

Are you prepared to ask something significant?

If you could have any one wish fulfilled. And you could ask for anything except money. What would you ask for?

How can you make your dreams into a reality if you have not examined your life, your aspirations, your relationships and yourself?

"I worked
like a dog
today"

"If I throw a stick, will you leave?"

Manners

civilized interaction

Manners are rules that are used to allow civilized interaction among people, relationships, and to facilitate diverse groups living together.

No matter how slowly I walked, it seemed that there are vast numbers of individuals who walk even slower. Walking traffic in the city was incredible. In many South American countries, especially Peru, people are always bumping into each other and starting fights over who has the right of way. In New York City, no one seems to crash into each other at all; instead, scurrying by, they step on each other's feet.

In most of the world, walking on the right-hand side of the Street is the proper route for pedestrians. If it is good manners to pass on the right, but in New York, no one seems to have heard of the rule. The same might be said of Universal egress. The person coming out has the right of way, whether it is a subway, building, or elevator. The fact that this is good manners and facilitates traffic appears to have escaped most people. Is it that they are unaware of these facts or is it that they do not know? Or maybe they just don't give a dam. Still, this is the city I love to walk in, despite the incessant noise and threatening vehicular traffic that no politician has the guts to improve.

I ambled to the gym enjoying the unusually warm weather. It was almost fifty degrees and a light leather jacket over a long sleeve T-shirt was sufficient. It was such a pleasure not to wear a thick winter coat or parka. Most of the time, I will try to be a considerate walker, but today people were cutting me off left and right, mobile phone dummies were stopping short to text or walking without looking and it changed my mood because, being a sizeable guy, one ninety and six feet, I could easily just step on them as they cut me off. It was always a conflict within myself whether to curb my aggression or teach people's manners. By the time I got to the place where I shop, I stopped short a dozen times to avoid stepping on people. Perhaps it was the shopping season, but that was such a lame excuse.

I stood aside as a line of people exited the store and then went in. The store was crowded with gawking rubber necked tourists who marveled at the high prices and variation of goods. Although the store probably had some of the highest rates in the city, it also had the best quality foods. I resolved long ago, considering I have so few expensive vices, that a small quality of good food with a good bottle of wine is preferable to a large quantity of anything edible.

I approached the bread counter, and the lovely woman behind the counter asked, "Can I help you, Mike?"

"I can use a scalp message right now."

"No! Really."

"I'd like a new Mercedes, a vacation in New Zealand, and a new girlfriend."

"I can't give you the first two but how about me, Mike?" She said as she smiled a slow, thoughtful beam.

Through my smile, I asked her if she would be kind enough to hold a large loaf of sourdough boule for me until I could pick it up in about two hours. "No problem." She said as she put the bread in a plastic bag and set it on the side and asked, "Let me know where we are going on our date, so I will know how to dress, or undress."

I bought the same type of loaf three times a week, so she knew me as a regular customer. We always went through a harmless flirting routine, and I am sure we both wondered how much we were really playing.

It took a while to get to the front of the store because people stopped to look at everything and not necessarily buy. The front door had a line of foreign tourists continually entering. After a while, I said, "excuse me" in a loud voice; my politeness barely registered, and I pushed past them.

When I got to the gym, there were two attractive girls ahead of me in line. Both were searching in their handbags for their identification that would allow them entry. One moved to the side after giving me a complete toe to head flashing look and nudging the other girl to look at me. The other girl, who had a beautiful head of shoulder length shiny brown hair, stood in the turnstile ahead of me continuing to hunt for her identification.

"Excuse me. Do you think you could step aside so I can enter? Since I knew I was coming to the gym, I have my ID ready."

Ignoring me, she continued to ransack through her bag and was trying to act pretty.

"Hello, earth calling, other people in the world, behind you. Have a little awareness, please?"

The other people in line behind me laughed, and the monitor at the door asked her to step aside. I flashed my pass and went in. I waited at the water fountain to hydrate for a guy to fill up his water bottle, lousy gym etiquette. Bending over I took a drink. I'm not sure if the girl who had, at last, found her identification did it on purpose, but when she passed me, she brushed against me. Had I been less alert and not changed the angle of my body she might have pushed me into the fountain and broken my teeth. Was she baiting me or was this her way of flirting? I would have none of it.

I finished my drink and walked toward the stairwell that leads to the locker rooms. Ahead of me, the same brown haired good-looking girl meandered down the two flights of stairs. First, she moved to the right, in front of me, and then she transferred to the left. All at once she stopped short and began looking into her gym bag searching for some unknown. Again, I did not know if she was doing her dance and routine on purpose and expected me to slam into her. I moved around her and in passing said, "It must be tough being retarded."

"What did you say?"

"And hearing disabled as well."

"You have a lot of nerve talking to me like that. Who do you think you are?" She said as she stared at me with her best snooty look.

"Excuse me tin man lady but I have a heart. It doesn't take any nerve talking to someone who is so totally narcissus and unaware of other people around them, and I know exactly who I am."

"I'm going to tell the authorities the names that you called me and report you."

"Oh, please don't say that I was politically incorrect and called you retarded." I said as I clasped my hands in front of me and feigned a concerned demeanor. "Just tell them I said mentally challenged. And I honestly doubt if you will remember any of this conversation five minutes from now, but you're free to do anything you want as long as you stay in the back of me. You know, you should not punish others just because you make love with rubber gloves on and haven't had an orgasm in months."

"You are such a pig." She said, positively bristling with hostility.

"Next to your anger Mount Pinatubo will be like an unripe zit, but, I suspect that you are a hardcore carpet cleaner, and you really need help."

"You male pigs are all the same."

"And the fact that you rapidly understood my put down reveals to me that you are a Lesbian and unfortunately a man hater. And I truly apologize for assuming malice for what stupidity can explain."

"What's your name?"

"Mellifluous Prometheus Satoru VonHantz, and good riddance to you."

If you think there is good in everyone, you haven't met everybody.

An Elderly Woman

An elderly woman walked into the Bank one morning with a purse full of money. She wanted to open a savings account and insisted on talking to the president of the Bank because she said, she had a lot of money. After many lengthy discussions, an employee took the senior woman to the president's office.

The president of the Bank asked her how much she wanted to deposit. She placed her purse on his desk and replied $165,000. The president was curious and asked her how she had been able to save so much money. The senior woman responded that she made bets. The president was surprised and asked, 'What kind of wagers?' The elderly woman replied, 'Well, I bet you $25,000 that your testicles are square.' The president started to laugh and told the woman that it was impossible to win a bet like that. The woman just looked at the president and said, 'Would you like to take my bet?' 'Certainly,' replied the president. 'I bet you $25,000 that my testicles are not square.' Done,' the elderly woman answered. 'But given the amount of money involved, if you don't mind I would like to come back at ten o' clock tomorrow morning with my lawyer as a witness.' 'No problem,' said the president of the Bank confidently.

That night, the president became very nervous about the bet and spent a long time in front of the mirror examining his testicles, turning them this way and that, checking them over again and again, until he was positive that no one could consider his testicles as square and reassuring himself that there was no way he could lose the bet. The next morning at exactly 10 o'clock the elderly woman arrived at the president's office with her lawyer and acknowledged the $25,000 bet made the day before that the president's testicles were square. The president confirmed that the bet was the same as the one made the day before. Then the senior woman asked him to drop his pants so that she and her lawyer could see clearly. The president was happy to oblige.

The elderly woman came closer so she could see better and asked the *president if she could touch them. 'Of course,' said the president. 'Given the amount of money involved, you should be 100% sure. 'The elderly woman did so with a little smile. Suddenly the president noticed that the lawyer was banging his head against the wall. He asked the elderly woman why he was doing that and she replied, 'Oh, it's because I bet him $100,000 that around 10 o'clock in the morning I would be holding the balls of the President of the Bank.'*

Free of the myth that marriage is a magical potion, we can all pursue the life paths that suit us best. Marriage is still there for those who want it. But now people who prefer to live single can come out of the shadows. The possibilities for meaning and fulfillment in a single life have gone largely unrecognized. It is time for that to change.

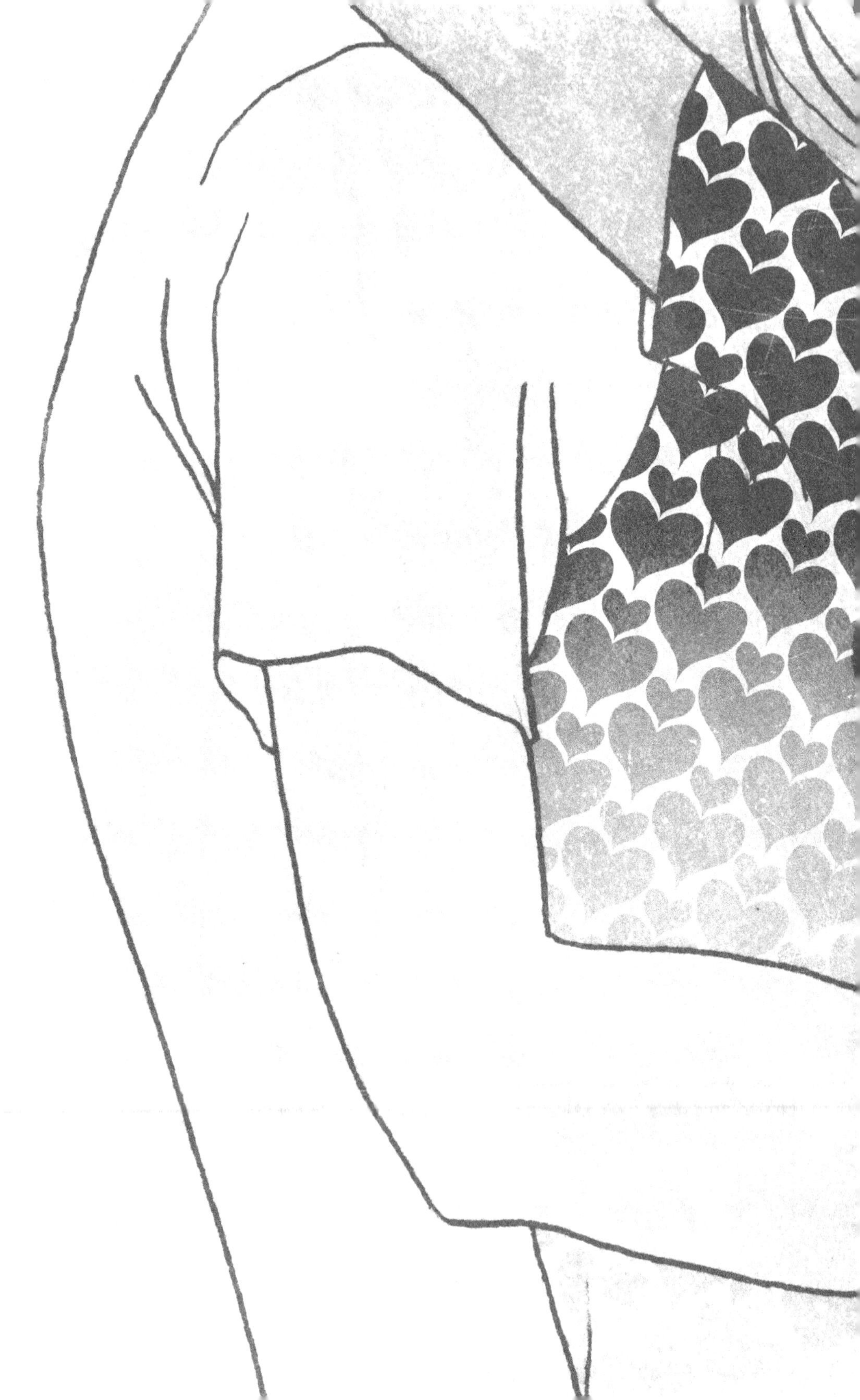

Change

Omni-a vin' cit a' mor

No one really wants to change. Everyone wants the other person to modify their needs to fit into the other person's schedule and existence. When a man and woman come together, they both want to improve their day-to-day lives. But, they have only allowed, or actually allocated, a small percentage of their time to interact with another individual. Since both have little reason to change, if their lives are relatively complete, the onus is put on the other person to modify their schedules. No wonder why it's so difficult to hook up with an attractive person. The trick is to relax and give the whole process much more time to develop.

Omni-a vin'cit a'mor.

Vin sit a'mor (Latin) love conquers all things.

Omni: a combining form meaning all-as in omnipotent and omnivorous

People cling tenaciously to their unhappiness. Why are the prisoners' chains so comforting when the door to the cell lies open?

Love and relationships are elusive because:

We do not reach out and take a chance.

We do not live fully enough in the present.

We do not compromise- and it is essential.

What men want from a woman never changes.

What women want in a man continually changes.

We are obsessed with what we had in the past.

We are committed to our own narrow self-interests.

We do not look forward with the proper perspective.

We do not continually change; find new interests,

and activities.

We want things our own way and do not respond when demands are made on us.

Another factor why love and relationships are elusive is because of a particular state of mind that applies more often to men than women. A psychological notable called the master of the universe phenomenon has often explained this reason. The more wealth you have, the smarter you are, the higher your educational level, the higher your status, the more you lose sight of the randomness of misfortune, and the effort it takes to interact, the lack of significant quantum opportunities, the more you think you are valuable and invincible. You also believe that you can control variables, eliminate risk, and if some problem does happen, especially in relationships, you will have the resources and means to deal with it.

Two of the women in the class that I was teaching were very concerned about meeting a guy that they could be loved by and love. The biggest problem they said was how to meet someone. I asserted that women were not aggressive enough when it came to initial meetings.

"But, I never know what to say."

"You don't understand. Say anything. Men are usually aggressive enough so that all they need is an opening. Ask the man, 'where can I get a good cappuccino.' This tells you immediately if he likes coffee, if he knows the neighborhood, if he is responsive to your questions, or even if he is shy. All you have to do is ask a reasonable question. Remember if he is unresponsive, he does not even know you, so you cannot feel rejected. Remember what my cousin said after divorcing her third husband, 'next.'"

If you have learned anything from this book, some of the bottom lines should be, don't quit a few moments or days before the miracle of knocking on heaven's door and finding a new honey.

Understand that the most significant perseverance involves continuously evolving, reinventing yourself, and changing your focus and attitude.

It does not matter how slow you go as long as you do not stop.

Don't let the fear of rejection shut you down, persevere.

When you change the way you look at things, the things you look at change.

The obstacle is the path.

What women and men do not seem to understand is that you need to become the right person for someone else, instead of only waiting for the right person to come along.

If you want something you have never had before – then you must do something you have never done before.

There is a theory, which states that if anybody discovers exactly what the Universe is for and why it is here, it will instantly disappear and be replaced by something; even more bizarre and inexplicable. There is another theory which states that this has already happened.

You better start to love this place in which you live. It is allowing us to stay alive. Throughout the past century, humanity did everything in its power to dominate nature. We dammed earth's rivers, chopped down the forests and depleted the soils. Burning up fossil fuels that had been created over eons, we pumped billions of tons of greenhouse gasses in the air, altering the atmospheric chemistry and appreciably warming the planet in just a few decades. And as our population began the year 2000 above the 7 billion mark, still spreading across the continents, dozens of animal and plant species were going extinct every day.

Teachers can only open a door. You must walk through it under your own steam.

People are so rattled by the speed and complexity of their lives that they need rock-solid certainty. They cannot live inconclusively. Religion provides one definitive answer; science provides another. The important thing for most people is to feel that the way they live is an inevitable outcome.

Right-to-lifers say abortion is a tragedy. The greater tragedy is the number of unplanned pregnancies that result in children born to parents who are financially and emotionally unable to care for them. These kids suffer abuse, neglect, and a host of social ills that underfunded social service agencies can't handle. The same people who stand outside clinics harassing women seeking abortions are opposed to increases in spending for social welfare programs, public schools, low-cost housing, etc. – services most of these women will need if they carry a child to term. They can't have it both ways. Either they support reproductive health education in the schools and communities, or they support the social-welfare system so that it can adequately take care of the babies they want to "save."

"There is a direct proportion between the lowering of crime rates and abortion." Steven Levitt, co-author of Freakonomics.

If you are not willing to fight for something, then you cannot change anything. So, pick a side.

A strong wind comes over me. I know this wind from Alaska where it was called the hawk. It bites into my flesh taking bits from my soul and courses through me. There is no color around me. I look back at my trail, a being crawling over a checkerboard. I was saving the game of chess for when I got older. Then I would have time and money to drink fine red wine and learn the game. When death came for me I could play him and forestall the inevitable. I waited too long. My body is just a hollow shell, coupled with diminishing strength and the death of a thousand cuts. But the wind now changes from an arctic chill to invigorating energy and I enjoy the feeling of still being alive. I look ahead and take one more step.

We possess nothing certainly except the past- yet to live we must exist only in the present. Satoru

The heart is a lonely hunter

I am probably too focused on finding a new love. When I was younger, I could pick and choose with such abandon and ease that the idea of it being difficult to find a main squeeze is an anathema to me. But with age, hopefully, there is a little wisdom, and I cannot settle or invest in someone that will only be around for the next two weeks.

The problem with the women I meet now is very apparent, especially when I compare them to the wonderful women of my past. The girls I went with in the past did not have a fully developed life. Therefore, they were able to adapt, and in some cases, dovetail mine. The women I want and meet today have worked at cultivating their existence, fought for years to be themselves, and refined their needs and wants. They refuse to engage unless they are immediately taken with a man and will not give a relationship a chance to develop. Trying to find a woman under these circumstances makes me think that I am sliding down the razor blade of life or backstroking in the toilet bowl. Ultimately the fault is not only the women I meet but also my choices. I have embedded a Sisyphus story that keeps dragging me up a hill, by my penis, with a beautiful face and then hurls me down into heartbreak and failure. How can someone so smart be so dumb? How come I cannot climb out of the sexually embraced idea that a pretty face and nice figure will fulfill my needs? Still, life is for living and I will have few regrets.

No
Gay Marriage
God...

Fuck
This
Guy

A KiSS From The Heart

When I awoke, my stiff muscles surprised me. I languished in bed stretching and trying to manipulate the soreness in my knee joint. The sky was overcast, and there were whitecaps on the waves. There could be no fishing this morning because the bottom sand needed hours to settle from last night's storm. I put some freshly baked banana bread into the toaster and poured myself a large glass of apple juice over ice. I decided to slowly walk the two-mile beach from one end to the other. The sky was the color of wet cement, and no sunlight shone through, an ideal time to stroll without getting burnt. I put on my comfortable sneakers, dark glasses, and locked the door.

The last hurricane had eroded the Queensland zones about fifty feet along the entire length of the Island beach. The dunes and hills that no one owned or used were intended to act as a buffer from the sea's storms. No one in the Caribbean could build closer than two hundred feet from the high-water line. It was smart thinking and good ecological planning. The zone is very useful in preventing damage to the homes that were on the beachfront property, but the Queensland had shrunk in many places to a few feet. As a result, the beach doubled in size and the Queensland sand was spread over the beach and on into the water. In some places, the beach was right up to the terraces of the homes. But, what saved the beach and was responsible for the development of the island was that the entire shoreline is cloaked by hundreds of small fringing coral reefs, which ring the east side of the island like a giant horseshoe, absorbing the force of the sea's waves. Also, further out from the shore are banking reefs, impressive coral structures that parallel the coast for miles and reduce the wave impact on the island.

The wind died a little in the afternoon, and I decided to go fishing near the south bar. The wave action made the water a bit rough, but the clear visibility compensated for it, so the swim was enjoyable. It had taken about two hours before I spotted something edible. The antenna of a medium sized lobster waved from beneath a ledge of black lava. I dove down and smacked it between the eyes. After taking off its tail and tucking it into my vest, I evaluated my new diving gloves. I was tired of having the razor-sharp points of the lobsters' tail piercing my old gloves and sticking into my hand. The new gloves were neoprene thick palmed used by football receivers; expensive but they worked.

I covered a lot of territories and didn't see any other lobsters, so I decided to use this lobster's body for bait, catch a fish, and get out. My knee was bothering me so with this tactic I could just plant the head and float around. I put the bait in about twenty feet of water and began drifting in a wide circle. In a few minutes, the fishes in the area were tearing at the exposed antennas. A juvenile striped Grouper, too small to shoot, was first to the feast. Moments later a Queen Triggerfish with its colorful green and yellow camouflage started to feed. All the fishes were too small or too bright to kill. Although the natives eat all of the fish I was observing, I never could. Aside from being so pleasant to look at, there is no sport in the kill, and the fish are a hassle to clean.

A large tail showed itself under the ledge. Where did it come from? There must be a back door. It was a Nassau Grouper, a little too big, but perfect, if I could hit it accurately. I dove and pulled back my sling as far as it would go. When I got to the spot, it was gone. I knew it was hanging around and would be back. I swam around, diving every so often near the place, hoping I would be there when it showed its head. The feeding became more frenzied, as one of the fish broke the shell of the lobster's head. The large grouper showed its tail and was distracted by the food. I dove down on the other side of the rock, shook off the air bubbles, relaxed, and slowly pulled back the spear as I swam forward. I was low on the bottom so I couldn't move rapidly without my fins raising a cloud of sand dust. I lined up a good shot, but I was not close enough. The grouper was going to move under the ledge and into the hole. I let go of the spear and pierced the grouper in the body. It was not a good hit, and the fish turned and took the dart straight into the hole. I had grabbed the last few inches of the marine steel before it disappeared. The fish wiggled and made the sound of a resonating thumping beat. He shook furiously and pulled off the spear. Too bad, it would have fed me for days. I was chilled as I slowly headed back for shore.

Walking back to the beach shack would take about twenty minutes. I remembered the days when I would dog trot back. Now with my bad knee and lack of energy, I took my time. A few people were playing in the water. Apart, but with them, was a lovely, lithe young woman. She was standing knee deep in the waves holding her upper garment so that it would catch the wind. The bottom of her bathing suit was no more than a thin handkerchief and a piece of dental floss. When she turned her back to me, her round bitable rear end was revealed. I stopped for a moment to enjoy the view before walking home.

I just finished washing the equipment and taking a shower when someone rapped on the door. It was a tall African about six feet five.

"Hello," he said, "You are tough to find."

"Here we go again," I mumbled under my breath.

"Reggie, the cabman, told me where you were hiding. This is truly a hard place to locate."

I knew Reggie would screen anyone before he told him or her my whereabouts, but I couldn't be sure.

"I did the whole survey and planted about twenty markers."

I walked over and unlocked the door. It was Tasso Theophilus, the surveyor.

"Tasso, you were supposed to call me on Friday. When you didn't call, or show up, I assumed you weren't coming."

"My eighty-two-year-old mother was sick, and the phones were out where she lived."

"Welcome to the islands."

"What?"

"Nothing, go on."

"Then when I called you ... Do you have a foreign language answering your machine?"

"No, Theophilus, just English. But, why would you call me when you knew I'd be leaving? Also, you were explicitly told that I wanted to be there when you did the survey."

"I couldn't finish it on time and contact you first. We looked for you, then started yesterday and just finished today."

"For someone, I haven't slept with Theo; you certainly fucked me. Sit down, my friend. So, I can tell you the bottom line."

"Do you want to see the survey?"

"In a while. First of all, my lawyer set up this appointment and study, right? If she didn't know we were going to contract on the land, she would not have set things up."

"Yes."

"Ok, first it's hard for me not to get excited about this but Brett Knight, the man who owns the land, now tells me that he sold it to someone else."

"Maybe he's just unscrupulous or sold it for more money."

"I'm sure he wouldn't sell it for less. He knew he had my price and put it up for more. At any rate, it looks like he might have sold it."

"Well, that person needs a survey anyway. Maybe he could pay me."

"Brett said the person buying it is going to use his survey. From what you have told me, that doesn't seem possible or legal."

"The Government said that any foreigner who buys land, since 1983, must have it surveyed."

"Let's look at it anyway."

As soon as I saw the advanced satellite survey that Theophilus had done, I knew that it was more difficult negotiating with Brett Knight. The survey was excellent. The old survey maps were off about thirty-five feet of beachfront times the two acres of frontage. The road dividing the parcel was smaller. Both sides of the land, on either side of the road, were buildable sites. The main site, the one where I wanted to build on top of the hill, now became more accessible, because the new survey included the entire hill. The land now changed into a very private hilltop retreat.

My rough measurements and perceptions were accurate and as Knight saw the survey, he knew the land was worth more. My anger at Theophilus, which kept increasing, was redirected to the lawyers. After all, if they had done their jobs correctly, then the survey would be a minor error. There was nothing I could do, I was apprehensive, angry, frustrated, and couldn't sleep. What was my island beach shack dream to them, but just a few more bucks? How could I be so unwise to trust in lawyers? Superimposed on the situation were the momentary flashbacks and blurry mental snapshots, I was getting from ordinary sights. Could the strains of the city and the past hallucinogenic experiences last for so long?

Waking up every night was making me grouchy. My mind was not shutting down for the evening, and I could not turn away from the anger of my thoughts. I kept getting more aggressive feelings toward both my Caribbean and New York lawyers. I had to do something, an action that was positive and anxiety releasing before talking with Brett Knight again. I decided to become more social and find a woman to sleep with, two goals easily accomplished on a small tropical Paradise. But first, some swimming and neutral buoyancy to relax my body and mind.

Walking down to the beach, I set out to fish and work the reefs on the north narrows side of the island. There was usually no one else on the beach at four o'clock and the feeling of having this three-mile beach almost to myself was expansive. Just to stand alone and turn my back on civilization, forced to stop thinking by the vastness of the ocean view, pretending that this was the last block on the edge of the world, was unrestrained and invigorating. But, my mind would not let go of the self-judgments and dichotomies that dove in and out of my consciousness. I want to be a better Zen Buddhist. I must be the change that I wish to see in the world. The unity of our existence consists of perpetual change. All things change. Hold on to nothing. But here I am trying to buy my island dream and build my ego with some intimacy.

A few hundred yards away, a semi-nude woman wearing a Walkman was sunbathing on her stomach, her feet swaying up and back to the music. When she saw me approach, she threw a towel over her bumpy behind.

"Hi. Did you just purchase this house?" I asked just to make conversation.

She smiled a young, scared, strained smile. In broken English, she tried to answer, but her faculty for the language was limited.

"Ruska?" I said.

"Da Russian." She replied.

"Have a wonderful day and Spasiba for the view," I said into my smile.

"And good-bye."

"Vonderful? And how you know thank you in Russian?"

I waved goodbye and continued up the beach. It didn't matter how young or beautiful she was, being smart and perhaps spiritual came first. Was I at last learning? Further down the beach, a skinny naked woman got up from the blanket she was sharing with another woman, and walked into the water. "Damn, another flat tushie," I said out loud to myself. A big navy blue boat was beached near where the women were sunbathing.

"It works much better in the water, you know," I said to the charming smile.

"Do you think so?" She answered me in perfect clipped English with a hint of a German accent.

She was so comfortable with her body and so unpreoccupied in her attitude that I hardly realized that she was bare breasted. She asked me a few questions about the gear I was wearing and asked to see my knife.

As I took the dive knife out the sheath, I held her hand and placed the handle into her open palm. I watched her face, and she wet her lips like a porn star. I laughed and told her to be careful.

"You stab sharks with this?" She said jokingly, as she felt the heft of the big dive knife.

"It's more for the monofilament fishing line that you encounter in the ocean. Fishermen leave long spools of it when they lose a game fish. Also, I use it to cut the tails off the lobster."

"You catch lobster? How many?"

"Enough to have a big lobster dinner for my friends. But, I used up all the ones I had in the freezer when I gave a party in my place up the beach."

"Oh, we're having a party on Thursday in that big house in the back," she said as she pointed with her breasts toward the large house on the hill off the beach. "Why don't you come? My name's Julia."

"Okay, Julia," I said smiling. "What time?"

"Nine."

"See you then."

The water was rough with big swelling waves and white caps. I would be over one spot looking for a telltale antenna sticking out from under an overhang. Suddenly and sporadically, I would be lifted ten feet and transported twenty feet by a powerful wave. This was slightly dangerous and coupled with the waters increasing number of suspended particles; it was approaching a no lobster, no fun, and no swimming situation.

I saw a fast-moving large fish in the distance and soon realized it was a White-bellied shark. Aside from the fact that seeing this predator always engenders a rush of fear, I just didn't want the hassle. I changed direction, lining up with a nearby reef to become a less conspicuous silhouette, and pumped my fins more deliberately. The silt was becoming denser by the agitated current, reducing my visibility rapidly. Many shark attacks occur because of obscured vision and the shark, whose vision is close to humans, bites almost by mistake. I wasn't going to take any chances in this murky water. I was spooked by this predator's speed. A few minutes later the shark cruised by me again. A coincidence? Yeah, right. Some species of shark cruise by very slowly in a straight line. This one moved rapidly and veered off in an unpredictable pattern.

Below me was a hole I had passed over an hour ago. Inside was a lobster, so big; it resembled a giant underwater insect. I was unable to shoot because it moved around a corner of the cave. Since I knew that it was there, it was worth one more dive. I lowered my sling and cleared my ears. The sea had grown so opaque that I could barely see into the overhang. Just for a moment, the water cleared and I aimed and shot.

The lobster pulled the spear so far into the cave that I grabbed my shooter and surfaced. It must have backed up into a small opening in the cave and jammed its tail in a wedged position. I dove down and tugged on the spear, but it wouldn't budge I reversed my grip and plunged the weapon forward. When I was sure it had gone through the lobster, I pulled slowly with all my strength knowing that the swing piece of steel at the end of the spear would open and make it possible to pry the spiny crustacean from its safe hole. I pulled it out and swam for shore looking around for the shark. It was nowhere in sight, but I stayed in a defensive mode all the way to shore. That night, I wrapped the lobster in tinfoil for the party, put on my best blue hospital scrubs and used up the last of my tiny cologne sample.

This party had the most beautiful slim young women I had seen in a long time. It turned out that the house was rented by a group of models and that they invited another modeling crew to join the party. The rooms were filled with very pleasant and attractive people. The aesthetic of some of the women and men was lovely and a treat for my eyes. I was submerged in an entirely water oriented frame of mind for the last few days, and the contrast was a strange test of reality.

I spoke for a while to Julia, and after touching her arm lightly I could tell that she was not interested in me romantically. She spoke fluent French, German and English and lived in Paris.

I was having difficulty getting away from the cigarette smoke and was dismayed by the fact that so many of these beautiful people were destroying their health by chain smoking. Many of the guys were openly gay, and I wondered how many of the women were too. By the end of the evening, all the men had drifted off, and I was dancing with five energetic, beautiful women. To rephrase more accurately, the women were dancing with each other, and I was simply there. One woman was very attractive and spiritual, but her English was not very good. Every time I spoke to her, it was in competition with a blasting radio. After a while, I gave up. The fat kid in the candy store was very frustrated because all the sweets were wrapped up and behind glass and he could not even get a taste.

For the next few days, I'd meet the girls on the beach and talked for a while and waved hello, as we passed each other on our golf carts, the preferred means of transportation on the island. Somehow, I could never hook up with the two ladies I preferred. It was ego deflating not to have them flirt or give me any encouragement. It was also true that the beautiful faces never showed the need to cultivate their social and conversational skills.

I had only a few more days to interact with them before a hurricane closed down the island. The storm suddenly shifted course toward the Caribbean, and the two modeling crews hired a private plane to get out before it hit. The large hotels evacuated their guests, and the tourist left. The whole island went into a high-energy preparedness for the hurricane. Constant hammering of plywood over windows and vulnerable openings built like a crescendo of giant woodpeckers and hammering was heard well into the night. There were only two days left before the hurricane hit. Everyone was nervous and scurrying about.

I went to check out one of my friend's house. It had a glass panel missing from the front door. The wind driven rain would forcefully spray through the opening and destroy the kitchen behind it. I authorized putting a plywood panel over the door getting it fixed. It was done in one morning. Record time for the Caribbean where under ordinary conditions, it would have taken at least a week. This was going to be the last night that I could move around freely before the wind and driving rain made traveling a chore. I drove to a native friend's house and asked if he wanted to bar hop before going to Sea Grapes, the only late night disco on the island. We shot around from bar to bar, but it was too tame and deserted. Pub-crawling before a hurricane was like playing handball against the drapes or as disastrous as making love on a water bed- there is no support.

In one of the bars, a lovely long legged dark woman in a sheer short dress was having a drink. My friend introduced us and after a while asked if she wanted to hang out and go dancing after we visited a few more bars. She said "yes" and it was good to carouse in the company of a beautiful Bahamian woman. At the disco, the few remaining tourists and some of the models that were leaving tomorrow were dancing to the deafening base and disco beat. My ego was raised significantly as they watched me dancing with this flashy chocolate-colored young woman. Her name was Dynamique, pronounced in French Dean-a-meek, or maybe I just gave her that name after she showed an interest in speaking French. She moved wonderfully, and every time my body or hands came in contact with her hips or butt, I smiled. I laughed a lot that evening. My friend who said he was getting something to eat, disappeared. After a few hours of dancing with Dynamique, we talked outside the disco until it closed.

"I can't believe you're as old as you say you are, thirteen hundred years?" She said to me looking me up and down with her mango eyes. "The way you move and look!"

"I can't believe you're thirty-five, the way you dance and look. You know your big eyes are very beautiful. You must have been cute when you were a child."

"Yes, I looked like a bug."

I was going to drive her home, but somehow her directions led us to the vacant Maritz beach house. I thought that I was going to get lucky, but I could not be sure. I was trying not to be aggressive, but it came too naturally. We laid outside on the deck in the chaise lounge and I touched her hard runner's legs all over. We talked and listened to the waves lulling us to bed. The breeze was warm and invigorating and made you feel good to be alive. As we went inside she said. "I have to leave soon." Did she want me to rush? Did she have some place to go or an obligation? She lay down on the bed on her stomach and repeated,

"I have to go soon." and appeared to go to sleep. I pulled her dress up and stroked her fat plump behind. My fingers slide between her legs and I gently smoothed and teased her lips. Her closed eyelids fluttered. Even though she was tired, she moved her pelvis to the rhythm of my fingers. I moved her bikini panties aside and tickled and teased. She was hot, wet and juicy. I slid my fingers into her, and she was tight and beautiful. Dynamique's hands strayed back and stroked and touched me.

Somehow my precognition, which seemed non-existent for the past few weeks suddenly, focused. I pulled back to interpret what I was visualizing and decided that I'd rather be safe than sorry. I did not have any condoms with me, although I never did like to take a shower with my socks on. My dread of Aids became primary. My body reacted to the fear and Lazarus would not fully rise from the dead, even though I wanted this woman. I tried to tell myself I am not going to catch Aids. I'm not going to make it with a gay bisexual intravenous drug user from Haiti. But my rational mind ruled my body. We played for hours. Even though she was a bit passive I felt close to her and her potential. I brought her to a pumping orgasm with my fingers and she sighed a full release. We finally fell asleep as close as two spoons, her favorite position, and mine.

The next day I called unannounced at her home. Her sister told me that she was indisposed. I wasn't sure, if she was rejecting me outright or busy. Such is the male ego, locked into the physical act of penetration, just as most women are her emotional and procreative instincts for the survival of the world. That afternoon Dynamique called, and we talked for a while.

"What are you cooking tonight? If my car radiator cools, I might drop over."

"I hope your other radiator stays hot. I'll surprise you, at least with my cooking."

I was a little drained that evening because of the long swim in the afternoon. Not being able to fish liberated me from wearing equipment, my wetsuit, and weight belt, carrying a spear, shooter, and knife. Being so unencumbered I was able to use my arms and hands. The water on my bare skin was almost a new sensation, although it was a little colder without my shorty wetsuit. I swam for at least two miles using the breaststroke and occasionally the crawl. I could easily have floated for two more miles, but it was getting dark. I decided that unless it were totally dangerous, I would swim in the hurricane tomorrow.

The last time I swam in a hurricane was in Manhattan Beach, Brooklyn. The waves during that storm thundered in. Although they were only twelve feet, they were the most brutish force I ever encountered. The wave undertow pulled me out into the breakers and then slammed me down, pinning me against the sand. I could not move until the crush of the water flowed over and past me. Then, I kicked to the surface and took a deep breath before the next wave crashed over holding me against the bottom with tons of seawater pressing down. I could move in or out of the sea a few feet at a time as long as I didn't fight the undertow. It was an exciting Zen game for a swimmer, and I enjoyed the experience remembering that the ocean was my first love. There is nothing that makes you feel more alive than engaging in a high-risk activity that, at the same time, utterly focuses your mind. I didn't know what the reaction of these Bahamian waves was going to be. Brooklyn was in a relatively enclosed huge bay and northern waters. This hurricane was in the open sea in the Caribbean. I'd have to test the waters carefully, especially the rip and crosscurrents, less I be pulled out to sea off the island. Tomorrow will be an engaging day.

At about ten thirty, I put some of the terrace lights on and put a tray of barbecue sauced chicken thighs and veal sausages in the broiler. If the electricity went off tomorrow, I'd still have cooked food for two days. I was talking on the phone when Dynamique appeared on the terrace. Looking like the Tahitian woman straight out of a Gauguin painting, she wore a dark red parraya sarong contrasting with her honey skin. She grinned widely, her beaming slightly insecure smile, slide open the door and sashayed in. It was a warm evening, and I was sure it was going to get hotter. We dined on the terrace under a starlit night; the warm sea breeze cooling us.

I woke up groggy because Dynamique and I were holding each other in changing positions and playing all night long. I was too focused on being a good lover and was too tired and wired. If only I could relax, everything would have been fine, but I was too anxious. It always takes time for me to adjust to a new lover. It was frustrating because I wanted to impress Dynamique with my creative skills and prowess, and here I was weak. She left at daybreak, and I stretched out troubled and fatigued. I awoke two hours later in a tent; Lazarus has a mind of its own.

Out onto the terrace, I studied the drably desaturated palette of different blues, grays, and greens of both the water and the blustery sky. The breeze was steady at a refreshing fifteen knots, and the sea was white with the wind and a mass of chop and whitecaps. Along the horizon, a dark gray wall of clouds extended thousands of feet into the atmosphere. I took a walk on the beach, but the wind driven sand stung my skin. The first fifty meters of the ocean was a bubbling mass of foam and sand. Beyond the breakers, the water was milky and agitated. Further out, the swells rolled into the reefs and pushed the sand over the beach and up to the crown lands.

I had the entire three-mile beach to myself. It was not as if I was alone; it was splendid isolation. Along the dunes overlooking the beach, most of the houses were vacant and boarded up. Still, some teams of workmen attacked the remaining homes with full sheets of rough plywood, covering the windows and glass doors, and hammering the plywood into the sides of the cement buildings with big cut nails and heavy sledgehammers. Since the three island hotels evacuated their guests and were completely closed, the beach was mine, just like in the off-season golden days in August, before European tourists discovered the island.

The water was undulating and chaotic. The wind shifted from its normally eastward direction over the water now coming from the North, the wave action was twofold. Getting past the heaving breakers was the only challenge. I walked slowly into the sea testing the undertow. I had to evaluate navigating the open water currents carefully. Sometimes a rip current stays in one place and sometimes it moves down the beach like a vacuum cleaner. The slight current was pushing south. I dove in and under the first big breaker and came out into another frothy wave. The force did not yet rise to a dangerous level because the hurricane stalled off San Salvador two hundred miles away. Tomorrow would tell a new tale depending on which direction the storm took. Coming out of the water, I realized how simple my life had become on the island. All I had to think about was the water and Dynamique, who I now sleep with every night.

Dynamique sneaked up on me, while I was reading and having a beer. She laughed at my efforts to suck frozen beer from the bottle. She had a great sense of humor. She was wearing a long dress. For a moment, I thought we were going out dancing again. Instead, we went out onto the deck to watch and listen to the thundering waves pushed in by the storm. We sat next to each other on the chaises langue's, held hands and drank wine. We talked about the island, old lovers, and new friends. My hand slid down her leg and onto her crouch. She was not wearing any underwear and the thrill of touching her sent an electric charge through my body. I squeezed my legs together and ooowwwed out a long moan. She was so sexy and unexpected. Each night with her was better than the last. After a while, she got up and kneeled on the bench surrounding the terrace. She leaned on the railing, alternatingly looking at the sea and me. I pulled up her dress and felt her delicious table tushie behind. We rubbed and talked and kissed ever so slightly. I sat down on the bench next to her.

"Don't your knees hurt?" I asked her.

"No. Not really."

"You might consider getting a pair of Monica Lewinsky pants."

"Why?"

"They have built in knee pads."

We laughed, and she straddled herself across my legs. She kissed me on the forehead, eyes, and lips. I tried to grab her head and kiss her hard. I did once, and she leaned back.

"No." She said. "You're kissing with your lips. You have to kiss from the heart."

I looked up at her. For the first time in years, I felt emotionally sad. I closed my eyes and hung my head. I stopped and took a deep breath letting go with a long sigh. I relaxed and took my mind and body totally into the now. I tried to breathe slowly and deeply changing my race with myself and my predisposition for control. I had had sex with numerous women, loved many, lived and loved with a few but somehow I had forgotten that what I was pursuing in a female were softness and love. This island woman was letting me be alive, and getting to me emotionally, completely disproportionate to the short time that we were together.

The timing certainly has a lot to do with being emotionally open or ready I mused to myself. I kissed her from the heart and caved in emotionally. It was as if I was rapidly drinking the wine just to quench my thirst and forgetting to savor, smell, enjoy and taste it. It had somehow been a long, long time. I could not keep my hands off this woman, and she welcomed my touch and undulated her entire body to the movements of my hands. I looked into her eyes and bent toward her to kiss her mahogany lips, but she turned her head away. I learned slowly that she did not like to kiss, but she loved to be touched, she was rather passive. I could, however, move her any way I wanted and she'd pick up the rhythm and sway with me. She was a cowgirl and loved to ride the pony to music, even if it were the rhythm and symphony of the incoming storm.

"Listen Dynamique; I have an idea. Meet me tomorrow for lunch at The Shores Hotel and wear that fantastic red dress."

"You know I don't like to walk around in that dress. It's too sexy."

"I know. But I want you to join Brett Knight and me before we have lunch and I need you to look hot and good."

"Just for you."

The next day, through the binoculars, the Breakers looked like miniature tidal waves rolling in. These fourteen footers certainly would have caused damage to the shore and the beach homes, if not for the solid miles of reefs that stretched from one end of the island to the other. The huge waves broke against the reefs a mile from shore and rolled in dissipated and flat. People who consider building on the "prime real estate," beachfront properties, should see what the beach is like during a mild storm. There is no beach at all. The waves wash over the entire seashore and break against the Queensland, only fifty feet from their homes. One good hurricane, of medium force and cross current to the beach, could take out many homes if the conditions were right. The last storm that stayed over the island for a few hours took out thirty-five feet of shorefront.

I went down to the beach to swim in the hurricane. The sky, beach, and tops of the white caps all turned pink as the fireball dipped below the trees. The long crash of the waves intermingled with the howling of the wind and the storm music was strong and compelling. I'm so burnt out. I have less love to give, and my heart is paper-thin, but the sorrows of my heart vanish when I swim.

I plunged into the water and was turned sideways, first by the undercurrent and then by the incoming wave. All the force of the slow-moving hurricane seemed to be concentrated in the last fifty feet of the surf. The wave held the power of a thousand miles and a billion tons of Atlantic Ocean behind it, so swimming to it was hitting a wall of liquid force. The only recourse was to dive to the sand, hold my breath as the weight of the wave hit, and advance a few feet at a time. Once I got out past the first few breakers, the sea was manageable but rough and sandy. The storm was moving away. The ancient mariners' adage was true: "Red sky at night, sailors delight. Red sky in the morning, sailors take warning."

I wrote and alternately read, waiting for Dynamique to join me. I'd try to plant a seed in her mind today and convince her to consider me in her future, since I was going to spend a lot of time on the island in the coming year. I was not sure if she had much faith in deferred gratification. She might have some idea of how I could perhaps fulfill her dreams, but I doubted it. She was ambitious, shrewd and opportunistic. I had to let her make up her independent mind. I would ask her to write a letter to me that was a test. My foresight told me that the correspondence, or lack of one, would be significant. If she did not write back, she just wanted to play with my soul. To make it easier for her, I composed a letter that I would send to her after I left to which she could reply.

Dear Dynamique,

I still reach out at night and look for your softness. I love the way we fit together when you turn your back to me- like two spoons in a drawer. I miss you pulling me close to you, letting go some of your cares, falling asleep. You told me in our conversation that; "I'm thirty years old and not a kid anymore." You make me feel young when I'm with you. I enjoy being close to you and look forward to interacting with you on a multiple of levels. You are a very special lady. Hope everything goes well with you and that your dream house is progressing. Don't get frustrated about the speed or cost since it will be the best investment you have ever made. This is going to be one of the hardest performance years of my life. It will also be like living in a taxi with the meter running. The only great thing about getting through this year is that I will never have to work this hard again. I look forward to laughing a lot with you and learning about you. I hope that the fates look kindly upon us. I think of you and await your communication with me that will keep us connected.

Affectionately, Mike

We arrived at the Shores Hotel and asked Brett's wife if I could see him. Dynamique got some tall glasses of ice water at the bar, and we sat down in the main building on the sprawling, open dining room terrace. Dynamique was wearing her short red dress, and her airy red and tan straw hat contrasted her long beautiful tan legs. She had been a runner all of her young life, possessed an athlete's figure, and a movie star smile. As soon as Brett Knight came in, it was evident that Dynamique distracted him. Previously when I had met Brett I judged him as a tough negotiator and a good businessman. He waited twenty years to sell this land. Because of my lawyers, I jerked him around for a year. I am sure he was disgruntled or a little angry. He was an older man of about seventy, a fighter pilot in World War II, ran his hotel with an iron hand, and could not be reached after five o'clock when he retired to his fourteen-acre estate. We talked for a while about tourism and customs in third world countries, particularly Nicaragua. I was trying to negotiate using every modest and incremental approach possible. At last, we connected on a point that we agreed on, lawyers. "My contention exactly. But, customs officials are like lawyers, they get paid regardless of the job they do, and if they screw things up, we have to pay."

"Well, this new one I have is much too busy."

"Brett, first let me apologize for all the delays and the terrible lack of competence on the part of my lawyers."

"That's all right. I'm going to get a new one too. Either he is too busy or too lazy. Bahamian lawyers all take three-hour lunches."

"But, I tell you, I was dealing in good faith. It was my Caribbean lawyer that procrastinated and perhaps even lied about communication with your man. Also, my New York attorney appeared to be handling the details but did not."

"We let lawyers handle the details and lose control."

"But, not at the expense of the entire transaction."

"True, but all they care about is their fees."

"I still want that piece of land. What can I do?"

"Well, this man has priority now. I believe he wants it and I sold it to him."

"Has he put any money down?"

"No."

"So, I still have a chance."

"Not at the old price. That was over a year ago and everything on the islands gone up."

"What's the price now?"

He named an amount that was many thousands more than the original contract.

"Those lawyers are something else," I said out loud. To myself, I said, "Those stupid assholes."

"That's the new price if the other guy doesn't want it."

"I'm so angry. If my Caribbean lawyer were a man I'd punch him in the nose.

"I walked over to look at the land, and someone said that they were cutting it, and I was very pleasantly surprised."

"Well, the surveyor wasn't supposed to touch it without me being there, but he's a Bahamian. Considering that it was not my fault, Brett and that you haven't gone to contract, let's renegotiate."

"No, that's a pretty hard cost because I'm sure I can get it."

"In ninety days?"

"Everything on the Islands gone up since the storm. Land just off the beach is more valuable, and this plot is a rare find, high and private. Also, that survey shows it's a much bigger lot."

"All right, I'll give you your new price, but make it gross rather than net."

I knew he was accurate about the land assessments going up. I also thought that property values were soon going to explode. He thought for a while and looked at Dynamique's legs. If he agreed on the gross price, I'd buy the land for significantly less and her long legs were distracting him.

"Remember, I'm talking about ninety days on the contract. No more fooling around."

I wanted to keep talking, while he was thinking, negotiating and staring flirtatiously.

"Just to be fair we'll split the survey."

"All right. That's if he doesn't buy it."

"Listen, Brett, I'm going to send you a check for ten percent just to show my good faith."

"That's not necessary."

"Well, I'll do it anyway, just hold it in escrow until you know. Let me know this week either way."

Good I thought, if this guy buys, it won't make any difference, but nobody likes being pushed, and maybe he's not quite ready

"OK, I'll see you next week. Thanks again. I feel like I'm talking with someone that speaks the same language."

"That's because we're both from New York. By the way, Mike, what do you call two thousand lawyers, chained together, on the bottom of the ocean?"

"I don't know."

"Not much, but it's a start."

I shook hands with Brett, and we left the bar to have lunch in the Terrace dining room. He watched Dynamique walk all the way out.

I called my New York lawyer. I had him rewrite the contract, as he should have done in the first place, and send it to my Nassau attorney with a check. I called the Island lawyer and told her to sign the contract for me with verbal authorization. Knight would have the new contract and check in a day or two. A good sign was Knight had already called his lawyer and informed him of the new terms. If someone else were interested, he would have waited, or Brett figured why bother, I have what I want and this guy is in earnest.

I went spear fishing that afternoon. In a long valley, on the inside of a small reef head, I discovered two spiny lobsters. I shot the big one. To my surprise, when I grabbed him, he did not put up a struggle. He was a free skin and had shed his hard armor shell. During the lobster's rapid growth period, they shed their skins and in weeks grow new armor. He was soft all over and had more meat like a soft-shell crab.

The sky became dark, and a long rolling cloud drifted through the center blocking the sun significantly. The hunt was over because the shadows cast underwater were obscuring. I started my swim back to shore. The large cloud fragmented filling the sky with hundreds of small puffy clouds with infinite purple shades. It rained and the water became a bed of needles. I liked being in the water when it rained. I dove to the bottom, perhaps thirty feet, and fully exhaled. Lying back on the soft sand, I looked up at the exploding seas surface. The rain shattered the face of the sea, a wondrous and amazing sight. Liquid water is the real miracle of life on this planet and the universe. This was the first time I took it easy in days. Relax I told myself: "try not to be so preoccupied and wired, loosen up." I swam slowly to shore the free skin in my vest feeling like a soft sponge rather than the usual sharp, hard lump.

The sea was a clean aquamarine green around me. Toward the horizon it turned turquoise and then light purple. The sky was a vast field of slate blue, a shade I had never seen. Across the expanse of space, out at sea, an entire rainbow appeared that formed a semicircle along the horizon. In all my years in Alaska, where after every summer rain, rainbows appeared, in all my travels, I never saw as full a rainbow, let alone one with such vivid colors and magnitude. I looked behind me and realized that I was standing in front of the highpoint land that I wanted to buy, on a deserted beach, in the middle of the rainbow arch. My spirits uplifted as I observed this treat and I fantasized that this is the point in time my luck will change. In its simplicity, the sea, beach, and rainbow were so basic, yet so overwhelming to behold that time paused. I found myself standing in a daydream and an hour had passed.

I was at a point high enough to see up and down the entire three-mile beach and to peer several miles out to sea and observe the reefs and boat navigation. Overhead, two sparrow hawks, with a white spot on the underside of each wing, zigzagged and did loop de loops in the air to catch insects. Looking at the reefs that circled the island, I decided to try my luck tomorrow in the outer reef straight out from Maritz's house.

I swam enjoying the softness of the water and the privacy. A small Hogfish, which Brock Forgeman said is the best eating fish in the water, passed below. I went down to smack it. I lined up a shot, but after getting close realized, it was too small. It was also the beginning of my three-hour swim, and if I speared it, I would have to go in because of sharks. The increased effort that I used to fin down to shoot the hogfish made me aware of the stiffness in my knee, so I decided to cut the swim short. On the way back I hit a medium sized Chubb with a lucky shot. I filleted the fish on the beach using my dive knife and threw the remains into the ocean. It was late, and I felt as if I was growing older by the minute because I was limping.

The next day I walked lamely about the highpoint land. I thought back to my youth when I wrote a check for one hundred dollars. When did I write my first check for a thousand? I remember thinking that writing checks for a thousand meant I had made it. Now, I was writing checks for a hundred thousand, but I didn't feel wealthy. Just for fun, in the memo field, I will write in very tiny script, "for sexual favors."

I walked into the coconut forest down the road from my land and searched for some recently fallen coconuts that had sprouted leaves. Many had already sent their taproots deep into the sand and were too difficult to pull up. Others came out more easily with just a few short roots showing from the coconut and tiny crisp green leaves already developing. I made several trips and piled them up near the driveway entrance. As I explored the area, I came across a dozen fresh turtle shells that were salted and left to dry in the sunshine. They smelled of decay and were covered with flies. In my enthusiasm, to pull up the trees, I pulled a muscle in my deltoid. My shoulder ached as I carried the palms. I reprimanded myself for not learning fast enough, "use your legs and ass, not your arms," but my mind just refused to catch up with my body.

I dug holes, with a small gardening spade, every eight feet on both sides of the center road that divided the plot of land. It would take years for the palms to mature, but even now I could visualize how majestic the driveway would look. I thought about my Kamikaze Rita and how she would get a thrill out of planting some of the trees along the road, not realizing for the moment that she was gone. A pang of pain shot through my soul, and I tried to let it flow out of me. I finished planting a dozen shoots. Should I plant the entire parameter? Here I go again.

It started to rain, but I was happy. I did not have to water the plants and their chances for taking root increased considerably. It was pouring torrents. I walked back to the Maritz place, feeling proud that I had planted coconut trees on my own land. The trees that I planted today, because of the lawyers, had cost me a thousand dollars each. I resolved to send them a letter requesting them to make up the difference in what they had cost me, considering it was cumulatively their fault.

The rain let up and dissolved into a mist. Across the sky, another rainbow appeared, but it was all in shades of blue. I never knew colors could look this way. I walked, hopscotching the puddles and in my mind composing the letter. Dear Sirs, no. Dear Lawyers, no. Dear Incompetent Hacks. I was redundant. Is it worth the time and trouble to send them anything? After all, paper work is their forte and what will I accomplish besides venting. It's best to let it slide, create and disseminate more lawyers' jokes. Like, why did the United States Postal Service cancel their lawyer stamps?

The people didn't know on which side to spit. Or, two lawyers are dining in an expensive restaurant. A cute waitress passes by. One lawyer says to the other, "I'd like to screw that woman." The other agent replies, "Out of what?" Or, four surgeons are discussing the merits of operating on different types of people. The first one says an electrician is best to operate on because everything is color-coded.

The second surgeon disagrees and says that an accountant is the easiest because everything on the inside is in numerical order.

The third says a librarian is easiest because everything in alphabetical order.

The fourth surgeon says you're all wrong. A lawyer is effortless to operate on because they are gutless, spineless and their brains and asses are interchangeable.

Dynamique never answered the letter.

Don't waste one moment on your past mistakes. All flowers need manure.

A flower falls, even though we love it; and a weed grows, even though we do not love it.

We fabricate our illusions, basing our perceptions on thoughts rather than realities. Perhaps it is because thinking is more entertaining than knowing. And although we think in generalities we live in details. So, we focus on the details of planning, compiling and refining lists, calculating variables and alternate scenarios, and dreams of improvements and expanded life styles. This lack of objectivity in our thinking manifests itself by allowing us to become emotional attached to possessions, expectations, and situations. But the real quantum leaps of improvement in our lives escapes us because we are not detached enough to simplify our existence to concentrate on the absolute priories and look at the world with fresh interest.

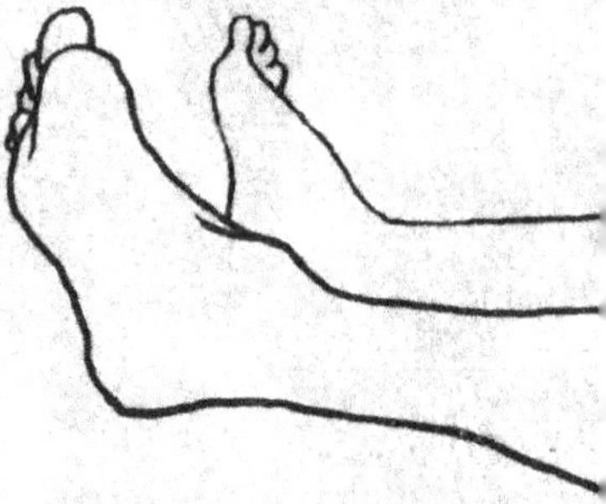

Whochee Kooche Lady Trying To Be Park Avenue

Tell the Truth and Run

She was talking to a salesman when I first saw her. Her high-energy level was so apparent that I was immediately attracted to her, to understand why she was so wired. Since I'm peripatetic myself, I visualized that together we could make people crazy trying to keep up with us. I was also talking to a salesman, but his answers to my questions were not fast or specific enough. I leaned over slightly, since her back was to me and said, "Hi, I'm sorry to interrupt. I know how busy you are, but if I don't say hello now I'll never see you again. I love your energy level."

She turned her head toward me, and the overworked salesman gave his attention to the people next to him. She looked at me with a quick head to toe glance. She focused on my face; I just came from the gym and was warmed up, and was probably wondering why my face was so red.

"All right, write your number down here," she said as she took out a pad and pen from her crammed full of stuff purse. Her pen did not work, so I used one of mine and pulled out an index card for her to write her number. She seemed preoccupied but wrote it fast and large.

"What's your last name, Sandy?" I asked. She wrote that down too.

"Would you have time for a cappuccino? I casually asked.

"I'm too hungry to stop, and I've been drinking coffee all day"

Twenty minutes for a cappuccino is my usual rule pattern when I meet someone. I can screen them in that time and not waste an entire evening. I've learned from experience that everyone seems normal when you first met them, but soon after the craziness comes out. Still, she was so attractive. My ego took over, and her pretty face, slim body and tight tushie suckered me in.

"OK," I said, "We can grab a bite in Chinatown if you like." **Violate your own rules, and you get what you deserve**, I thought to myself, but also **chance favors the prepared mind.**

She came closer to me and at the same time untied her hair. The long reddish gold locks fell to her shoulders, and she moved her head from side to side shaking her long hair loose. A moment ago she was attractive, but now Sandy became very good-looking.

"All right, but you know it's starting to rain?"

"My restaurant is close, and I guarantee the food will be fine."

We made our way out of the store into the rain. She took out an umbrella and walked with a good pace next to me. I took her arm and guided us around the puddles and human traffic.

"I like your hand under my arm," she said. "It makes me feel that you can catch me if I slip."

"So Sandy, what kind of work do you do?"

"A little of this and a little of that."

Uh-oh, the first warning sign.

"From your conversation with that salesman, you're into computers."

"Yes, I just bought an Apple and I'm learning, but I want to do it all myself."

We reached my restaurant, and she looked in with dismay.

"It doesn't have any tablecloths, and I don't think I could get a glass of champagne in there."

"I understood the tablecloth, but champagne with Chinese food?"

Dam, now I'm in trouble. Why don't I listen to myself and just go for a cappuccino?

"Yes, you're right, but the food is delicious and very fresh and authentic."

"Let's go to my place instead," she said, as she turned and took control.

"Is the food there good?"

If someone is competent, why not give up control and relax? Go with the flow and let's see where she leads. After a few blocks she said, "Oh no, it's in the other direction." Although the rain was beginning to soak through, I didn't mind. I was now watching from outside of myself, as this beautiful woman transformed herself from a lovely person with potential to an incompetent, unclassy, trying to be in control, freak.

We finally got to her chosen dining place. To me, it was a typical Chinese restaurant that catered to round-eyed tourists. We had to stop at the entrance for a few minutes, while Sandy combed her heir and adjusted her white suit. When we entered, there were many empty tables.

"Sandy, if you don't mind, I need to face the entrance."

"I like to face the entrance too."

"Really? And why is that?"

"I don't know. I just like it."

"Did you just make that up?"

"Alright. Let's sit here."

She chose a table too near the entrance where everyone's coming and going would bother us- or maybe just me.

"Can't we sit further in the back?"

"No, I don't want to have to look at a family."

All is lost. This is going to be a dead date. I could just get up and leave now. I probably should, but... I know, take it as research for the A Way to Love book. You can't make this stuff up, and there is no way this encounter is not going to get worse. How about a chapter on dates from hell?

We sat down and the waiter asked us if we would like a drink. I declined since the tea smelled good. Sandy had white wine.

"Can we order some ox tails and little birds? You can just have a taste, and I can take them home."

"Oh, I thought I was ordering dinner to stay? All right. We can order some real food after we taste your selection."

I asked her some questions about her job and life, but she was defensive and evasive. (So I stopped trying and drank my tea.) After a while, she started to philosophize about life and injustice and talked without making any sense. The ox tails and little dead birds were served. She dug in as if she had not eaten in days.

"You know that these birds are very fresh" I joked. "They are probably pigeons just caught in the park."

"No, pigeons don't have as much meat on them."

"How would you know that?" I inquired.

She reached over for her wine and spilled my tea. The waiter came over to put some napkins on the wet table, and I ordered some scallops, rice, and vegetables. When the dishes arrived, and she tasted them, she said, "These plates are so good. You eat so healthily. I guess my order of food wasn't as tasty as yours."

"Unfortunately all the food was a little overcooked and not hot enough," I answered.

"Why do you think that happened?"

"My guess is the regular chef is off tonight, and the relief cook just wants to get the orders out and has the flames on too high."

"Oh, let's ask the waiter about that."

"No Sandy, I don't like to bring attention to myself, and it doesn't serve any purpose."

She called the waiter over, complained about the food and asked about the chef. The waiter, who was probably a relative of the chef or owner, told Sandy that the regular cook was off and that the proprietor of the restaurant was cooking tonight. She said that the food was overcooked and that the owner has the gas on too high.

"I told you what I thought, Sandy, because it was in our conversation. It was not for public announcement. And I said not to say anything. If you can't control your mouth, you can't control your life."

She relaxed and started to tell me about her life, which was a train wreck. She meandered aimlessly from one subject to another. Her lack of a good education was apparent by her discursive commentaries. She was needy, insecure, and used men for what she could get from them. I was not about to hook up with a basket case. She said that if I took her home, she would do me. Hooker vernacular. I walked her to the subway and said, "Good night, it was interesting meeting you. You know you make a bad first impression... but it's an accurate one." I was disregarding and overriding my prescience, as I have done too many times, for a pretty face.

She called me a few times, always leaving me a message and asking me for something. I never returned her calls. The last time she called she asked if I was dumping her.

This experience slapped me in the back of the head. When will I stop making decisions about the women I meet with just my eyes? Was it a lack of maturity on my part or just habit? But I don't have time to make an in-depth analysis. Life is not a dress rehearsal, so there is no time to practice. I like to jump right in. If it is a mistake, I'll survive. I could never be with a woman whose skin and body I did not like to touch. Even if she is an incredible woman, but does not feel right, or is not sexual, it ends before it begins. So, I guess my screening device, sex, still works for me. I just thought of a new title for a chapter. Making love and music, at New York Speed.

Don't expect life to go in a straight line.

Sign-in, Password, Search, Send

One of **the games in life have changed, and you must be part of the times you live** *in or be condemned to exist only in the past. The opportunities to meet that special love are as near as your desktop, laptop, smartphones, and now Google-glass. Nearly instant response from smart, beautiful women who realize that having an old-school "Sponsor" is not such a bad idea. I was skeptical at first, but after experiencing so many relatively short relationships that started the old-fashioned way of my youth, I figured that I would take the advice that I give on my blog and to my students and,* ***cast away your remaining Luddite ways and peruse a digital future.*** *The most interesting and unappealing factor I discovered on the Internet is, everybody lies about his or her appearance and lives.*

How you think dictates how you build your character and enjoy your life. If you're thinking is not clear, organized, or negative, then your life will be muddled, disorganized and underachieving.

The last thing many people want to know is themselves.

Sometimes not getting what/who you want is a strike of luck.

Life ain't easy; nothing is free, and nothing is without meaning.

Life is not a sprint, so it does not go in a straight line; it's a marathon, so pace yourself.

"He who settles doesn't tangle, since 'a bird in the hand is better than two in the bush.' And I say that a woman's counsel is bad, but he who won't take it is mad." Cervantes, Don Quixote.

Her eyes promised sweet nights. "If she doesn't kill you sexually she will make you stronger." What? That's not the Nietzsche quote.

Your eyes are an exposed portion of your brain. They allow us to form interpersonal bonds and become social beings. The have evolved in humans to become prominent in appearance, nonverbal communication, and to navigate the world. Because they can show emotion, they are critical in expressing feelings and evaluating trust, fear, love, and a multitude of emotions in those whom we interact.

Don't trust a man/woman who doesn't close his/her eyes when you kiss.

Classic Love Songs

Astrud Gilberto – The Girl From Ipanema

Elie Karam - BAADIMA (Buddha Bar)

B.B. King - Since I Met You Baby

Benny Goodman - Yours Is My Heart Alone

Carousel the Musical - If I Loved You

Cole Swindell - Hope You Get Lonely Tonight

Etta James - I've Been Loving You Too Long

Fats Domino: My girl Josephine

Frederic Chopin - Nocturne InE Flat Major, Op.9 No.2

Tavares -- Heaven Must Be Missing An Angel

The Penguins - Earth Angel

The Del-Vikings - A Sunday Kind Of Love

Neil Young - Unknown Legend

Perry Como - Till the End of Time

Ray Charles - Come Back Baby

Willie Nelson - Always On My Mind

Zac Brown Band - Sweet Annie

The Mailman Retires

It was Gregory the Mailman's, last day on the job after 35 years of carrying the mail through all kinds of weather to the same neighborhood. When he arrived at the first house on his route, he was greeted by the whole family who soundly congratulated him and sent him on his way with a tidy gift envelope. At the second house, they presented him with a box of fine cigars. The folks, at the third house, handed him a selection of terrific fishing lures. At the fourth house, a strikingly beautiful woman met him at the door in a revealing negligee. She took him by the hand, gently led him through the door, and led him up the stairs to the bedroom where she gave him the most passionate love he had ever experienced. When he had had enough, they went downstairs, where she fixed him a giant breakfast: eggs, potatoes, ham, sausage, blueberry waffles, and fresh-squeezed orange juice. When he was truly satisfied, she poured him a cup of steaming coffee. As she was pouring, he noticed a ten-dollar bill sticking out from under the cup's bottom edge.

"All this was just too wonderful for words," he said, "but what's the ten dollars for?"

"Well," she said, "last night, I told my husband that today would be your last day and that we should do something special for you. I asked him what to give you." He said, "Screw him. Give him ten dollars."

"The breakfast was my idea."

Saved

A young woman in New York was so depressed that she decided to end her life by throwing herself into the ocean. She was down to the docks and was about to leap into the frigid water when a good looking young sailor saw her tottering on the edge of the pier, tears flowing from her eyes.

He took pity on her and said, "Look, you've got a lot to live for. I'm off to Europe in the morning. If I can stow you away on my ship, I'll take care of you and bring you food every day."

Moving closer, he slipped his arm around her, pulled her back from the edge of the dock, and added, "I'll keep you happy, and you'll keep me happy." The girl nodded yes. After all, what did she have to lose? Maybe a fresh start in Europe would give her a new life and meaning.

That night, the sailor brought her aboard and hid her in a lifeboat. From then on, every night he brought her sandwiches, fruit, cheese and wine. They made love until dawn. A week later, during a routine inspection, the captain discovered her. "What are you doing here"? The captain inquired. "I have an arrangement with one of the sailors," she explained. "I get food and a trip to Europe and he's screwing me."

"He sure is lady," the captain said, "This is the Staten Island Ferry."

April Tender Heart

To gain freedom, we have to move toward it in our actions. We have to go from restricted, to differentiating between our needs and wants, (throwing our garbage out because we wanted it but do not need it,) through encumbered, to less is more, to unencumbered, to more time, to focus, to unrestricted, to freedom. Of course, we all define our own freedom.

April continually carried either two pocket books or a purse and shopping bag. She carried at least two novels and magazines with her just in case she needed to wait on line or travel. She carried a kit of preparedness of cream, water, flashlight, extra clothes, wallet, many credit cards, check book, identifications, perfumes, some makeup, and assorted other "stuff."

One day while we were taking a break from work, and having a cup of tea, I suggested that she empty her huge purse on the desk and separate the contents into her needs and wants. On the outside of her purse were several hearts and metal animals hung from the leather handles on her purse.

"These have to go first," I said because it's just added weight.

"But they're sentimental." She replied, "They remind me of my children."

"Put everything back into your purse," I said. "You're not ready to make your life easier or unencumbered because you refuse to differentiate between your needs and wants."

The first time I met April I knew that she had just fallen out of a Christmas tree. She was such a strange combination of romantic and undefensive intellect that I knew that I would find her interesting. Her natural layer covering was extraordinary. Although she was somehow out of my range of reference, I knew immediately we would get along. We spent an hour over lunch and mutually decided to see each other again. April appeared to be the first real winner I encountered in my search for honey. She has piercing, light blue Irish eyes, and a warm demeanor. In business and contract negotiations, she was smart as a whip. Her level of perception was also excellent.

The next time we met, I realized that she was also very giving and generous of her emotional energies and her time. It was a pleasant change from all the selfish women I met. I was going to take her out to dine for her birthday. She was born on the fourth of April, the fourth month of the year, and was forty-four years old. When she told me this information, it was as if I had déjà vu and amnesia at the same time.

It was easy to see that April was strangely organized and very impractical. She has mistakenly, and no doubt without a lawyer's consultation signed a divorce agreement that gave her ex-husband control over several important aspects of her life. It would soon become apparent that some of these restrictions would become obstacles to our smooth interaction. For now, however, the relationship was accelerating rapidly.

The strange thing was that the only thing I cared about was that she treated me in a warm nurturing manner. She did, and there was nothing else that mattered. Perhaps in the past, I put too much emphasis on the pretty package and did not see the beauty on the inside of the women too clearly. Somehow I just wanted to stop and be with someone real, someone beautiful on the inside, a woman who could feel and treat me well. I was going to stick around and build her up and make up for some of the pain she had felt. I would treat her excellently and see how she would take it. Who knows, maybe I just could make both of us happy.

"I still don't know what you are doing with me," she said.

"I told you. I like you for your warmth and your smartness."

"But, you're so much smarter than me."

"Oh, I love when you build up my ego. But, don't butter me up; I'm not a baked potato. But even if it were true, so what? At least we're going to be together for two more weeks."

"Two more weeks? That's all?"

"You said you want someone to love forever. Forever is two weeks. Eternity is three weeks."

"You're teasing me again."

"Absolutely."

"I don't know why I'm so insecure with you. You have me wrapped around your finger."

"Yeah, right. You manipulate and control in such a sweet way. You're so subtle that I would almost miss it."

"I know. But in my heart, I'm an optimist and in my head a pessimist."

Unfortunately, April was encumbered, and it became a problem. April had two children whom she spoiled silly. She raised them in comfort, ease, and luxury without giving them any reference to work. She did not know how to give the children boundaries or consequences. She had no understanding about developing the boy or girl's character or of parental tough love. April bombarded her two kids with gifts out of some past guilt and gave them affection unconditionally. Although they appeared as pleasant looking kids, because of her overindulgence, they didn't behave well, and they were both brats who were tough to control. Her ex-husband was also a negative influence, and a wrong model, never teaching them how to treat others with dignity or respect. After observing her children, how they interacted with others, I attempted to suggest some alternate ways in which to raise them.

"You know April, if you give them everything, they will wind up with nothing. You cannot give them presents continually, especially if they have done nothing to deserve gifts, no matter how they behave. You're training them to insist on instant gratification. If they want something they get it, instantly, regardless of if they deserve it or not. Life is not like that, and **life pays greater dividends for deferred gratification** and in time punishes instant gratification. If you want to build their characters, you're going to have to stop the free flow of presents. You're going to have to live and imbue them with more reality. Wake up and smell the chemicals."

I was so involved in attempting to improve her relationship with her children, and at the same time frustrated by their demanding and selfish actions, that I had nightmares. I dreamt of her girl child Debra. In the dream, I went to the door and answered an urgent ringing. When I got there, her child was in a basket with a note pinned to her little coat. Please take care of my baby. It was signed Lucifer.

I told April to scare and tell her children over dinner. "Due to your unpleasant actions and the economy, we are going to have to let one of you go."

I really like April, but every time I spend time at her home in Scarsdale, I return a little sad and angry. Not so much at April herself but about her children and some of the people around her. At one of the lovely Thanksgiving dinner parties, she gave, she cooked for a dozen people. When I arrived, I immediately went to work helping her to prepare and serve. If I did not help, everyone would have been eating cold food. At the end of the meal, no one so much as took his or her plate into the kitchen. The kitchen was a mess that would require hours of cleanup. I felt terrible for April having initially done so much and now having to clean up.

The first time I went out there and spent time with her and her children, the same scenario was present. The children accepted my presents without any enthusiasm, saturated with presents given to them continuously, without them earning or deserving the constant barrage of gifts. The children were not trained to help, and both of them played upon April's motherly love and warm heart to do whatever they pleased. They were little monsters that continually burdened her. They both were extremely messy, spilling food and seating on counters used for food preparation. I remember her son eating the heads off a community bowl of strawberries and throwing the part he did not eat back into the bowl. He walked away when I tried to correct his manners. April was totally used by her children without regard to her time or sensibilities.

I was angry that her children were so spoiled and untrained. I could not really help her, as they were not my kids, and she was emotionally unable to withdraw her love from them in exchange for control. I was so sad to see her used and it seemed that she was not even upset by it. April defined herself almost entirely as a mother and could not understand how encumbered she was because the children were untrained. April had inflicted psychological damage to her children by her inability to give up the role of caretaker and become an authority figure. Her children should have been an asset to her and not a liability. Of course, they needed nurturing, time and patience. But they also had to understand that they have a responsibility to the family and must help. At least they should be taught to help themselves.

Of course, April was also difficult at times to deal with. If she conducted her personal life as well as she ran her business, everything could be okay, but that was impossible for her. I would try to solve some of her problems, but she would only create more. For example, she complained about her high heating bill. Her sunroom, surrounded by windows, was losing heat all winter. So, I bought and put up quarter inch sheets of clear Plexiglas over all the windows and sealed them inside and out with silicone. April's heating bill dropped dramatically. The next time I visited I checked out the sunroom. It was cold again because April had installed an uninsulated skylight that negated all my efforts.

How could I add my needs to all the demands that April filled? I could not be just another person that took from her. It made our future interaction questionable, and I became discontent with myself. April, on the other hand, was euphoric with me. I would constantly tease her about being addicted to love and mush, mush. She enjoyed my idiosyncratic behavior and the fact that I was an artist with all the accompanying accouterments. In spite of my extreme honesty with her, she accepted, no, even enjoyed my blunt honesty and emotional frankness.

I, however, realized that I was totally tapped out emotionally and was using her closeness to replenish myself. After a while, I realized that I was just burnt out emotionally and it was impossible for me to give anything, anymore. All the women that I tried to date, be with, bed, love, or just be friends with, disappointed me with their inability to commit to an emotional depth, that is a prerequisite for love. The overwhelming self-centeredness of so many people that I met burnt me out. I had nothing left to give. I was finally and at last content to be alone, to work on my writing, my sculpting, my learning Zen, and my survival.

I could love April, but I could never give her what she wanted... pure, intense, love with a capital L. I didn't know if I should stay with her and try to save myself by letting her nurture me, for which I felt guilty, or leave her so she could find someone who could give her what she wanted. She wanted a romantic, idealized, old-fashioned true love. She also had more heart than any women I have ever known. She would never find contentment or fulfillment until she got what her heart needed. I didn't know what to do.

I didn't know if April realized how insulated she and her children were living in Scarsdale. Some parents can't own up to the fact that their children are mean and stupid. But, April could not own up to the fact that she was a super mother and sacrificed much of her adult life and happiness, indeed perhaps even her health, to give her children everything. Giving the children everything was such an ingrained habit and a source of emotional satisfaction that she insisted on drowning while holding her children over her head instead of teaching them how to swim. April could not change her role from total caregiver to a supervisor. It was driving me nuts, and she did not seem to understand the word survival when it came to her giving just a little more to herself.

The strange thing about April was that I just surrendered to her. I just gave in. I was so used to being aggressive. With her, I allowed myself to become passive, receive love, accept her and relax with pleasure. It was almost a regression. I was trying to rejuvenate and let myself go and be as soft and as hard as I could. April is waiting for her children to grow up, get a better job, get into shape, clean up the house, etc. She spends much of her life waiting to start living. In the meantime, she spends her money and future savings on decorating.

I struggled and endeavored to build April up and succeeded to some extent. In the end, however, she was just too encumbered for me, would listen but not take my advice, and I was too burnt out. I had to change the relationship, but I did not want to lose her. She went on to be a successful literary consultant, Chairman of the Unicorn Writers' Conference and friend.

I buried my love in her up to the hilt. Vibrating with passion, she said I was making her eyeballs shake.

All right. That's it. I am so tired of the game that I will have to try to evolve. It will be difficult to modify my fault and move from physicality to emotionality. That may be what a woman wants but it might be too hard for this too long male. Continually searching and not finding the food that nourishes my heart and sexuality just may be the way I have to live. Sometimes a tough experience is necessary to push you forward in your maturity regardless of your age.

When everything goes well, we do not learn. We believe, "that is the way things should be." But when adversarial or severe conditions or experiences occur, they affect us emotionally. We learn on a deeper level, in the same way surviving hard winters make a tree physically powerful, the growth rings inside it grows more compressed, denser and stronger.

"Knowing that the game is fixed, doesn't stop the urge to play anyway."

"Passionate people always get in trouble, and that's their curse." Jan L. Kardys

Approach love and cooking with reckless abandon.

A reply from a writer and millionaire

Dear Young and Pretty,

I have read your interesting post. Many women have similar questions like yours. Allow me to examine and dissect your desires as an inspirational writer. My annual income is only a hundred thousand, which does not meet your requirement, but since I have many millions, I hope everyone believes that I'm not wasting your time. From the standpoint of an independent, sensitive man, businessperson, it is a bad decision to marry you. The answer to your inquiry is very simple. What you're trying to do is an exchange of "youth & beauty" and "money": Person A provides beauty and Person B pays for it. However, there is a practical problem here. Your beauty will fade, and you will get older. My money will not only be gone but will increase. In fact, my income will increase, but you will age and will not become better looking or stronger. From the viewpoint of economics, I am an appreciation asset, and you are an exponential depreciation asset. If your only assets are beauty and youth your value years from now will be much less. Every trading position has a position. It is not a good idea to keep a long-term trade if the value drops and that is pertinent to your marriage position. Any assets with great depreciation value will be sold or "leased." Men see only with their eyes but are not fools. If you said you were nurturing, intelligent, attractive, a young and pretty woman with the potential to work hard and better the both of your life's you could find a mate, no matter what age, and be happily married. Forget about looking for any clues to marry a rich fool.

Carotid Doppler

I walked out of the elevator and approached the counter to one of the receptionists in my physician's complex. A lovely, silky black haired, Asian woman behind the counter asked me, "Can I help you?"

"Yes please, I'd like a Mercedes, a vacation in New Zealand, a hummingbird tongue sandwich, a pound of hundred dollar bills, and a new girlfriend."

"Me too."

"You would like a new girlfriend?"

"No, just the other things. Anything else?" She asked.

I paused and said, "Well, I could use a foot massage too. So, can you help me?"

"I guess not."

"Just like all the other women in my life. First, they offer to help; then they are too busy. So why did you ask?"

"Which doctor did you want to see?"

"No, I don't want to see a witch doctor. I'd like to see a surgeon."

"Do you have an appointment? When is your birthday?"

"The same time every year."

"OK, how are you?"

"Fine, if not I change it."

"That's such a good attitude."

"Well, I wrote the book."

"Really."

"Yes."

"Can I read it?"

"Certainly."

I reached into my back pocket and took out some cards. Looking through my cards, I asked the smiling receptionist, "Would you like the key to health, and happiness, A Way to Live Zen or relationships?"

"I thought you were kidding?"

"Do you think I'm the kind of guy who would pull your leg and just joke around? There ain't no slack in my act, jack. I was really something in my day, but that day is long gone."

"Definitely. Is everything on your chart the same?"

"No, I've gotten older."

"Will you take a seat?"

"No, I have enough chairs in my home, how about the water dispenser?"

"Are you always like this?"

"What's a like this?"

"What kind of job do you work at?"

"I'm studying to be a part-time gynecologist?"

"No, really, what do you do?"

"The best I can. But honestly, I stood on the corner trying to give away a bar of gold, but, no one would take it."

"I would."

"Yes, but what would you do for it?"

"Depends."

"Isn't that an adult diaper?"

"You are so loquacious and fast."

"Speaking of fast, I'm sorry, but you're taking up too much of my time,

and I have a doctor's appointment. So, if you could just take the information you need, and stop joking around…"

She smiled a practiced smile, that was a little too good to be true, and asked, "What's your name?"

"What? That's it? You're the one who asked if you can help me." I told her my name is on the site, on the card I gave her.

"All right, we will call you shortly."

"Oh no, please don't call me shorty. First of all, that's politically incorrect. Diminutive of stature perhaps. But it's an incorrect nomenclature considering I'm six feet tall."

"OK, we will give you something special." Moments later, a long-legged tan woman, in a mini skirt and white lab jacket, with a thick European accent, approached me and told me it would be just a few minutes. I sat down, but before the seat was warm, she came back and said, "Follow me please sir."

"Anywhere as long as you feed me. Excuse me, could I possible trouble you for an emergency cappuccino?"

She turned slightly, adjusted her bra, and signaled for me to either kiss her ass or follow her.

I followed her down a corridor and into a room where one entire wall was made of white smoked glass and acted as a divider between the next room. The room next door had lights on and the wall glowed pleasingly.

"Please put your things on the chair and make yourself comfortable on the gurney."

I did as I was told and adjusted the pillow. She unbuttoned her white labcoat, put on rubber gloves and raised my sweater and undershirt.

"Hold it," I said. "If you're going to get kinky, I want rubber gloves too."

"That will not be necessary, and I'm going to shut the lights off now," she replied as she opened up a tube of clear lubricant. She turned off the lights, sat down on a stool next to the gurney, spread her legs uninhibit-

edly to balance, and proceeded to attach white cloth squares with small metal centers to my stomach and chest.

"Now the fun starts?" I inquired.

She answered, "Please don't move and can you turn your neck to one side facing me?"

I turned my face to her, closed my eyes, and puckered up my lips, feigning a huge kiss.

She chuckled indulgently and countered with, "That won't be necessary right now, perhaps later. You have to stop talking, moving, and relax, just put yourself in my hands."

I resisted giving her a great retort, although she feed me the perfect line, breathed a sigh of relief and relaxed.

Dr. Cole, as a writer I cannot help recording and utilizing new situations and characters. I thought you might get a laugh from this perspective. Thank you for your excellent professionalism and your personal caring. Please look at my website.

Cheers, Mike

A Way to Live.com (Please click Like)

Note: Carotid Doppler is a procedure, administrated by a technician, where an ultrasound mouse is slid along the carotid neck artery to investigate the speed of the blood flow and search for any anomalies. It is one of the tests used to help diagnose and analyze any possibility of a heart problem.

"I like you. You remind me of when I was young and stupid."

"I like that wagon your dragon, tushie."

Kiki

To the love light one more time

Good morning, Mike, I am not good at dating and expressing what I think. Sometimes I am shy and quiet, but not because my intention is bad. Because of this characteristic, I missed some good chances, and some people misunderstood me. The conversations with you made me think about myself. I still have confusion between my culture and myself. Some don't think about it at all, but I want to have my notion whatever I choose. At least I want to express myself and have freedom from some uptight restrictions. I hesitated to call you, but, then pushed your number.

Older people are respectable; we don't really hang out with them in Japan and can't be friends. That's why your suggestion that we date was a surprising one. At the same time, I didn't think it was all of the sudden. Everything is connected. I couldn't reflect on any possibility that I could be your girlfriend. When I think of you, I was considering my cultural confusion and my passive attitude regarding dating. Since I don't find any reason not to go out with you, I want to get to know you better, having a good time. Going out with you is not that big a culture shock because I found you are younger than the young man in my dreams, energy, and mind. So, I think you're energetic, not crazy. I am not sure if I explained it well enough. Hope we build a good relationship.

WHAT A NICE SURPRISE.

If you don't mind the analogy. You are like a tree with strong Japanese roots. You will always have the solid roots and always be a Japanese tree. But now you cannot look down or back to your roots for you to grow. You must look up to the future and the sun.

I have an endless supply of water to share with you. But it will be difficult for both of us. We are such opposites. It will be difficult for me to have enough patience because I move very fast into change. For you to grow, you must change.

Change, in turn, means giving up something to gain more. But for you to give up shyness and a conservative attitude can only lead to having a richer life with more happiness, a good trade off. It is important to me that we try to keep our relationship private. I really let very few people into my life and like my privacy. I hope you don't change your mind by the time I get back next month.

P.S. I dreamt about you last night that we went shopping to buy you shorts.

I was talking to Kiki one evening over drinks on the terrace. And the topic was her sense of humor and the difference in cultures between the traditional Japanese and American perceptions. She said that the most interesting joke she ever said was the observation that Richard, my best married friend, was in total control but next to his wife he could not belch. Somehow, I don't remember how I brought up the topic of kissing. I told her the best soul kiss, swapping tongues, I have ever seen was in the movie Species. I told her of the scene where the alien woman kissed a man and put her tongue through the back of his head killing him. Her dry reply was "That's because Americans and Aliens are too direct." This is the woman that I could love. I was risking it, but the chance for failure makes our love more meaningful. I laughingly look forward to having my stomach hurt from her mastery of the understatement.

Hi April,

Thank you for all the information. For the next few months, I must concentrate on building the deck on the land. But not to waste time, and to consider all you have taught me, this is my plan. I have hired an excellent designer and Webmaster. Her name is Kiki. She is just starting a master's degree in New York City. I have given her my website to redesign and improve. I will now let her work on designing the A Way to Live–Zen book jacket and book. By the time I'm finished with the deck, in about six weeks, she will have upgraded everything. I will then concentrate on the book and website and coordinate with you. Naturally, you will see all the results and if you want you can hire her for yourself and your authors. She is a rare find, but she eats too much. So, I hope you like this plan. Cheers, Mike

Hi April, I have been away for a few weeks. My webmaster/designer did the book cover and the pages. I must say I never realized what a professional could do. I was very impressed as you will be. We have a winner for designing books, cover jackets, and websites. I will be away again for three weeks and if all goes well ready to print the book. I am sure we will be working together soon. I hope all goes well with you. We will get together when I'm back. Much love. Mike

Mike, I hope you don't change your mind as well. I'll practice speaking and expect what we'll have. Let's have lots of water together to grow. The interesting dream I rarely dream. I spent some time responding to my mail. Although I have the same ordinary day, I feel a little bit different or weird to be involved with you. Kiki

Kiki, I will not change my mind, only you can change my direction with you. I do not care about how well you speak English now. After a while, you will become more fluent, and there is no rush, especially because your vocabulary and comprehension are excellent.

My prescience tells me that we are going to have some problems, but nothing that we cannot work out. I'm so glad you're feeling different and weird about our us involvement. New feelings are always fun because they change our way of thinking. Then we alter our actions. No feeling is bad if you know what to do with it. And we have not even kissed, and this is only the beginning. What fun.

Mike, I respect who you are, what you have and where I am going. I know I am not an easy person. I think because I always try to do the right thing. So, I need someone who is mature and has a bigger picture and can lead me to other directions. As you know, you may require some patients with me. I just hope I don't make it hard, having a great time together. Besides that, I'll look forward to what we'll face.

Kiki, I hope I did not raise unrealistic expectations. My biggest fear is that you have been holding back for so long that you cannot let go. I'm going to give you options that will short circuit your emotions and jump-start you into womanhood and life. Of course, only if that's what you want.

It's good that I'm leaving town or else I would eat you up. I love having to look forward to seeing you when I return. Looking forward to our first kiss. I forgot to tell you. I'm a romantic.

Mike, you may be busy, but I wonder if it is possible to build the terrace first. I guess it is good that you are away from here for a while so that I can take some time. I may forget you and us when you return. And you need to answer some questions for me. It's about realistic expectations. I'll let you know when I find out my new roommate's nationality. Hope you don't forget about a shiny shell for me. Kiki, The Bronx Chick.

Kiki, just went on-line again everything shut off when I left. I'm back for a month. I thought a lot about you-us. I'll be happy to answer any questions you have about expectations. That's such a hip expression- Bronx chick. If you have not changed your mind lets touch base. How about dinner, any time after seven, on Friday night? You can stay over if you like and we can spend some time together Saturday.

Mike, Nice to hear from you, again. It's been a month already. I've taken care of the plant you gave me thinking about you. It's strangely alive. I used to kill any plant around me. And now I have five small sprouts as well. It's a little fun I have. Welcome back. I'd like to have dinner on Friday. I'll come to your place around seven. I'd love to spend time on Saturday with you, but I'd rather not stay overnight. See you on Friday. Kiki

Hi Kiki, Dinner out on Friday- any preference for place or food? Drinks and sunset watching here first. We both have had over a month to think about getting together so, something for you to think about. **How will you ever learn to swim if you do not jump in the water?** How much of our human lives and our love lives are lost by waiting? Looking forward to seeing you. M

Mike, I got a long letter from you in a dream. I was sleeping while reading it. It's funny. Any place you like. I'll bring a bottle of wine. Looking forward to seeing you, too. Kiki

Kiki, Sorry you are not sleeping well. I know how to fix that, but now I am not sure where you/we are now. No need to carry wine I have several bottles. Also, since you will not take pay for the drawings you have free wine and dinners forever. We have much to talk about. But I am so aggressive compared to you I have to be so careful with you. I wonder if you will surprise me?

Mike, do not be so careful with me. I wasn't sure if I was ready to see you. While exercising every day, I've thought about this a lot. So, my choice is that I'm going to walk with you and keep up. If it is too fast for me, I'll tell you. I know you meant a lot of things in your E-mail. I am concerned, but my intuition tells me you/we are on the right track. See you tomorrow.

Kiki, you make me jump back and forth between hope and apprehension. I have to curb my natural enthusiasm and understand where you are and what you want. I can hardly walk, but I would like to fly with you. I appreciate our communication. Tomorrow. Mike

Hi Kiki, I thought I was going to be disappointed. I was going to write, all you see, and all you touch is all your life is ever going to be. And a third of your life is already over. This is not a dress rehearsal. But instead, I can write.

You surprised me. What a wonderful 22 hours together. A solid beginning and opening up to each other. Looking forward to hearing your funny laugh again. Your skin is heaven to me. I hope you were not too overwhelmed. Thinking about you. Now we can both relax.

Mike, I guess you had not gotten my E-mail since Saturday. I had two other lovely e-mails. I wrote that I was glad I was not alone anymore.

Hi Kiki, you have me worried. Usually, your communication is rapid. Too much too soon? I'll understand. Think of me. If you change your mind, I'll understand. Just tell me you are OK.

Kiki, What's going on here? I ask you if I can fulfill any of your sexual fantasies and you turn around and achieve mine. Forty-four hours of straight lovemaking? Do you want to hurt me? Remember I'm 1,300 hundred years old. I can't do this anymore. My tongue, my hands, my salami and even my eyelashes are sore. We are going to have to cut down to no more than twenty hours, and with frequent breaks. Sneakers next week.

Mike, I feel good I still smell of you since we used the same soap. I'll come home, after taking a shower at your place. My fantasy...I was curious about how people are crazy about each other in the first period of their relationship. I felt strange because I could see a different myself with you. Although some parts of my body are sore as well. I'll try to give you a good massage and lead a diligent day. I also want to study carefully, after taking a good rest.

Mike, I had a quiet day enjoying the sun, reading a book, and thinking about you. I miss you, too. Like when I decided to be with you, I want to follow my heart. But I come up with some worries because I have few things I can share with you. You may want to say something. I know. I need to borrow your 1300-year-old wisdom. I forgot I have a book about foot massage, and I'll practice.

Mike, I just got home from meeting my friend. If you'd called me, I would've come to you. I was in SOHO. Are you not working? Because you miss your lollipop so much? I'll come tomorrow. You make me feel like a different Kiki. I blame it on you. I am picky. Your cooking has been excellent so far, so keep working on it. I'll tell you when you are qualified, and I fall in love with your cooking. Kiki

Mike, how was your day without getting a massage? I've thought I need to express myself more. I don't mind telling you something, but I still have shyness. Miss you, your smile, your hands, and your eyes. Kiki

Mike, sometimes you deserve massages. I always have the assignment I get to know myself. I am still in the middle of building myself. Your mail reminds me of something that I have forgotten. I was too stressed out when I was a designer, and I am still stressed out surviving here. My problem is I don't know how to manage both stress and relaxation at the same time. I can deal with only one. I have something like your lumpy pillow; I don't depend on Japanese food, and I don't use an instant messenger. I use an agent, and I need to eat rice sometimes, but now I can control myself. Being alone with my baby English in a different country makes me lose my pride and confidence. However, I am not struggling to figure out fundamental issues anymore. I want to work hard to be someone I want to be with. And I want to make a plan with you. I feel comfortable and safe when you hug me. Thank you, Mike, my funny face.

Kiki, funny face? I'll get you for that. I miss you. I want forever to begin tonight. Tonight? Tomorrow? My dream/reality? You give me a message. I let go. I crash. We hold each other. I fall into a Zen sleep, Heaven.

The Secret of Life

"Please tell me the secret of life."

"Mike, I read some of your new book, Zen. I am so impressed with your wisdom."

"Well Kiki, as the book says, since I am old all I have is the wisdom of a lifetime. But, what I left out was that your memory slips, as you get older. So, even though I have these great flashes of wisdom by the time I get to write them down I forget them."

"You are such a character. So, do you know the secret of life?"

"Yes."

"Will you tell me?"

"Yes, the secret of life is to live now because we all die."

"That's it?"

"What more do you want?"

"I want you to tell me using the wisdom you have gleaned in all your years."

"How much do you really want to know? And how much are you willing to pay?"

"Everything, nothing."

"The secret of life can be found hidden in a variation of the prejudicial old Polish joke, 'how many Pollock's does it take to change a lightbulb?'"

"How many?"

"Three."

"Three? How come?"

"One to hold the bulb and two to turn the ladder."

"That's the secret of life?"

"You didn't listen carefully. I said a variation on the old joke."

"All right I'm paying attention now."

"How many psychiatrists does it take to change a lightbulb?

"Please tell me?"

"But, you did not even think about it. You just wanted to be given the answer without doing any work. This is not the Zen way."

"I'm sorry. You're right. I'm just impatient for some wisdom and want to improve my life. I do not know enough and by the time I learn I will have moved through many years and have wrinkled skin."

"Good, you have begun. The answer is, it only takes one psychiatrist to change the light bulb, but he really has to want to change it."

"So the joke is that a therapist's patient can only progress if they want to change, but the more profound expression in the joke is that change is what it's all about."

"Correct, go on."

"So the secret of life is change. But change what? And how? Oh, I see. Wanting to change is the first step, and everything else follows."

"Good. The first step, since life, is linear, but it more often than not does not go in a straight line we can see, is to consider giving up your dreams for reality."

"But, everyone's dreams are different, and we all define our own reality."

"Forget the philosophical arguments. We are talking about your dreams and your realities. How many of your dreams were given to you by your parents? How many dreams has the culture you live in indoctrinated you with? How many dreams are based on wishes and serendipity? And most important of all, what are the chances that the countless dreams you have will come true?

"So, even though I'm living in this world and I'm part of the culture of today, my beliefs are based on past experiences, which have their roots in dreams, and I have to change to give up my dreams?"

"I did not say change to give up your dreams Kiki, but the converse. Abandon your dreams for authenticity and that will produce the positive change and make you more open to grasp the opportunities.

Most people will not give up their dreams for reality. So instead of compromising and fulfilling much of their lives and aspirations, they insist on believing that one day, or soon, or under the right circumstances, or if I just wait a little longer, etc. What usually happens is, they lose both their dreams and the opportunity to move forward."

Would you trade your dream for reality? Would you trade hope for truth knowing that hope is not a plan?

"But I love my dreams, and I don't want to give them up. And genuineness depends on who you're talking to."

"I think it should be who you're talking with and remember the answer to the psychiatrist joke. What you have just said is typical. You want your dreams, independence, and control. As long as you hold on to these assertions you will never change and even though you have been told the secret of life you were not ready; so, you learned nothing. Come back to me with your regrets in twenty years and we will try again."

"Mike, please tell me the meaning of life."

"Why do people insist that life has a meaning?"

"Mike, please tell me the secret of life now. I don't want to lose twenty years and have regrets, and I want to learn."

"What makes you think that there is only one secret?"

"Please tell me some of the secrets of life."

"One of the secrets of life is that there are tens of thousands of choices and chances to which you are exposed. **Even small decisions can have enormous consequences. But there are only a mere handful of options that can give you a quantum leap forward or help you find the happiness you seek."**

"How do you know which one to choose and if you are making the right choice?"

"That is not the problem. The choice is right in front of you; you only get one chance. If you pass up this offer or opportunity, it will take you twenty years of work to make it up. You will also lose your youth and your time. What do you do?"

"You grab the opportunity."

"But the opportunity demands that you compromise, change and give up some of your preconceived ideas and dreams for reality."

"It is only my reality that I give up or define. It does not matter what anyone else thinks or cares. I do not have to please anyone else since my life is not a dress rehearsal. How can I compromise what everyone else will see as strange or different? It's so hard to change and not know if it is a change for the better. And how can I give up my dreams?"

"This is why most people are wage slaves all their lives." "Explain please."

"Because of a failure to modify our behavior and reject contingency with all its permutations. Also, compromise is not capitulation, and you can compromise for eighty percent of what you want and still have a good life. **Remember all you touch and all you see is all your life is ever going to be.** And that is only one of the secrets of life."

"It seems so hard."

"Where does it say it's going to be easy?"

"It's going to take a long time for me to understand and gain some wisdom."

"Now you have started. The first step is the hardest."

"Show me the path. And make me your girlfriend."

"Good. You have been listening."

"The various situations and conditions of time and space contain latent within themselves opportunities whose influence and power we must enable ourselves to exploit, if we are to make the most of what fate offers us." Chapter five, Potential energy, The Art of War by Sun-Tzu

From Candyman To Selfish Super Pervert

Kiki was an extremely young looking lovely woman with incredibly clear skin and kiss me eyes. She was tall for a Japanese woman and possessed a beautiful, lithe shape, perky perfectly formed breasts, a sweet ass, and long legs. Her legs, however, were thin and long with little shape. But her long legs dovetailed perfectly with her long stride, which made walking together synchro meshed. Her demeanor was a bit shy, demure Asian girl. Of course, I knew that she was an ambitious, independent, assertive, dry humored, creative, talented, woman. I knew when I took her to the lake house that jealousy would be rampant. I told her that all the women there would automatically hate her.

"Why?" She asked.

"Because it would demonstrate that if a man, an older man like me, could get a beautiful young woman like you, then their husbands might stand a chance of having the same. This is a threat to their marriage, and the women will hate you. The men, of course, would flirt and love-to-love you and that will further antagonize their wife's. So, what will you say to the women who will ask you in many subtle ways, "What the hell are you doing with this old man?" Of course, they will say instead.

"How did you meet? How long have you been together?"

And they will ask other leading questions all moving toward answering the same old man question.

I prompted Kiki to answer with the response we rehearsed, but she was reluctant to use any of the lines I gave her. At the lake house, it was at the dinner table for twelve that the woman I referred to as the unhappy bitch, who on a tender day rises to the level of vicious, and whose demeanor was like a smiling cobra, asked the question.

"What is a young girl like you doing with an old man?" She said, a diabolic smile rising from her lips with a hiss.

Kiki answered, savoring slowly, "Well, he is a selfish pervert, but he shares his fine wine, has broad shoulders and a big dick."

The women around the table froze with their mouths open. One of the men suddenly and dramatically spit his drink onto the lawn. Some spit food into their napkins and exploded with laughter. Kiki's place in the evening and the history of the lake house was assured, and I was surprised, and content.

Then the unhappy bitch's best friend incredibly wanted to pick up the theme and asked me loudly, "But you know everyone is haunted by death and you are much older than her. What happens ten years from now? You know death comes to all of us."

I answered, "There is nothing I can do about it. I'll cry and be sad, but if she dies, she dies."

"Kiki," I said, "Get me a drink."

Maggie chimed in and said with a raised voice, "PLEASE."

Kiki answered her. "Please stop trying to impose your American standards on our relationship. A master does not say please to a slave or a slave to a master."

Maggie looked at Kiki incredulously, as if she was a betrayer of all women's liberation and rights.

Kiki continued, "And since he is my slave, I resent you trying to retrain him for your use. He is mine to deal with, and you should be polite enough to ask permission if you desire to have him modified."

I was so proud of Kiki and enthralled by her dry wit, quick humor and her growing sense of empowerment. I reflected, **pompousness needs to be punctured.**

Mike, we had a short and essential time together. I have many things that remind me of you. Is this also your plan? You absorb me little by little. I've already memorized and brought your smell.

I like your disposition. We are so different. I have lots of things I am not good at. But I want to yell at the rude people who try to put us down.

Dear Desert, you surprised me again. How can you open up so fast? I plan everything you know that. Yelling back at rude people is just a game. But, if you don't open your mouth in NYC, you get stepped on. The big question is... Have you fallen in love with my cooking? I'm still smiling. I think of you too often. I know in the short run I can help you and bring you out. Over the long term, I am just an iconoclastic unconventional male who has found an emotional, vulnerable woman of whom he can take advantage. My last spring or can I change your life for the better with my interaction? Sleeping with you means everything. Am I losing it? I love our communications.

Mike, you know what? I have to become stronger. The beginning of working out is you, Mike, If I can do anything to be healthy, especially with you, I will study and try to work things out. Your instinct may not work in the long term, or I made your vague because of my quietness. What I do know is that you are a part of my life. Being with you is an unusual adventure for me. I believed my strange intuition about you and your place. That's why I didn't care about our big age difference. I am vulnerable. You have too much thought. Let's say this is a beginning of your golden years with me. Too cocky? My firm hope. Miss you.

Kiki, a message every day would spoil me.

I sleep on a lumpy pillow every night to remind me that **stress is always self-imposed by desire.** I am a student of Zen Buddhism.

My conflict is wanting, not leading a simple life but being able to afford luxuries, irresolvable but interesting. You must express yourself more and talk more for you to become successful at whatever you desire. But since English in now the international language and the language of money you are way ahead, all things considered. I enjoy your quietness and your talking. But life is action, and you jump right in. Excellent.

Hi Kiki, I can't seem to get the energy to complete my projects. I think of you. Am I taking on another project? But my ears become full of sound when I think of you. The background music is always the same, Andy Kim singing "baby I love you." Am I careful enough with you? Maybe I'm just tired. Love Mike

Mike, Yes, you are careful enough with me. I appreciate every one of your concerns, but I don't want to make you tired. I am waiting for you finish your work to see you more often.

Just because you are taking time doesn't mean you are not moving. Save your energy for a while to fly higher. Many things are so new with you. I don't even know how much I can miss you. Thinking about your funny face.

Mike, you must have gone to bed.

HOPE you are full of beans after a long sleep. If you are still not feeling well, let me stay next to you and make some soup for you. As you said, take care of you first and then take care of me. This is our deal. Nobody can be energetic all the time, especially because you are an artist, so your flexible plans would be the best. I'd like to see you with satisfying work. I love our emails, too. I just worry about my insufficient English. Fortunately, you are a good mind reader. I love your cooking!

Kiki, I'm trying to watch a sunset, but my eyes are tearing and itching. It must be an allergy. Unfortunately, I think that being a first responder to the World Trade Center disaster may have triggered the allergy I developed in the army. I will look into the problem when I return. I always have anxieties when I travel and leave the country. I can only imagine how difficult it is for you. I am drinking good wine in a crystal glass. I look out at the sunset and the magnificent city skyline. Still, I am only a speck of dust. Our contact civilizes me. It is the only intimacy I have. It stops me from becoming alienated. Can we see each other before I leave? Dinner and... I hesitate to get together with you because all I want to do is sleep. Still, to hold you again and hear your funny laugh.

Mike,It was comfortable, fun, and lovely day with you. I liked your unexpected invitation, your cooking, and your taciturnity. I apologize for my foolish interpretation. But because of this, I could see you and get to know you better, and I like you more. Your ex, Kiki

Dear Kiki Taciturn, that was a lousy fake fight. You're not supposed to laugh all through it. I did not realize how long you must have been holding back. It must be a big relief to let go. Now that the cork is out of the bottle you can never put it back. Good.

But I'm angry with you for sandbagging me. I'm supposed to be the older and wiser one. I'm expected to call the shots and be in control. Instead because of your feminine wilds, you made me your slave. But even though life is trouble and sorrow I guess I will get used to it.

Have I got a voluntary slave? I am the luckiest teenager in the world. I am an owner who is manipulated by her slave's plan. I'll change my nail color to a light one. Beautiful weather to think of you. Love.

You are terrific.

The dam phones do not ring because they are not digital. I have to get all new phones since I switched to fiber optic cable. You staying next to me put me in a trance. Talk to you tomorrow.

PS. In about ten minutes I'm going to give you a little uptown show. Some wind, rain, thunder, and lightening. How's that for manipulation?

Now I believe that you have special abilities. What a lovely display. I like this crazy and unexpected weather. Don't make me laugh alone.

Kiki, you're driving me crazy. I can't stop thinking about you and your sweetness. The potential of our future conversations, your laugh, your skin. I still don't understand how you have any smooth skin left after taking boiling hot long showers. But at least you are clean if not sterilized.

Watching TV shows becomes another meaning for me. I used to watch shows to learn the culture and develop my English. But now I think some conversations could be ours. I appreciate your smile, patients, and generosity. You don't know how much I feel safe with you. Why did you go to the World Trade Center when everyone was running away from it? And what did you do there? I miss the coffee ice cream with the cute little demitasse spoon.

That's it, I have had it. I send you emails that are serious, and you answer me back with jokes. I am going online to a dating service. I am going to use the cover from one of my new books about love and online dating. Here is the cover. Do you get the jokes? Do you think they will accept it?

I had a girlfriend that worked in one of the twin towers. She was killed. The first day I just helped the firemen carry heavy hose lines from the river down Vesey Street. The lines were massive and all the firemen, who are the greatest guys, were crying at the loss of so many of their comrades. As crazy as it sounds, everyone was waiting for another building to fall. It did because the basement was full of the FBI stored explosives. Having little to do for a while, I went into the American Express building and took out trays of cookies and gave them out. Then I just went back some other days to help.

Kiki, Come to me early on Wed. We will go out to dinner with some friends in Queens. They love raw fish. We can do a little shopping before we see them. Be hungry, you can stay over but no sex. I am tired of being your sex slave. But you can hold me all night always.

Mike, my email was not a joke at all. Seriously, put your ad online. I want to know how many women will Email you. I am not competitive, but let's see what happens.

Meeting your friends makes me nervous. If I don't understand your conversation with them and cannot be part of it, what will they think of me, you, and us?

Hi honey, don't be silly. What can they expect from a seventeen-year-old? They will accept you because they are friends. It will be good just to hold you and perhaps just play. At last, I can get a little massage and fall asleep, which is just what I need. Sleep well, you have no worries about being with my friends or me. You can relax; they have good karma and a great sense of humor. All you have to do is be yourself and laugh, which you do naturally.

Mike, I was trying to reply to your email, and it went into send now mode. Sorry. I just wanted to say that I am looking forward to seeing you tomorrow for dinner. Later, Maggie.

Maggie, Me too

I'm bringing my little 17-year-old friend, Kiki. She likes to listen to improve her English and she doesn't eat much. See you around 7.00. Love, Mike

Mike, since you made a good excuse to see me, I will try not to be nervous. I don't have doubts your friends are kind. If I make excuses for my English not to see your friends, I may not see anyone. What kind of clothes should I put on? Are we going to go shopping for a tattoo?

Remember me? Can we get together one day? Remember when you used to answer my emails instantly? I guess the honeymoon is over... Jeans and sneakers. Maybe a light sweater in case the AC is high? This is very informal. I think the tattoo may have to wait.

Can you get here about 5:30? I need to pick up some stuff at a store near Stephens and Maggie's house. Your weakness is only in your head. We have a nice ride where we can talk. And considering how pretty you are, and that you are so new to the city, guys must hit on you all the time. So here is a good comeback for an often-used line.

Man, "I'd like to call you what's your number?"

Woman "It's in the phonebook."

Man, "But I don't know your name."

Woman "That's in the phone book too."

My beloved teddy bear, I still feel today is Sunday. Since you have many books for me, it's too scary to believe your prescience. Everything would be new for me, but I always appreciate every small change with you. I admit today was my fault, I hope you can make your schedule up. See you on Saturday.

Kiki, you're making me crazy. Be a bitch. Stop being so sweet. I hate you. You are destroying my life. Go away. Come to me. Missing you will be hell/good. Do I sound ambivalent? See you at eight. Love, your slave. M

You sounded very ambivalent. I don't get what you are talking about. You make me crazy; preoccupied, smile alone, having expectations, Most of all, you forced me to wait for you for a looong time. You'll be punished by my kisses. Love, your Honey Bitch

Kiki, you win; you make me, laugh so hard my stomach hurts. You're terrific. It was wonderful seeing you tonight. I never saw you dressed up. You look so lovely and much older, almost 23. Interesting that you thought our conversation was slow. That shows how fast you are learning. The time will pass. Try to remember me.

You are not alone. Remember alone is also all one. Although spending some time uptown would have been a nice change. Thank you for the compliments. You must be starting to like me, soon you will be so busy, but then, one day, your slave will return.

Your trip is like a break time that divides our play. How we met, how was the beginning of our relationship? Who ever thought Kiki would've kissed Mike at a 57th street bus station? What's next? I feel sad, but I am supportive of you.

You are so excellent. My life must be charmed. It is good that we concentrate on our work. I have been thinking about you all day I must focus on the island and my work. This break is good for us even though I think about holding you continually. We have time for some more emails. Thank you for taking a chance; you make me feel things I have almost forgotten. Be aware of who is walking behind you and drink a lot of water.

I feel the same way with different reasons. A conservative culture, responsibility, stubbornness, whatever we had, I appreciate that we are looking at each other.

Kiki, there is no sadness about us being apart; it is too intense, too good. We need to be apart or else we would burn out like a shooting star.

We must become like a planet revolving about the sun with a moon to light us up Slowly. Just think of me at sunset when I watch the orb fall I will think of you. I know a pilot who flies in from Japan once a week. I will ask him to bring us the most expensive Green tea in Japan, an aphrodisiac. **You know the opposite of love is not hate it is indifference.**

You fill my mind with fantasies and expectations. Be careful, if you stay so sweet, I will attempt to consume you.

Mike, A planet... we compare the earth to a pot that is made of stone because it saves heat for a long time. We compare the shooting star to a pot that is made of metal because it saves heat for a moment. I like the planet story. I think of you all the time, fondly, deeply, and quietly. I think I won't have a problem because I have your smell on your t-shirt. Someday, I will dress up for you. Anyway, don't worry. I'll be your bitch. Your owner, Kiki

Kiki Honey, what are you talking about? I don't know of any mistakes you have made. And even if you've done them they are not irreconcilable I'm sure. Also, don't tell anyone it was a mistake and no one will know. Everyone makes mistakes. The trick is to try not to make the same one again. Life is for learning. I hope you liked my little lecture on errors. I still like you just a little tiny bit. You are getting better in every way every day. I guess this is our last communication for a while, Stay well. The weeks will fly by, and we will fight and scratch soon enough. I can't wait to show you off and make enemies of more wives.

I think I'm much better wearing high-heeled shoes. I'm still too short for you, though. I think of your warm belly, big arms holding me, your sensitive blue eyes filled with my face... I am with you, even though you are not here, hoping I speak fluently and you plug your ears. You said you were a risk-taker, but am I worth taking a risk? It's still odd when I think of how I got together with you. I can't think of any better encouragement, can you?

Mike, like this time of a day in solitude, right to think of you. Spending time with you was like a dream, a good dream in a short nap. You were with me, but you are not. Still, I wonder why you come to my mind all the time. I can't help but define you were a dream. If you are not a dream, do not make me think more. Simple and complicated thoughts. Fear and expectations and things I can't describe. Things I don't want to explain. I'm learning.

MISS, YOU. School started... People looked good after a vacation. But I wasn't happy to see the mean girls whose behavior hadn't changed at all. I am sure I don't have any energy for them. Mike, how are you? Are you still busy? I see the weather in the Caribbean; you may be tanned a lot. There are thousands of men who want to go out with me in the Columbus Circle right now, but I'm writing miss-you mail to someone. I'm still with you, without you. I am afraid I depend on you. How's, is the weather over there? When a hurricane comes, America looks so small.

I want to have little pleasures with you. The Queen of Night takes plant roots in the water, and the leaves of Jade become tight. My karma must be changing in a positive way. I used to kill plants next to me. Or the plants are unusual, and they can survive in any circumstance? Then now I'd miss you more terribly? I believe it might also be one of your plans. Although you are not here and nothing exciting going on with me, the feeling of missing you is better than the time I was alone. It makes me full, safe, expectant and thinking of our lives.

I'm back. I was going to send you a joking message starting with...Do you remember me? We had some very intense, good, days together. If you do remember perhaps we can get together again someday. Etc. But when I saw your emails and read them, no time for games. It looks like from your schedule that we can see each other soon. Let me know when. Missed you.

What's wrong? We only made love for six hours. And you left after we were together for only 20 hours. Are you leaving me? Do you still like me? I hope you don't mind picking your birthday present out early. But you know how I like to plan. Besides, diamond earrings are basics. Your slave, Mike

Feel like I spent a long time with you. You want me to have everything good, but you can spoil me without them. I don't need to have something shiny or to go somewhere exotic but I will accept your present since the earrings are the first present from my slave. Being with you is already a special gift for me.

Be careful. **Expectations can destroy all we have and all we can ever have. Live in the now. Do not compare. Most unhappiness is caused by our desires. Alone is also all one.** I take all the blame.

Mike, a few expectations, but no comparisons and no complaints. Just grumbles for candies when I can do it. Tomorrow is a holiday in my country (the full moon of Aug.), kind of Thanksgiving. So, what is the best WAY to be happy?

The best way to be happy is to give up all desires. Of course, in this society that is imposable. **Everyone wants more. My way is to be glad to begin and to change your disposition.** If I am not in pain, if I have a few good friends, a good lover, enough food, exercise, and can feed my mind with chess, Zen, and music, I am a euphoric man.

Dear Loser Mike, I was sure you didn't remember my birthday, but you're right. You're the first person to congratulate ME on my day. You'll get some punishment, and I'll remember it. Still, thank you. Work hard, slave.

How can I not remember your birthday when I already bought you your present? **The most important thing that rich and famous people crave is privacy.** Why is solitary confinement the worst punishment? Why are people so afraid to confront themselves? And when you are alone you have it. So, you have something positive and good when you are alone. Thinking of you.

Mike, since you gave me a lecture on mistakes, I'll remember what you said. I thought I didn't talk about something when I was with you. Also, I don't know how much I can talk to you. You said I could speak to you about anything, but... You sent me your two pictures after we had dinner with Richard's family. Your picture was hidden with my previous Email. After you had left to the island, I happened to see your picture. I didn't know I missed you so much.

Kiki, if we see each other too often, you might get tired of me. But I miss you, so I'll take a chance. If you're not too busy running around town, dancing, dining and partying with all your friends, could I please invite you to dinner and a great personal wine tasting? Wed. About 7. If you don't want to stay over, I'll understand but you're welcome.

Kiki, My Honeybee, I'm not sure about what you meant when you wrote "Grumbles for candy." some time ago. But I have decided that I will no longer be your slave. Instead, I will be your candy man. I bought all the shampoo stuff you like and a lot of excellent wine. Went shopping for food after a doctor's day out. Great salad and BBQ thighs. And I almost forgot me for desert. I have a little surprise too. Girl, I miss you tonight. Your candy man.

Mike, Honey is funny. It's sweet, I want to eat more. You just call me, baby. Hope the thighs are not greasy, but you're a good cook. The surprise is we have telepathy. I'm hungry. Yours.

Kiki, does this message mean that you still like me? OK, if you can take it, I'm your candy man for two weeks more. Looooong day but both doctors gave me an excellent health rating. I hope you understand my sense of humor, understatements and sandbagging, and jokes. Your writing is poetry.

Mike, Be my boyfriend for two weeks? But you are always saying two weeks. What does that mean?

Forever is two weeks. Eternity is three weeks. And this is the last time I use this particular term because you are my last special woman.

Thank you for the pants. Thank you for the many things that you try to spoil me with. I like your thoughtful and caring surprises. So, I want to be spoiled for two weeks more, if you don't mind. Everything is new with you; bagels, chicken thighs, the air, taking trains. Please don't wake me up when I dream about you.

Your smell and voice linger in my mind. Have a wonderful day with me and without me.

Instead of reading boring books, I was reading "Newsweek," an article about brains, but merely, all emotions and psychological processes come from our brain. Did you know about this?

Did you have to ask with all the nature shows, thunder and rain, I have put on for you? I guess I have to prove my prescience to you significantly.

Nice to hear that you are super healthy. Keep working on your good shape.

No one would guess from your writing that English is your second language. I'm sending you good thoughts for today. Drink more water. I feel lonely tonight. I don't usually feel this. Would it be insulting you? Making you lose face...Thinking you are undesirable. If I just held you one night without sex?

Mike, you're always welcome holding me without sex (read, not in your life.) I rather feel your heart growing in me. I'm still trying to find excuses to be with you. Waiting for candies. When you feel lonely again, call me; I'll grab a taxi. Now I miss you. I need your warmth.

Baby, What a lovely answer. I don't want to use up our intensity. It would be like living in a desert. Good and sweet but not for breakfast, lunch, and supper. Thank you for being so ...you.

Mike, as long as we move forward in the future, our intensity would change. More solid, deep, rich, and an authentic one, like your wine, like your sculptures. We would not consume our energy in a moment unless we are shallow. And we can create candies all the time. Because of our opposite qualities, others would never taste.

Kiki, I am saving all our emails for the book. Your writing is very evocative, like music or good poetry. I'm proud of your intelligence and facility with English. Sometimes I just write to you because I need the connection. Sometimes because I miss you. I have a problem with you. I don't want to miss anyone. It takes up too much thinking time. Still holding you in my arms means everything. I'm lost; I'm lost in you. I never believed I could feel so young again. Well, what could I expect being so close and intimate with a seventeen-year-old?

I want to appreciate our every moment. Although I hate that I have to live like a young emotionally vulnerable girl. I worked at school yesterday, in my favorite classroom. Working in that room is reminiscent of the last semester, which was too harsh and too unsatisfying to handle everything. What I realized was, I worked too hard and still work hard, but I felt different. I am laid-back and happier with my candy man. I am still discovering myself. I am grateful to be with you.

Your words, as usual, are soothing. I am angry today that everything is going too slowly. Work, cleaning, friendships, plans the necessary mundanities of life. Too many people call and ask me. I have to **get rid of the neutrals and make room for the positives** like you. But sometimes life gives you traps. It's hard to be patient and wait for change instead of instituting it. Did I tell you that I'm crazy about you?

How are you today? I cannot define what life is, I don't know what's going to happen tomorrow, but at least I know I want to be with you until I could. Working for my dream company, coming here, meeting you, my intuition was pretty good. Now, you make me blind. You're weirdly tempting sweets, and my expectations make me blind. Thank you for being patient with me.

Kiki, **we are all blind until we learn to see.** See you at seven.

Mike, even if we hadn't gone out to dinner, we hadn't eaten a special breakfast and coffee, and we hadn't spent time together, twenty-one hours, and I would've had a great time with you. But you gave me more than a great night, morning, and afternoon. I couldn't resist having your smell on me, your warmth, and your sweets. Although I keep telling myself I have to accept my reality, just thinking about you makes me joyful. Strangely I feel better since I've told you, my friend, my worries.

Kiki, it's not strange to be able to tell a friend your troubles and share. That's what friends are for and it helps to talk and relieve the stress.

My definition of a friend is a kind of honest, loving, light revealing, mirror in which we learn to recognize ourselves and are shaped and modified. We are lousy at being objective about ourselves, where we are going, whom we are going to be, what we will desire a decade from now, and most of all how and if we have changed and in what direction. **A real friend can tell it to you bluntly and straight and perhaps save you some grief.** Don't marry that so and so, that's an ill-advised tattoo, consolidate, don't make another purchase and lousy financial decision. But it is so hard to listen that we usually don't.

Even though you don't promise anything or run away from me, I still appreciate being with you. If you didn't know because of my quietness, I am telling you now. Hope you are having a good time with Steve and Maggie and good wine.

Kiki, I'm getting it done, but things always take too much time. Even when I give it twice as much time as I think it will take. But **work always expands to fill the time.** You make me happy because you fulfill my needs. Contact, communication, intimacy... I am content. I can take care of everything else.

Mike, I never want to make your life complicated. You only make my life better. I take full responsibility for everything in my life so only I can make it more complicated. No guilt.

Kiki, your mail was poetry but saddened me. Perhaps I'm not fulfilling my role if you are alone. You know you have access to me if you need to. It is just that I cannot have you here without touching you. Then no work gets done. Perhaps that's better. Candy man

Mike, you already have me. I didn't mean to sadden you. There are always the fights between the rational Kiki and the emotional Kiki to be with you. I cannot cheer loving Kiki to be a winner every time because she is already with you. Although I need to control the fights, I just bite my nails. Your voice is always pleasant to hear. I've never been bored when I think of you. You keep saying my mails are poetry, and I just hope your English is not getting worse because of me. Your honey-bitch.

Kiki, your sense of humor really made me laugh at this one. Notice you are making fewer errors. Also, when you can joke in another language you are on you're the way to mastering it.

I was going to leave you, because I didn't want to go to jail. But since your birthday is so close I guess I'll stick around. I don't think that they can prosecute after the fact but I will find out.

Yes, our mails might make a wonderful book about love and life and action. We got together so fast and with such intensity. It's great. You have coined, (Invented,) a new phase never heard before in the English language. Honey-Bitch Congratulations, Your candy man.

Mike, no matter how much time I spend with you, I feel it's too short. It is always too good. I liked yesterday on the terrace holding you or sticking to you.

I still can't believe you hugged me in the morning after 14 hours in bed.

While I was hearing your snores in the morning, I thought about this... Everything I like about you is from your unconventional qualities.

Your warmth, sensitivity, generosity, enthusiasm, your dreams, your smile your sense of dignity. Maybe your buttocks are the only things I can barely complain about. I like the fact that I am free from being uptight myself when I am with you. Thank you for the many things that I can't even count. Hope your doctor gave you an excellent result as well.

Doc gave me 95% OK. But I need a little surgery where I was shot in the ass. I asked him if he could add a little while he's down there. After I come back, he can operate- all minor stuff. I'll miss my honey tonight and my cover thief. Soon, CM

Hi Honey,

Thinking about you. I'm so proud of you and the way you are coming out of yourself. I know Kiki means blossom in English and I must say you are blooming, opening up, communicating, touching. I know it is a mistake to feed into it, but I cannot help myself. Still, I think those months from now it will pay off in conversations and communication. Of course, I am a fool waking a sleeping tiger and a quite woman.

Hi Mike, Spoke to Beverly this morning, she looked up the joke and said that she got it from her sister. Her sister got it from? Got it from? Who got it from? It would be virtually impossible to get to the source that way. I wish that I could help you, but I am sure this e-mail is viral. Also, note that I asked Stephen if he could recommend a way to find out. He responded that he had seen that e-mail before. Bev also said that she "thinks" that she has seen that before. So, unfortunately, you are on your own. Will miss you and Kiki over the New Years. Have a good one, and hopefully, we will get together soon. xoxooxoox, Maggie

You made me open up to you.

You have not only opened up to me, but to the world.

When I find that I am not shy anymore, doing everyday life with you, it is not explainable. You are the source of my weapon. Still, it is amusing to me, when I see my changes, and when I can't control my tears because I like you. I say that I knew something how it would happen (only about myself), but I never knew every step of being with you and every thoughtful care. I expect our conversations and communication as well. Thinking about you, wearing the cute cat-shaped glove.

Tell anyone about the cat oven mitt, and I'll have to kill you.

Did I make an obscure meaning again?

Absolutely. Buckminster Fuller's Intuition has nothing on you.

I have a few merits. One of them is I always try to have a bigger picture.

You are such a funny, strange person and so cute. You will go far because you are camouflaged. They will never suspect.

Everyone thinks that if they change they will get better. No one ever really changes. I like you the way you are. All you have to do is become more of what and who you are. Of course, when I become perfect I will expect you to become perfect. I'll let you know when I reach perfection, certainly not for a while. Crazy about you or maybe just crazy.

No one ever changes? I think an environment changes people. This is what I want to study through interior design, color, and architecture.

Like rats in a maze? Modifying your actions to integrate with the environment is not changing.

I am a good example. I could be more of Kiki since I've had an American culture.

That's growing and expanding, basically not changing.

Even though I have a predicament, I am happy because I am free from my uptight culture and I have a candy man who spurs me to be myself. Because of this, sometimes I worry if I can adapt to some of my cultures again and if I depend on you more than I want.

You rely on me exactly as you want. And you will or can always adapt to your culture because you have grown and now you can be more objective about influences and prosper.

I didn't ask you to be perfect.

I know that's my problem and a joke.

I just thought that small changes might make you smile or feel happier and different because I am.

Yes. True.

You can say you are just crazy. Then, I'd believe you could be mad about me.

More poetry. I thought I already said that. I always look forward to your emails

The two days last week spoiled me more. I think you put something in your food. The memory of watching you cook boosts the taste as well. I am getting worried about this. Spoiler! I want to cry.

Stop crying so much, you sissy. I told you, you would fall in love with my cooking. Now I got you.

Hi Mike, You sound good. I'm inviting you to a wine tasting in two weeks, let me know what your schedule is, and we can dovetail. Kiki looks like a keeper, Incredible, and you sound happy, but remember trust but verify. And remember the economist Minsky's financial instability hypothesis where he said, "Success can morph into a virus of overconfidence." You can extrapolate this theory to many other applications, especially relationships. Richard

Richard, You're right. This ability to go with Kiki may represent the triumph of hope over experience or just irrational exuberance. However, you know that I'm a voluntary optimist, grounded in reality. So, while my feet are in the mud, I still reach for the Moon. Take care of yourself and remember we will try to lose 1 pound this week. Cheers, Mike

Hi Honey, did you understand the words in the ad? I want to use it for a cover on an Internet dating site. Richard and I are having dinner tonight since his wife is still In Italy.

Mike, No, I don't understand why your ad is so funny. I don't know about the bell ringers and your cousin. Tell me about them later.

The Hunchback of Notre Dame (French: Notre-Dame de Paris) is an 1831 French novel written by Victor Hugo. It is set in 1482 in Paris.

So, is Richard getting punishment?

I'm also going to punish you. I've asked Steve to invite us to the lake house this weekend. Have to wait and see if they have room for us and recovered from your last visit.

So, according to your ad;

I don't know about the genetic relation of Quasimodo's hunchback, but there is a possibility you could be a hunchback. You're deaf, blind, and interested in and aggressive young cowgirl who is sexually into corpses, (necrophilia). This means you're an awful mentally deficient. Did I study well enough?

Yes. Thank you and do you think I'll find true love on the Internet dating sites with this ad?

Mike, Oh, I saw the trees in front of my apartment are turning to butter yellow and barbecue red. When we go to the lake house, the scenery this time must be evocative and beautiful. I'm looking forward to experiencing inspirational nature. HB

Kiki, I miss you now.

My entire day was spent with Stephen. I was his law assistant. Aside from being one of the best criminal lawyers, his sense of humor and intellect makes him a pleasure to hang out with. But I can't complain because I learned a lot and he worked on my case for hours. He told me as far as your concerned 16 will get me 20. And he changed your name to Kiki Statutory. But that's better than Kiki Chlamydia. He told me of a statutory case where the accused man testified in court and said, "But she looked much older and matured even though she was sucking on a lollipop." Do you get the Jokes?

I put love in our food. I told you I would get you through my cooking. Didn't you believe me? It's starting to get dark earlier. Is it always safer in the light?

Were you an excellent assistant? I want to hire you soon.

You have already hired me as your everything. **If you had more, everything, where would you put it?**

It was hard to believe because I've never had a natural food effect.

What does this mean?

Do you know how pitiable I am, during the five days I don't see you?

No, but that is going to change.

I'll come to you as early as possible.

I can't wait to feed you again. Honey-Bitch is going to be a chapter in a real love book.

When I think about you, when I see a beautiful sky, when I see my shorter hair, when I find I'm using a green pen, when I feel safe with you, I also want to give you a smile and safety.

Our hugs are satisfying, our relationship is getting stable, more precious, then you take your bitch deep inside. Miss your human back.

WOW, No mistakes in English. More poetry. What's next? You make me take a deep breath when I read your email. How can my seventeen-year-old be so mature? Then I realize you are a woman with a great hard body of a teenager. I have what every man wants. And your sense of humor is excellent.

Do you realize how much we laugh together? Let's paint our toenails matching colors next week when we are together again. I plan to have dinner and drinks with Richard before his wife, Fran, gets home and he has no time. My nose is stuffed tonight. I'm going to try to go to bed early. I never do. If I could do you, I would rest.

Time to rest when we die. **Burn the candle at both ends with a flamethrower.** Black caviar for breakfast.

Mike, you make my heart leap up and drive me sad at the same time.

More poetry. But I feel the same way.

We both have to accept our reality?

I think we are both too tired with too much work to go to the lake house. If we just hang out on Sat. Rest, see a good movie, hold each other, and rest. The coming week will be easier for us. Will decide tomorrow.

It's more fun when an aggressive candyman wears a pussycat glove. I like the fact that we are intensely looking at each other. It's a big present of my life. Expressing something out of my mouth about you sounds too light; words are not sufficient to describe how I feel about you. I want to care about our togetherness and grow the plants you gave to me. Since the moment we have become us, I have the same notion: I appreciate now with you.

Yes, Kiki, it was good, but keep in mind it can never happen again. Four times in one night? It must have been a dream we both had. You have to stop crying so much. Except when it rains.

Hi, my candyman, I like this cold weather because I can hold your hand more tightly. Although I can't see your shape through layers of clothes, I like that your eyes become robust. I'm comfortable with you even if we don't talk to each other. I feel safe even when you are in the next room. I am happy only thinking of you.

I think you are getting to like me.

OK, No four times, no crying, and no biting hard. I'll come to you around seven. Today is a drafting day. I haven't had this much fun for a while. Now I have to worry about how I can make the drawings better.

I think we will eat in because of the rain. Had a great and lousy day. Good news to sleep on. Fresh sheets with stratospheric thread counts and fluffy towels. Just hugging. Maybe a kiss or two.

Hi Baby, I have to crash with you after we do some work. I went shopping for some interesting food as usual. I have to get you interested in me somehow. Your comment about "I hold you in me." It's an example of the double entendre that I told you about? Unfortunately, it is a French term and thereby sucks. It will be fun trying to work with you without biting or sucking. I'm looking forward to any improvement in my web page no matter how small. What fun. Love (smack myself in the face...shut up)

Thank you for the delicious dinner,

Thank you for the inspiring movie,

Thank you for the lovely hugs,

Thank you for the comfortable night,

Thank you for the tasty breakfast,

Thank you for spanking me,

Thank you for the pleasant conversations,

I am satisfied with all the time being with you. Your HB

HB, Thank you for the lovely email.

Thank for the excellent massage.

Thank you for helping me clean up.

Thank you for being you.

Thank you for giving me a new spring.

Thank you for giving me just what I want when I want it. Thank you for opening up to me so wonderfully. Thank you for your funny faces that make me laugh. Thank you for making me so hard.

Damn... I'm so used to winning and being competitive. I have to learn to lose to you. You have much to teach me.

I opened your mail all day long and could feel you even in your typing mistakes. We have different reasons and lives, but we both want the same thing. As you said, **we have what people look for in their lifetime.** I believe we are always with a smile looking at each other.

We can be at Steve's at about seven. Don't rush-no stress. Save all your drawings if they are on good paper. Sometimes it is great to go over your old work with a different medium, or even upside-down using the old picture for texture.

It's good to work hard. **The ability to work and love is my definition of mental health.** Looking forward to spanking you again. Yes, we have something special.

You may want to test our relationship, taking apart from each other.

I never test you. I accept you. Being apart is just business.

I cannot tell you everything in my mind in any language, but I feel safe with you. I won't be lonely at all. I am filled with you and your smile. Your craziness makes me happy.

This makes me feel great. I guess I'm doing my job right. Also, I'm crazy about you, but you know it because I show it.

I talk with my friend from time to time, and I haven't thought of the cultural conflicts we have. Since I've been here, watching the problems that she has with her colleagues makes me reflect on myself. While I haven't noticed cultural conflicts with you, it's because of your concern. I remember what you do for me, while I am unconscious.

How do you know what I do if your unconscious?

I want to enjoy everything that I have with you because I know I am the lucky one. I believe in you.

I hope you are going to the ultra-conservative NYC Halloween parade. It will be good for you to see what rational people and the fla'neurs are like. My gay friend once told me that it took him days to dress up for the parade. When I lived in the West Village, I used to dress up as Hermes the Greek messenger, with a winged hat and roller skates, and thoroughly sprayed with silver paint. In those days, the parade was only down Bleecker Street but expanded over the years.

I saw many people, who wore Halloween costumes on the way home, I envied them. Those who could express themselves without caring about how people looked at them. Have you done your packing?

Hi honey, I thought I would get so much more done before I left but... Work always expands to fill the time anyway. I'm glad we saw each other so much with so much intensity. It gives us a good foundation.

Mike, I think of many things that I have with you. Things that I haven't thought I'd ever have, I'd ever feel. I have much to learn from you and us. My roomie asked me if you were fictitious. I've just found I have 120 emails in the box with your name. Have we known each other that long?

It's like a dream that the sun is really warm and amber leaves are floating in the sky. I cannot imagine the dreary weather of yesterday. People seem to like to have a bleak life. I think people make others cold and indifferent. I miss our time, enjoying the sun. I'll work holding you in my heart.

Hi, my candy man,

I'm reading one of the books that you gave me about chess and poker. The city turns gray, and it makes everything calm. The class for tomorrow canceled and this weekend will be cold, so I'll be a homebody. Since I am free tomorrow, I'll take a nap a little bit to dream about you. So, come to my dream. Thinking of you playing the harmonica.

Kiki, everything went like clockwork today. I guess after so many trips I have it down pat. Still, subtle change always makes it better. But giving up comfort for experience always produces stress. But **what is life if we cannot modify our positions? Change is what it is all about**. I was just thinking about our sweetness. A warm feeling rose from between my legs, and I had to pull my thighs together. I figured I had lost a segment of my maleness and desire. That book you are reading is about conceptualization. Chess has no bluffs and poker is luck and bluff. That is the difference between the Russian and American cultures. Think about the Cuba missile crisis.

I'm back, beat and haggard.

Do you know the Christian Bible story of Job? Everything that could have gone wrong did. We have a date for Tues. If Stephen and Maggie can get together with us before they leave for SA, then we will have our sushi in Queens. If not, the evening is ours or yours to choose.

Missed my honey bitch more than you know. Reading some of your emails, it occurs to me that you spend too much time worrying about things that have not happened and of which you have no control. **Solve the problems when they occur. Worrying is not productive.**

Here is my formula for dealing with problems. Divide up what you want to do, learn, solve, or be. The steps are,

A-Inception. What is the idea that you want to express, change, work on, explain, and do?

B-Incubation and imagination. Think about it, dream about it, state the problem, and draw plans in your mind or on paper. Take your time and write down everything first. Dump it all out of your head, and you can refine it later.

C-Practical application. Work with it. Practice, make a model and pull the ingredients together. Dissect any aspect that appears too complicated. Approach the same question from different perspectives and issues.

D-Culmination. Keep going until you finish or find a solution. If it's too arduous or complicated, a project, start again after putting it away awhile. Do it. Soon, M

Kiki, the communication gap between us is sometimes infinite. It is also frustrating. I want to see you. My world is cold without you. I am tired but not dead. Holding you means everything.

Mike, Because of your email, I've read Job story in the Bible. I am not a Christian, but I have a Japanese-English Bible, of course, it's a present. One thing good about this Bible is that there are brief explanations about the scenes. The end of Job, there is a good sentence." The Lord blessed the latter part of Job's life more than the first." Could it help your fatigue? Maybe not.

Kiki, yes it helps. But I think that a new modern air conditioner that dehumidifies, with great filters might help more. I'm looking into buying one. She gave me you as a reward. Most people do not know that God is a black Porto Rican Lady. I have always wondered **why when we speak to God we are said to be praying, but when God talks to you, you have schizophrenia.** Sometimes I think people are just jealous that the voices only speak to me.

Kiki, I'm worn-out cleaning up the mundanities of life. I got up very early and started to clean with a vengeance. Not enough time in the day or days. Looking forward to letting go with you. The only time I can relax and stop is when you put cream on my back. I'm making my famous chicken soup tonight for us tomorrow.

Mike, why do you so struggle to clean things up?

Because I want to be nearer to that Puerto Rican black woman we call God. Don't they say cleanliness is next to Godliness?

You can be more relaxed. You don't like being lazy, right?

I like to be lazy after some quantity of intensity.

Or let me know if you need any help.

You help me enough already

I am all yours after the New Year.

I thought you were all mine now?

MIke, I learned one minute could change the mood of our comfortable day. I also realized I feel I'm really in a relationship with you.

It's about time.

I've never thought I could be a woman and have an unpleasant moment with this kind of subject. Is this a proper response?

How do I know? Men are a different, less evolved species, and not fully developed emotionally. It seems to overly sensitive to me. But it must be a sore point in your private thoughts. Be careful of this, it is part of your unresolved pre-mortal memories.

You can say I am stubborn. I am open-minded, but I also have some standards of morality.

Imposed on us by society before we can formulate our opinions.

Good night, my candy man. Thank you for the hickey and wonderful weekend as usual. Your chicken soup, your hugs, your breakfast, everything was more than extraordinary.

You are too sensitive. I love it. Stop worrying so much. I love your moans.

Kiki, I went shopping today for our food on Sat night. I know it's the only way I can keep you. It's a lot of work, but life is trouble and sorrow when you want to be with a seventeen-year-old. It's good that you are more motivated to learn more English. But you are smart so, **"you have nothing to fear but fear itself."** Have a comfortable evening.

Mike, My candy man, You gave me a unique and warm day as usual.

You get what you give. A woman that tries to make my life easier? How unique.

I'll be more relaxed and charming next week.

No need to be more than you are. I'm more than satisfied. I'm content and satiated. I finally cleaned out my paint room locker. Now I have some room upstairs for your bath stuff. I fight for inches of space. It was an enjoyable, satisfying, loving weekend. Thank you.

Hello, my candy man. I've worked thinking about you among lots of your faces.

Are you saying I'm two faced?

Your world is not dry and lonely; I'm always with you.

I can't take it...

The bagels are the same ones I had with you, but the taste is not the same when I have it alone. Because of you, I'm more relaxed this semester.

After multiple orgasms, I would think so. Me too.

They were much easier than I expected.

That's what happens when you study.

I got some good compliments about my presentation from my teacher, and I could remember only a few images. Learning is also about discovering my ability.

Probably more than you know. Once you lose your insecurity and gain confidence, you become a menace. Keep your feet in the mud but reach for the moon. If you fail, you will still have learned and possibly gained more if your goals were higher.

Talk about it to your Dominican God.

No. She's Puerto Rican.

I'll go to bed early tonight and see you in my dream.

Kiki, worked for a few hours today on the stained-glass window frame. It will be a long time until I create the window, but it uses up a lot of wood, which helps me to clean and gives me more space. My Honey bitch, Ha, now that you told me your innermost secrets. That food means so much to you. I am going to make you not only my Honey bitch, but also my slave. I'm going to cook Italian Saturday night. By Sunday you will be talking Italian and using your hands to express yourself. You, like so many others, will kill for my Pasta Primavera. You are lost. We are going to the lake house again soon; it will be cold but fun. You give me flashbacks of when I was a teenager with my first girlfriend. I am laughing at you thinking that you don't communicate.

A quiet woman that is affectionate caring, and sexual. Are you kidding? I can't tell anyone anything. But if I could they would be so jealous because everyone wants what we have. It's just a pity you eat and drink so much. Please don't get fat. I want to spend some time with you just listening to music. It will be good for both of us and fill our souls. Hope you enjoyed my "sausage." In obsolete french, that's called a double entendre. Since I believe that the french are snobs, and their language is spoken much less, I have programmed my computer always to spell french with a small f.

Hi, my candy man, I know the literary meaning of "I am crazy about you." But I am not sure about the degree of intensity.

How much more intense can it get? I hold you so tight I am almost on the other side of you.

Do you see it's snowing?

Lovely large crystals.

The weather in your neighborhood can be different from here. I still like when it's snowing like a puppy.

Do you mean raining like cats and dogs?

Did you have all of the pasta?

I made it especially because I will not be able to chew after the implant tomorrow. Remind me to tell you why my teeth were knocked out in the rock scrambling accident. When I was growing up, it was better living and experimenting with chemistry, (read drugs,) but now it has changed to better living through modern surgery. My prescience tells me that I am going to have a lot more titanium implanted in my body.

I feel like I have been experiencing many things that I cannot count on in one semester. Are you going to answer about orgasms or screams?

I deny it altogether. What?

Your existence, your world, my world, our present, and our future. You make me a wealthy and happy bitch, despite some of the difficulties. I couldn't see you that well, but I felt so good when you called me on your terrace the other day. Still, miss you. What's wrong with me?

Nothing.

The new fallen snow covers the garden flowers with bits of ice crystals.

More poetry.

Call me or email me if you need to fuss about your pain.

I will have little pain. I will knock myself out with Hydrocodone. But I may not email you tomorrow night.

I'll be hoping your surgery goes very well.

You get what you pay for.

Hope you don't get hurt anywhere anymore for me.

I always hurt for you.

Mike, even though you gave me a contented weekend, I'm not that impressed with your mindful patience.

What the heck is mindful patience?

I'm not in love with your food especially your secret ingredient love.

Ha. I laugh at your causality. I give you all I have. And you say you are not impressed. From now on we go out. That will teach you to appreciate me more.

Even though you keep me in your bed, and you always want a massage, having you in me gives me peace and tranquility.

My dream woman. Isn't that enough?

It's not because of your food.

Ha! I laugh at you. You took seconds of my incredible sauce. You are lost.

I am afraid I will be found out I eat a lot...

That makes you strong for me.

It will be your fault that you take me there.

I accept full responsibility. You're just what I want.

Kiki, what am I going to do with you? A Woman who relentlessly satisfies me. A person who about I can't find anything to dislike. Cute, smart, ambitious, demonstrative, and lovely. I'm supposed to be too smart to fall in love. But I'm going to keep you around two more weeks. Then you will probably turn from my honey bitch to a talkative, assertive, stubborn, take me for granted, self-centered princess.

Kiki, My Honeybee, I mixed some of your crocus powder with honey and took it. So far my congestion hasn't cleared up but small flowers are growing out of my ears, and the ginkgo is driving me nuts. You never told me how to prepare it for consumption. First I mixed the powder with honey and ate the mixture with a spoon. But I reasoned it would take too long to consume a decent amount. So, I dumped a whole bunch of powder in a mug, put some honey in and poured in hot water and I finished the whole thing. Now my hair is straightening out and turning dark. My skin is turning yellow, and I have this great desire to speak Japanese. CM

This is the funniest mail I've ever gotten.

I love to make you laugh.

We don't have "a decent amount" of something.

Who is we?

"Amount of whatever you like." is a decent amount. But, I think I told you to eat it one or two times with a spoon like candy.

Some candy. Like Plaster of Paris.

I also mentioned, "at least for two days." So, do you feel like a crab or not?

Where did a crab come from?

I called you, but your line was busy.

People are calling me, but I can't talk. It makes me choke, and I can't hear with the flowers growing out of my ears. I was out today and walking helped drain my sinus. I feel better in some ways, and I'm going just to stay in and do paperwork and rest all weekend so I that I have the strength to beat you up.

Are you still coughing?

Only when I talk or laugh or eat or drink or lie down.

When I was about to send this, I got your funny email, and I'm still laughing.

Good.

It was for several days, and I don't know what to do. I can deliver the rest of the powder.

I didn't take that much. I still have more than half.

I went to the MOMA, but too many people came there to see the building and the people, not the artwork.

It scares me. Too many people too crowded, to uncontrolled.

You are the only one who is interested in my expressions and what is in my heart. I appreciate you.

But your constitution is too weak for you to fall in love.

After you get stronger, I'll think about being with you.

If you are still in bad condition, why don't we go to an acupuncturist?

Why don't I paint my feet red?

You may not trust Asian treatment. I didn't know about it either until I had a serious allergy two years ago.

Last time I went, she gave me an infection in my lip. I took a lot more of your stuff. I still have no results, but I trimmed the flowers from my ears and filled a small bud vase. So, it's not a total loss. All seriousness aside, I'm not sure if your flower powder brought on a deluge of phylum release or perhaps it's drying me out. Either way, yesterday sucked.

Ascribing to one of the mottoes of my existence, **anything worth doing is worth overdoing.** I'm going to finish your flower power today and hope for the best. I'm also going to go out for a while and buy more drugs to dry up my sinuses. I feel like an old lady complaining about my health. I'm going to wait until tomorrow to decide about going to the lake house, but I'm not optimistic.

HB, thank you, you are my sunshine. I'm fine. Just down for the count. I do not want or need you to share my minor inconvenience.

I need you to be happy and active. There is nothing you can do to take care of me. I'd keep you up all night. The flu must run its course, and if you got it you would miss weeks of school, and work and I'd feel terrible that I gave it to you. If the flu does not kill me, it will make me stronger.

Mike, I know you're realistic. You force me to think that I'm afraid of being alone without you. I'd been thinking of it, but I'd forgotten for a while since you made me too happy to think about it. It took some time to get over and accept "why I'm with an older man" Because you're Mike, you are the man I've always wanted to be with. What am I going to do with you? What do you want me to do with you?

Like me a little bit.

Bite me more lightly

Pick on my bumps

Hug me, let me feed you

Let me make you laugh

Allow me to see your funny faces

Keep me civilized by holding you

You don't have to do anything for me

Just live and be happy.

The sunlight was warm, and I thought about the afternoon when we took in the rainbow holding each other. Are you still good? Your voice sounded good without choking?

Better but I cannot be around people. I blow my nose every few minutes. And have suffocating fits when I can't clear my throat.

Glad you can invite me; I was going to ask you anyway.

I am determined to beat this. I can't lie down because I choke. But I have some new drugs. I have had many mugs of hot water all day long. But I can't complain. You can only complain when you are in pain. I'm drinking our great wine, listening to good music and playing chess. Although, I sound like I'm dying when I choke.

I hope I will not let you talk alone on the phone. My resolutions are keeping you healthy and becoming your talkative honey bitch. How about that?

Healthy is good. Talkative is wrong. Honey Bitch is right. Honey, I wanted you to know a part of me, so you will not throw your hands up and run screaming into the night. This is an email that I sent to Richard.

Richard,

I'm so glad you're functioning. Keep up the honey and cinnamon, and it might help. I have not taken this many drugs since the sixties. In those days, we took everything. But the aim was different--communication was the goal. But I am feeling sad, and I thought I would reveal a part of my character to you.

I am upset. Why? Because I am a practical entity. I feel sorry because I am not a good Zen Buddhist. I want so badly to have the energy to cough in the faces of my enemies and all the garbage people who have ruined so many lives. What an incredible weapon and they cannot arrest me. I have always thought that the good die young and the bastards live too long. Am I sick? Of course, but if you are not in pain, it is only a lesson. Love, Hydrate, Mike

Hi Kiki, I hope you do not take advantage of my weakened condition and try to have your way with me. After all, I am a respectable older man. I can't wait to bite you, tomorrow anytime.

You take advantage of my tenderhearted, sincere love.

Absolutely

Do not pretend to be weak, and be a super healthy candy man. I'll give you one more week.

I'll take it.

I may be at your place around 7:20. Can we see the firework display at home tomorrow?

It usually starts at 9.30 in the summer. I'm not sure when it starts tomorrow. I can't wait to see it. I can't wait to be with you. It's all I think about. Disregard the above sentences; it must be the drugs talking.

Hello, my candy man.

Are you happy without me? (Absolutely)

You are getting too smart, predicting my answers.

Thank you for inviting me despite your inconvenience. I enjoyed being with you. I always feel I spent a time somewhere in Oz with you.

Kiki, everything is good because I'm starting to feel better. But not fast enough, so I took more of your witches' brew to accelerate the healing. We had such a good time together that I am left with a residue of contentment. I started to try to clean up my g-drive today, and it would not turn on. The G-drive is too finicky and sensitive for an external drive. All the connections are right, but there is no way to turn it on with the computer. Life goes on.

My wish that I wanted to be with you more affected my physical condition. But I still don't know the exact reason.

Life gives you problems to solve.

I had lots of problems with my first computer, which was IBM. Despite all the connections, IBM would not work sometimes. So, it's about your system G-drive.

If you have a problem, and you can throw money at it, you can usually solve the problem. I have another G-drive. Tomorrow I will disconnect and plug in the other. So, if it works, it is the other G-drive. I'll play with the connecting wires and find out.

I've been thinking about you as usual. With you, I don't feel lonely in the middle of luminescent streets.

I think you mean luxurious sheets? You ain't seen nothing yet.

How's the condition of your G-drive?

You would not believe it. I have been working on it all day. Finally, I had a brilliance after several consultations. I dumped the entire photo backup, 8,500 photos. Then I'll plug in the G-drive to copy the 1,500 that I have.

Still, I feel sorry that I couldn't take care of you as much as I wanted to.

I need you to take care of me when I'm healthy and active. I take care of myself when I'm sick or injured.

I'll finish your butterfly before I go back to school.

Thinking of your skin.

Mike, How's your day with your persistent coughing?

EVERY DAY ABOVE GROUND IS A GOOD DAY.

I found out you have been sick for a long time. It has taken too long time to be cold. Do you think you can be healed entirely, as time goes on?

Honey, it's influenza. We call it the flu. That's similar to the 1918 flu pandemic that killed 50 to 100 million people. Three to five percent of the world's population was eradicated, making it one of the deadliest natural disasters in human history. It spread around the world right after the end of the First World War. By contrast, 16 million people were killed in the war. That's why we wash our hands and take off our shoes when we enter our homes. And just to add a positive note about cleanliness, fleas in two Arizona counties have tested positive for bubonic plague. (Time Aug.2017)

Thinking of you, as usual, wondering why you like me.

Who said I like you? It was the drugs talking. I was delirious. I am innocent. I didn't do it. I wasn't there. I don't remember saying anything. I didn't see anything, and If I did say or see anything, and if I was there, I was sleeping.

All I do is work on the Apple all day. Then for a break, I go to the Apple Soho store and hang around with the excellent manager, David, and ask him for help. At any rate, I'm learning a lot and turning a negative illness, into a learning experience that's positive. Unfortunately, this flu is hanging on like a monkey in a coconut trap.

I feel I haven't seen you for a while, worried about your flu.

DEATH IS NATURE'S WAY OF TELLING YOU TO SLOW DOWN.

Hope your coughing doesn't affect your mental illness.

I am getting better slowly. I have not been this sick since 1986. Before that, when I was government property, I received a dozen "vaccinations" in a few days. I was a precursor of bionic but very sick. Was Nietzsche right when he said, "If it does not kill you it will make you stronger?"

Kiki, this is a way of saying that even when something goes wrong, we can still benefit from the experience by learning from our mistakes and sometimes it can make you stronger. It's called post-traumatic growth. You have become important to me. I don't know what to do about it except to bite you.

Mike, I would let you do anything except for biting me.

I would sing songs next to you to please you. I would allow you not to connect with erotic websites. I would give you black coffee when you enjoy the sunset. I would stop up your anus when you make fart tones. I would have you cook for me in morning, noon and night. I would take you even though you are mentally ill. I would do anything if I can expect a longer time together. I would never ask anything except for your health.

NAG, NAG, NAG

Be a bastard.

I solved the G-drive and have hundreds of gigabytes more. I am trying to get a special meal together for our reuniting. But my energy is down. Maybe we'll just have bread and wine.

Giving me bread for dinner is punishment.

It's a joke. It would never happen.

But, don't make hard on you.

I love when you talk dirty.

I don't need special food. We can go out around your place.

Yes, but not on Saturday nights.

Or, I'll cook some Japanese food. You can prepare some ingredients, vegetables; I'll only bring the main ingredient.

What can you make with shrimp? Can you make shrimp patties?

Glad to hear you solved the G-drive. You must have learned a lot.

How are you enjoying your day?

I enjoy every day.

I can cook something that includes shrimps. Have you coughed less than usual?

Much less. I'm getting better, but it is still making me nuts. I have been close to death many times. I have been injured beyond your comprehension. You remember when I fell off the mountain? I have spent months in hospitals close to death. But I do not remember ever being this ill. It makes me more aware of my mortality. Unrecognizable.

I'll be aware of catching your flu. I have to be healthy so that I can take care of you. The weather is nippy, so I wanted to walk with you somewhere, anywhere.

Big storm approaching. Several inches of snow expected. Wear your boots and dress warm with thick socks.

I think my choice of the word, 'fool,' was wrong. I wanted to say that "Don't make me crazy, stop being so lovely," like what you often say to me. I spent time with Karen, my new friend. I had a chance to talk about many things with her, but I felt an extreme lack of the expressions I need to express myself. I always think of and appreciate your generosity and patience.

I'm going to try again to go to bed early. You're terrific. Don't worry about your long chicken legs. You can always wrap them around my face, and then it will not matter, Love, CM

Mike, I finally found out that I may be able to edit your website here, at my place.

You know your stuff. I am so impressed. Will you be able to change, bring back, Vicki, my sexy voiced apple, back from lesbianism? I was able to make some other changes, but I just turned off the speech center for now.

Although we couldn't find a nice wool sweater, I had a good time walking with you today.

Called LL-bean and they are sending a new winter brochure.

After I said good-bye, I always regret that I talk too much.

You never talk too much, or is that remark a joke?

You always make me comfortable and convenient, and I never have enough of your deep concern. I also love working hard like you. But sometimes, I work hard not to feel lonely.

That's what all of us do.

Kiki, I am rejuvenated emotionally from the way you put me to sleep yesterday. It will ingratiate you to me incredibly. The butterfly you put on my site made me smile and be happy. Since my middle name is reciprocity, you will get yours.

Mike, I am glad you like your butterfly. When I was alone, I think I was desperately stressed out. I am being transformed by your warmth and relaxation.

You have not seen anything yet. Today I bought thick, aged, rib eye steaks for the weekend. They will spoil you more; make you healthy and more aggressive.

This is your entire fault, because of your selfish, inconsiderate kindness.

I keep telling you that life is trouble and sorrow.

I still think of someone whose existence adds meaning to my life, whose warmth makes me hold him and feel him. The butterfly is flying beautifully.

Remember **you will never fly if you hang around with turkeys.**

Went on the roof today and shot more sculpture. What fun I spent time editing and adding to my inventory. Soon I will shift to writing and music. Then my happiness will fall all over you.

Mike, say that you fixed the sites.

I already did that. But my sexy computer voice, Vicki, is gone. I turned her off, but she is lost forever. Her voice is not the same. I have tried to adjust it and make her come back, but she has turned butch and is gone. It's all right I can live without her. I'm out with the boys tonight.

So, I think my habit of pushing shortcut keys (for PC) might have affected your computer's voice Vicky. Sorry for making you lonely without her.

I'm never lonely. I just liked Vicky's titillation. Besides, I only used her voice for chess moves. She is gone. It is time to move on. Since you killed her or turned her into a lesbian. You have already taken her place. Besides, I never heard her laugh.

Can I take her place? My legs tingle because my skin is too dry and I scratched a lot.

I'll get you better lotion.

A body lotion is not okay. Instead, I need you to warm me up.

Sounds good to me.

I don't remember when we were together. What's wrong with me?

You're addicted. Have a good time with your friends.

I'm pretending to be a lawyer preparing for my Coop air conditioning case. I'm trying to do a lot of homework to make it easier for Steve. All the guys were nice, and I may be lining up a show in California this summer.

Mike, I never want to have a nice meal where I make you work hard. Even when you were in a worse condition, you cooked for me. Still, I remember and appreciate your efforts. English is not my friend. I'll hug you to plant potential energy.

I would prefer to plant my energy in you. It has the added benefit of making you happy. If you don't, believe me, I have the article. Remember, I used to be very smart. But now my mind works like lightning. One brilliant flash and it's gone.

I am not a princess who is only waiting for your care.

I know you are a helper.

Let's be lazy.

Teach me how.

Mike, I don't mind working with you, on you, and for you. You clean my stuff, shop and cook for me. All I do is go to your place and enjoy the time with you. Everything is luxurious and comfortable with you. I am just sorry I don't reciprocate all your thoughtful concerns.

Honeybun, I set out to take advantage of your seventeen-year-old youth. After all, what did I have to lose aside from a few years in prison, just precious time, money, and my paper-thin heart? But you fooled me.

You give me such pleasure to be with you. Your sick sense of humor and strange ways dovetail with my drain bandage. Can we be together for a little while longer before you destroy us? I have become your slave. I don't like it, but I am helpless to your 25-cent BJ's. Anything, everything I have is yours. I believe that I can make you stronger and smarter. Hang with me a little while and give me a chance. Let's do it again sometime.

Mike, I might have been confused again. There was the meaning behind your words when I consider what you said to me. I remember more than you know. I didn't think your mail was insane. Or should I say, "it wasn't funny at all."

I don't have prescience like you, but at least I know what is in my life. I don't want to think a lot because I see my solitude. When you are next to me, when I enjoy the hot sweat with you and when I enjoy taking a walk with you, everything becomes special. Even though you're smart, many things about us are unexplainable.

You are special, and you are right about the magic we have together.

I believe that we are learning from each other and we are completing each other. You make me want more, so I'll make you a good slave. I am willing to be taken advantage of in my youth.

I'm sorry if I made you worry. But I like to tease you. I'll try to be more sensitive in the future. Don't be concerned. We are together.

Mike, I don't have anything to worry about. Your email didn't arouse any concern.

Good.

I think I just didn't understand what you meant.

What's new?

I went on a field trip today to a famous architectural firm that is located on Lafayette Street. It was very impressive; their work, drawings, system, library, building, and everything. This would be one of the companies I want to work for. It gave me an impetus to work hard.

Aim higher, raise your expectations and do not underestimate your abilities to climb over obstacles and circumvent barriers. No not compromise by lacking self-confidence. Remember what I taught you; if you want to succeed and be a New Yorker, and successful, you must be able to say, "You will be kind enough, if you please, to place your lips on my gluteus maximus." Or "Kiss my ass." Submit a resume now. It is important to be ready.

So, your phone is working perfectly now?

My place is a wreck. The guy was here for three hours before he called someone else. But three out of four are working, and I connected the new answering machine. But I did not program it yet since the instruction "booklet" that it comes with is 125 pages long.

Being with you means more than your eggplant lasagna. When you are tired and busy, don't feel any pressure to reply to my email. My understanding is wide open as only a tiny piece of the sky.

This sounds like something I should have added to my Zen book.

I think I become much more sensitive to smell. Is it a symptom of any sickness?

No, that's what happens when you become more womanly.

I got home thinking of your pasta. Of course, thinking of you, too.

Yeah, yeah, yeah.

Although I'm worried about you spoiling me, I'll take a chance to be with you.

You're so good to me.

Working on your computers?

Vicki is a princess.

My work is due and coming up soon, and I have to be healthy. I think my stomach was just shocked since I had your good food with comfort. So, I blame it on you.

I guess I have to take responsibility for my actions.

Something that is usual for you is not usual for me. Good food, intimacy, taking care of each other, conversations, comfort, and numerous things.

I love it. I wouldn't be bored if I hugged you for all day long.

Six hours would be enough for me.

Thank you for the wake-up present. I smiled all day.

Hi honey,

As you know, I don't like sex, (yeah right.) I also thought that the beast was dead or at least dormant. But something happened when you complimented me the other day. After you had called me a super pervert, I felt a little tingle. Could it be that you have awakened a sleeping tiger? It was a good day above ground. I went to the gym. I shook some cobwebs from my system. I will be tired from the workout tomorrow but happy. I went to the Veterans Hospital to have them look at my sinus condition, and they said the fatigue I have is directly related to my allergies and sinus condition. I miss your funny faces and brushing your hair. It's wonderful that you **keep your feet on the ground and reach for the moon.** I'm home tonight.

I checked FedEx website and your scanner has just arrived at NJ FedEx location. You'll get it tomorrow. Would you let me play with it?

I will always let you play with it. Did you make a joke? Double meaning?

Mike, whenever I come back from being with you, I still have residues of your smell, your warmth, and your love. You made me so relaxed, and I didn't want to think about anything but enjoying our moments.

But I am sorry that I ordered the wrong scanner, and I forgot to take the roast beef you gave to me.

No problem with the scanner but not to take the roast beef-unforgivable. I make you relaxed, and you free me. Good exchange.

Can I come to have my roast beef tonight?

You are a gluten for punishment.

Thank you for the sweater. It was an impulse purchase, but I like the color that I've never had before. Why did you go to the Veteran's Hospital instead of a private doctor or NYU as usual? Hope the exercise refreshed you. Your sticky cuddle bug

Good writing as usual. But you are starting to show me a maturity that I did not see before, or perhaps you are growing at an accelerated rate. Either way, your writing is better. The gym was all right, but I just got home, and it's a late night, but it's necessary to do.

I went to the VA Hospital because I have a service-connected disability. "Subjected to extreme cold for prolonged periods of time" which I contacted while serving a hardship tour in Alaska, as a cold weather survival specialist, when I was in the Army's Yukon Command Headquarters. Glad you liked the sweater. I'm going to give these scanner people a little bit of Brooklyn. I don't like their customer service. And you are the cuddle bug, not me. I'm too macho even to hug. Love, CM

Mike, I am pretty quiet. I don't know what to say sometimes. I don't know some decent expressions of what I think, I am still a shy person, and sometimes I am not used to expressing what I have in mind. I'd been living in the Japanese culture where you don't show what you think to be a noble person or grown-up. Now I don't express myself not to be hurt.

Sometimes I enjoy listening to the silence.

In many ways, I feel free when I am with you. What makes me appreciate and happy is that we are relaxed with each other. You made me naturally talk to you, hold you, and smile at you. I can be myself. What a great present of my life?

I try to give you what I think you need.

I wonder if you are doing exercise.

Yes, this kills most of my day, but it is the only way I know to get stronger.

I have my lighting class at NYU today, so I need to leave soon.

Yes, you are the light of my life. Don't waste it by lighting up the course. They will not appreciate it. Here is a quote from Plato (ca.400B.C.) **"We can easily forgive a child who is afraid of the dark. The real tragedy of life is when adults are afraid of the light."**

Mike, there are many things we haven't had since you only want to eat, touch, give me work, and sunbath.

A millionaire's vacation.

But I also like to do the simple, ordinary and relaxed things with you. Once you mentioned about 'planet.' I hope we create the lighting that doesn't reduce the light.

Our whole planet and existence is a unique phenomenon. Everything in nature came together perfectly to allow us to live. Of course, it took a few billion years. So, the magic that we have is very fragile.

How are you today?

Angry at myself for having to sleep. I need another hundred years to finish what I want to do.

I walked around the factory where I work, and I saw lots of naked cabinet doors.

Shame on you.

Your cooking is always exceptional and extraordinary. I want to show you a little Japanese food.

You already have given me food for my soul.

I look back and see me more carefully into your eyes. I always appreciate your existence next to me. Don't say that I'd never said it before.

You never said it before.

I will remember today your sunbathing having behind the beautiful sky.

I will remember yesterday you beautiful behind and having you, the beautiful shy.

Hi baby, the telephone guys were here for five hours yesterday. I got nothing done all day. It was like a surrealistic comedy. But now everything is fixed.

Although it is hard for me to go from indestructible to vulnerable, it is the way of life. It is what makes every moment with you a treat, and every touch an ecstasy, and every experience with you a delight. How can you be sad about that?

Did you find some nice-looking girls at the gym? So many of them are wearing shorts.

I wanted to say, "Put on some long sweat pants until you lose the fat." Imagine a room full of totally out of shape men and women who are doing many things incorrectly with no one to show them how to get in shape without hurting themselves. A few instructions would save them from injuries, but I can't save them, so it's a little frustrating. At least there could be an ugly face and beautiful body, or at least a good tushie, but there is nothing at all to look at or distract me, so I keep my cardio down to a half hour.

You are a mean pervert.

Thank you.

Nevertheless, you are the only person who sees the individual qualities in me and who makes me special with hugs.

You make life better for me. I can get into my work, and I am more relaxed with little tension. Since I know I will see you on the weekend, I can focus on making progress. It is all right to become cold and indifferent to the madness and mendacities around me and in life because soon I will transform into a human again as soon as we hug. Remember you are my civilizing and humanizing facilitator. But, I decided that I'm angry with you.

Where were you ten years ago when I needed you? Then I realized that you were in high school or they're about. I would have to be a pervert to have grabbed you then... But... That would have been fun. But it's just as much fun grabbing you now. OK, I'm not so mad at you. You are terrific. I'm so in love with you that... I'm sorry. Please slap me in the back of the head. I'm a fool. I almost loused it up. I'm still angry with you. I'll think of some reason.

Mike, I think of my candy man. You make our connection beyond my conservative culture, beyond my restrictions, and beyond my comprehension.

So, you still like me. Your kisses save the world and me. What are fame and fortune compared to that?

I've been having a busy day without exceptions, a full day with your burger, (that's a new way for an inhibited Japan to talk dirty. Do you like it?) Do you realize how many euphemisms I use for your penis? Mushroom when soft, salami when hard, burger when fat, potential when your horny, carpet cleaning when you eat me, taking you for a ride when I am undulating. I'm developing a whole new sophisticated vocabulary because of you. It is a warm day having you in my heart, a tranquil day thinking of your smile, and a beautiful day as usual thinking of you.

One day you will speak like you write. When that happens everything in your life will change for the better, and you will have more control and power. It is such a pleasure reading you emails and connecting with you. One book ready to go. I'm going to start editing Dead Man's Float.

I am getting so much done every day that I am dizzy.

I appreciate your patience and your compliments about my short and straightforward emails. You make me think I am a lucky woman with you. My fast hands are not as harmful as you think, it's just your computer's voice, Vicky is too jealous.

Yes, I love your fast, small hands. They make me look bigger. Yes, that little rat Vicky is giving me fault moves that make me lose the chess game. But I have learned that she is a just phony lovely voice. So, I play my own game and beat her pantyhose off. But it is like taking the panties off a virgin. It takes a long, long time.

The black sweater you bought for me is already fluffy.

I spent hours with Steve in his office catching up. But he did the entire AC documents while I was there. He said he could not believe how prejudice and archaic my cooperative is and how they are stuck in the past and controlled by one manager. And all I want from them is a rational accommodation so that I can live and breathe. But it is a lesson for me about an entranced corporation that indemnifies its management that takes advantage to bend the law. But there is always tomorrow...I think.

I've been spending an ordinary day, working and researching, but I'm satiated thinking of you next to me. You're a special old selfish pervert.

Thank you again.

A special New Yorker, a distinct impression of America, I keep telling you, it's not because of your food.

Yeah, Yeah. Thinking about you-us-the fragility of life.

I had shocking news in the morning. A famous model in the 50-60's had her financial adviser who is also her lifelong friend. She found out he disappeared with all the money in her bank account. I thought about "trust" you told me about before. If people don't have friends and family whom they can trust, where can they find the meaning of their life?

The meaning of your life is all you see and touch. It must come from within and be defined by only you. Those who cling to life die, and those who defy death live. Throw out opinions, prejudices, and theories until there is nothing left. Then throw out the nothing.

Sometimes I wonder about your life. Your aggressive, energetic, and fun life... I admire you are energetic and enjoying your life, and you are younger than the young. I am with someone I admire; someone I want to bother all the time. Can we see each other five times a week?

What are you going to do the other two days?

I am braver now. My ignorance encouraged my bravery, and now I have a little bigger picture. Let's think about the greatness of the fragility of our life.

I reflect on that all the time. Why do you think you are so precious to me?

Why is the cooperative corporation you live in so discriminating against you?

One man, who is the Chief Executive Officer, Vice-President of the Board of Directors, and the Manager, an apparent conflict of interest that no one seems to realize or confront, runs the cooperative. The tail wags the dog. I ran for the Board of Directors, I lost by a small margin, on a platform of transparency against his political machine. I said that the board was just his rubber stamp and that the board of directors and the manager was like a baby's diapers. They should often be changed and for the same reason. They will never forget or forgive me.

Hello, my candy man.

I realized I could think more about you, me, our connections, and what a relationship is, as we talked about making love. When I become less inhibited and more free and relaxed, the scope of my consideration and sensitivity will be made more extensive. It is all in your lessons. My understanding is much better than memorizing. I'll work for you as a part-time secretary. You can pay me kisses. Is it too much?

It is far too much. Are you trying to ruin me?

Unlike what I said, I am not brave, I am not generous, and I am not open-minded. I try to be rational, try to give you space, and try to be a woman who can be compatible with you.

How dare you use the L word? I never said it. And if I did say or see anything, I was asleep. I have a brighter smile now. I took my dentist to lunch and taught him some Yoga. He is so stressed out he has four children and his father just died. I like him, even though he is a red head, he is so bright. You are the jam in my life's sandwich. Without you, it would just be bread.

MIKE, today I thought about our laughing together the last time and wondered about when I had this laughing. I can't help but loving your unconventional qualities your warmth, and you're many things... You said people want what we have. But I still have a fear that I have not completely overcome what I have to accept, although you made me brave.

Kiki, I was laughing tonight at some people who said they have some adversity in their life. I was comparing my life to others and my many injuries, although self-inflicted by exposing myself to risk, cumulative and significant. The deaths around me, by a rough count over a hundred, but we all die. And most of all, the people close to me who I no longer talk with. Someone must have cursed me, "Have an interesting life." But at least I have lived. And now you are a significant part of my life. We have what everyone who is alive wants, intensity, passion, integrity and real contact. The curse continues. Everything is good. Especially you. Your writing is very poetic and evocative. People born in this country do not write as well as you do. Stop worrying so much. I'm yours, and I'm not going anywhere.

I like using your expertise in computers. It makes me proud of you and your knowledge. Soon you will be as loose as a goose. You are the personification of the fantasy I always wanted to have. I am always honest with you, and I thought I'd let you know why I am suddenly getting older.

Prelude to Oblivion

In the darkness of the night, deaths shadow passes over me. It was not coming for me; it was just checking me out. Fear permeated my soul, and I realized that I absorbed one more of the thousand cuts leading to the inevitable.

It reminded me of the time that I met evil incarnate, the devil. He said to me, "Do you know who I am?"

I replied, "With that demeanor and horns how could I not know you?"

"Aren't you afraid of me?" he asked.

"No" I replied.

Satan was a little perturbed at this and queried, "Why aren't you afraid of me?"

I calmly replied, "I was married to your sister for seven years."

Yes, thirty years ago I was married to the devil's sister. She had a hot temper and a ruddy complexion and disposition. I taught her to draw and to infuriate me she would sketch caricatures of my friends and me. One afternoon she observed that I cursed her brother for allowing people with no taste to become productive. She never got along with him and was always angry that he burned everything he cooked on the barbecue. She was in a good mood for days, and she created an interesting drawing of me.

I never thought it would happen. I keep her drawing of me hidden in the back of my bedroom closet against the wall with two other pictures in front of it. For decades, much to my delight, the drawing aged in a way that allowed me to stay younger. The drawing took on new wrinkles, and my face remained more youthful. The drawings eyes became dimmer while mine still shined. My shoulders in the drawing grew less muscular, my neck slacked and skin tone atrophied at an accelerated rate, while my real body aged very slowly and with almost minimal impact.

My housekeeper changed all that. She decided to clean out the bottom of the closet that safeguarded my drawing. Accidentally, she put the vacuum cleaner hose through the drawing. In just a matter of weeks, I have begun to age dramatically. All the injuries I have gone through over the years have caught up with me. The multiplicities of health problems that I have avoided all my life now are incapacitating me. I am aging rapidly, becoming old.

I always tried to keep a sense of humor about death. Hoping that perhaps it will keep its distance a little longer. But, how can I have a sense of humor about the deaths of tens of thousands? If I reveal my prescience, I lose my privacy and become a freak. How can I warn everyone about the impending asteroid striking earth and killing thousands? Also, they will not believe me about the terrorist attack of small satchel bombs coordinated to explode in several cities at the same time.

Do I give a writer inspiration? Oops, it's more embarrassing about writing to a writer. I enjoyed your writing more today. I had a cold and hot day and having disgust at my roomie's one-night stands. Listening to music, the link between heaven and earth, copying some episodes of sexy TV shows, (for my English) another comfortable and satisfying weekend with you.

Got ya. Your writing is good and getting better. I thank you for coining a new compliment for me, "You selfish pervert." But to be truthful, you are giving me another chance, a flight toward health and happiness.

Then we'll curse each other for having an interesting life. A good curse indeed. Had a long talk with my dentist Neil. I will try to make him a new friend for the millennium. I sleep much better without you, but in the morning, I reached out for you and missed you. I stayed in bed awhile longer so that I could smell you near me. You are turning me into a mush, mush. You say such sweet, nice things that I feel guilty making jokes about what you say.

Hi, my candy man, Hot, warm, pleased weather, like you. I have no idea how to fix my strange kicking you in my sleep habit.

I already told you, an S&M leather harness.

You make me a woman, smart and attractive, I'll be more compatible with you.

I don't know if my body can stand more compatibility. Your magnetic movements always have me on the edge of ecstasy.

Hope your dishwasher is working properly.

I'm sure it's OK but don't sit on the door again. Amex resolved the scanner problem in my favor. I think it pays to have some power with words and use them aggressively and also have Amex on your side. Do you realize how much we laughed together this weekend? Your candy man super selfish pervert sadist. P.S. Please stop heaping complimentary names on me; it is taking too long to sign off.

I have a special memory of San Francisco. Because I still remember the unfamiliarity, the color of wood, the shape of the city, even the humidity. My friend's family added a good impression of the city, but it is nothing compared to NYC.

I walked around the city everywhere when I just got here. The city is getting much more special wherever we go and walk together. The cityscape you can look down on from your terrace, the small hardware store, and 18th Street where we were looking for the Gotham. New York becomes my love.

Do you believe it is our anniversary and you forgot? It has been six months of madness and feeling different and alive. To celebrate this is a Merlot and aged meat weekend.

You will be hooked forever, (what's new.) Another insane day of work and shopping because you eat so much. I have you, and many of my friends are dead, not getting any, or going to jail. The curse is bouncing off me. Are you running around town, dancing, getting drunk on our anniversary?

Who are you talking to? What anniversary are you talking about? Maybe the day when you realized I am not a cold fish. How do you want to celebrate? There is a reason why we have a spring sun together. I'm hooked.

Thinking of you.

Stop thinking of me... until tomorrow.

You are selfish. You are the meanest person I know. You always occupy me somewhere, anywhere inside of me, and do not let me alone.

Don't hold back. Let it all out.

I feel I am special with you. You encourage me to be myself, to grow. I hope I make you younger, healthier, harder, and happier.

Yes.

I believe in my insight that we are complementary to each other.

If is true that opposites attract we will be crashing head on.

My step was light with you, with a lovely weekend, and with sunny weather. Of course, it happens by accident, and it is not your prescience.

That's what everyone says when I improve their life by accident. I think that since we are from such different cultures, and even though we give each other a lot of space, getting to know each other well take a long time and a different dimension. Although we are unique, we are distinctive rivers flowing into the same aesthetic sea.

I only thought about me. You are the one who is in the frustrated phase. But I'm holding your hands, and we are looking at each other.

Let go of my hands; I can't type or get any work done.

You're a happy candy man, and I am a happy honey bitch. If you were not with me, I don't know where I would be.

Right, where you are now, but with more free time.

Busy today changing the world.

How did you modify the world today?

You have to be the change that changes the world.

I haven't heard any news on TV yet.

I don't like to tell the world all that they should know because they are not ready. **The light is too painful for someone who wants to remain in darkness.**

You said you're creative, but you always use my sources. If you steal from one source, it is plagiarism. If you borrow from many sources, it is research. Sometimes I think I should run from you with all my being. Sometimes I think that I need glue strong enough to keep every inch of your body against mine. But most of the time I say to myself, "Stop thinking and enjoy every moment with this beautiful, strange, exciting, sensuous, smart, creative, woman with long chicken legs."

What's this? Love?

Please do not curse in your emails by using the L*** word.

:) Is called Emoticon.

When I send an email or text message, I use it sometimes. It is like a small face.

Emoticon = emotion + icon

I'll show you simple things I use.

: -) classic smile with nose

:-D laughter

:-(classic sad with nose

: -S confused

:O surprised

:-@ scream

-.- The showing of annoyance, or when you don't know what to say.

^_^ (This is a Japanese smile emoticon.)

You are about ten years behind, but you can be ten years ahead compared to your friends.

NO, NO, NO, emoticons for me. I did not give up my religion, Luddite, to become a techie, computer literate, new, shorthand emailer.

All my education focused on learning to communicate. We think in words, not symbols. I refuse to resort to archaic pictographs and ancient symbols of writing to convey my emotions or feelings. It may be a hip thing to do, but it is as simplistic as the smiley face.

No shorthand for me. I'll take a long way home to express what I feel, and think. You can still be as progressive or modern as you want. I will still love you. In fact, I even put something on my blog about technology and its alienating properties. Here it is, **there are only people and things, and things don't hug back.**

Below are some of my notes that I use in my NYU class. So, you can see I think very strongly about this subject.

> This generation, children, teenagers and people under forty, have a tremendous ignorance gap because of the false science and values they have learned on television and from advertising since they were infants.
>
> Problems cannot and will not be solved by all–natural, pH-balanced, over the counter, 1-800, cure-all-dot-com. Even though you can use the net to meet, communicate, write and set up contacts with people, intimacy comes from contact, not dis-

tance. Don't let the soul-destroying power of technological advances bring you to a place where there is no room for music, nature, or real friends. Get off the Internet, hear the person speak, observe the body language, see the demeanor, and meet people personally.

I appreciate that you appreciate me even though I am imperfect.

Join the club. However, as soon as I become perfect I will expect you to become as perfect as I am. I think it may take a few more weeks.

I want to be with you more. Is that too much for you? Nobody wants a super selfish pervert, except for me! good. This is what I have been thinking...Nothing is definite. The class I want to take during the summer session is full.

This was done to teach you a lesson.

PUSH and they will let you in.

The lesson is in assertiveness.

I think I was too honest with my Philippine-American friend.

Probably. You have to **learn to keep your own council. But life is for learning.**

She is a smart girl, but what her boyfriend says is a rule.

She will learn the hard way.

I don't have the friend...

Trust no one you do not know for years.

About my friend, I want to be strong. I have a test tomorrow. Wish me luck.

Luck is when preparation meets opportunity. You are prepared I'm sure so don't worry. I'm sorry I can't just wave my magic wand. But you wore it out.

I found out you called me only twice this year! Including yesterday!

Lies, lies, lies.

You need to make things up with your lips.

I made that up with my lips.

I want to go to Central Park with my watercolors. If you are with me, it will be more than great.

All right, I can spit on your brushes.

I know you don't want to celebrate your birthday. Can we do something for me?

Nag, nag, and nag. Everything I do is for you. Shopping, planning, getting information, talking to people about you, etc.

Otherwise no, no morning greeting, no massage?

Be careful, I don't take ultimatums.

Oops, too harsh punishments.

Much. Take a break

Hi, Relentless Honey Bitch, I'm still loading software to the new pro Mac. It is amazing to think that I wrote books on a computer with just eight gigabytes and now I have a machine with over two terabytes. It must have been prescience when I wrote, "life." Of course, it was an accident that you spilled water on your computer but still that is what life is about. Study, hydrate, and rest. Your Candy Man Super Selfish Pervert with painted toenails.

HI, my busy honey, you can borrow my old Sony laptop if you need to. I'm off to Steve to do the air condo stuff. I hope we can win this judgment so I can alleviate my allergies, sinus condition, and breathe. But the Micromanager of the cooperative hates me and has hired an entire law firm, and will freely spend the coops money, to stop me from putting in a modern air conditioner. If I have the energy, I'll go to the gym afterward. I hope your computer dries out successfully. If not we can talk on the phone, which is functioning erratically. (I wish it were functioning erotically.)

Your Emails make me smile. Your sign is longer than the context.

That's because I cut & paste it.

What we have is much better and sweeter than I'd ever imagined and makes my heart hurt.

I wish I could make it sing instead.

I spent the entire afternoon with Steve eating sushi and working. I will be able to finish the petition and application on my own after I check the exhibits and proofread. By Monday we will submit and continue this insane amount of work, a hundred pages of evidence so that I can breathe better by putting in a split unit air conditioner with a superior filter. Who would have believed that a coop board of directors and management would be so archaic and unprogressive as not to allow a cooperator to install a modern unit that no one would ever feel, see, hear or disturb? But I am sure they will use the law against me, and with their assets, I may lose. I truly think that **the road to the truth is always under construction, but we should not abandon justice for a procedure. When injustice becomes law, rebellion becomes a duty.**

Hello Mike, my Candy Man Super Selfish Pervert with painted toenails

Hopeyouarehavinganiceday. <-This is how I can write right now without a space.

Funny but, Forgetaboutit, Missyourwarmth, YeseewhatI'msaying, Ain't no slack in my act, Jack. Everybody in Brooklyn talks this way.

It's good to walk with you.

Better to fly. I like you so much. You are a cookie baking, straight haired, Mongolian, with a super-sized tushie.

Mike, I always appreciate all the things you do for me every day and every week.

I love to be appreciated even though you use me up sexually and leave me a hollow, but content, shell.

I am not knowledgeable about relationships. But I learned at how people look at me is not important, since I came here.

A very big lesson. Soon you will say, "If you don't like the way I look, don't look, and you can "kiss my ass."

Big day tomorrow with Steve and the Air-conditioning case. I can't believe what I have to go through just to kiss you without a clogged nose. We just did all the paperwork perhaps ninety pages of text and photos. Now it gets submitted. If it is accepted and not rejected, as the last suit was not within the statute of limitations, then we have an excellent chance of winning since they have no evidence to the contrary. But the law sometimes is a gray crapshoot without compassion, and the coop management has unlimited money and octopus's tentacle political connections.

Life is what it is, not necessarily want we want or expected, and it seldom goes in a straight line.

Hello, CMSSPWPTN

Nobody could find out what that means. When you open the entrance door, ask me the code.

Maybe we should start from the beginning, and I'll call you honey B and you call me Candy M. That's it. You are finished. You will stay with me. Incredible wine, succulent barbecued steaks, healthy living, ha. You have no choice. That's the breaks. You have to learn to take the good with the good. I can't even tell you about my day. I'm dead tired but happy.

I had slept with that night guard you bought me yesterday so I would not grind my teeth. That helps a little, even though I had it only one night. I forgot Richard is visiting you tomorrow, and I have no choice but waiting my turn being with you.

I had a fight with my brother the other day. It was a usual occasion with him. He always looks down on me, because I'm different from his Japanese conservative point of view. Just because he teaches martial arts, he thinks he is a samurai. That's why I don't talk to him that much, but...I'll tell you later.

Tell him to kiss your ass and meditate, which will help him in his conservative viewpoint and he will get a glimpse of the new you.

Mike,

I like your consistency, your diligence, integrity, concerns about me, and numerous things. In some countries, near China, the consistency is hard to find, because it's a man-centered culture. Once men think their friends belong to them, they easily change their attitude and behavior. They make a joke that they don't give bait to a fish after they catch it. Tomorrow is my time with you. Giggle. When you asked me to go to Florida, and I didn't think of anything, but following you, I had a strange feeling; more reliable connections with you. I can't find a word that means more than happiness, more than comfort.

How about "We complete each other." As usual, you gave me more energy since you let me relax. It's good to have you in my life. I think we are so compatible. The world is yours. Grab it. Grab me.

I am sorry I don't remember everything like you. But I like your belly, your craziness, more than anyone. You are the one who makes me hear my heart beating.

I love when you talk dirty.

You always interpret my sincere words to dirty meanings.

I love your actual words, but they always set up a good joke. Besides remember I am your super pervert. I fluctuate between seriousness and frivolity. You have made my world smaller because I am content. I no longer have to seek and hunt. Is it a good thing to be satisfied with quality? Yes, I think so. You're the best.

I hoped you were not soaked from the torrential shower this afternoon. It was a long, and short day.

I went out onto the terrace and took a cold shower.

You've given me more than what I wished. Come to think of it, from our first meeting until now, and there are lots of things I can't explain.

Never analyze real magic.

Hope we have a sunset together this week, even though it is raining all week.

I will talk to God and order one for you.

I do not like the name of the main character in your book.

Let's try to live in the now. No problem. I always use a conglomeration of real people when I write. It makes it much easier to describe them, and since they are at least two people, I have more to describe.

Of course, you had your love life before. What can I say when I was on the other side of the world?

Stop remembering everything. You will make us crazy.

You give me love and pain at the same time.

You do the same for me, but I hide both and accept both.

I got my computer back.

Good.

The new keyboard has less softness, but it will be getting softer.

I only think of getting harder.

I am happy with having my plans, dictionaries, and the Internet back.

Sometimes less is more.

This is the email I sent to Neil. When he calls, or emails I will tell him sorry, she is too busy now. I have to read some books before I give them to you, classics to expand your mind. **If you stand on the shoulders of giants, are you truly taller?**

> Neil, I understand you want to control your website, but you do not have the time or creativity. Of course, you will have total approval before anything is finalized. When you bring your car to the garage, do you tell your mechanic how to fix what's broken or do you just say fix it? Kiki is a professional designer. She is between projects, and you are getting a bargain because we are friends and for reciprocity. Relax, she will update and improve the site. If you don't want to do a little snowboarding, how about a little Base jumping skydiving in Norway? Talk about control. Cheers, Mike

Did you work on the railing?

The satisfaction of a finished product is uplifting- but it was a little too much maintenance work.

Don't give Neil pressure. I always find that people or clients who don't trust a designer's work, never have a good website and it is not suitable for both a client and a designer.

Good insight.

Is this an essay question? I would want to stand on the shoulders of giants for having his point of view. I am still short, but I can be a giant in mind.

I know.

Once I was surprised when I hugged you, you were smaller IN shape than I thought. I am becoming your woman, and your strong arms; your hugs civilize me in every way.

That's what you do to me- keep me civilized.

And that amazes me. Miss your fur.

Only animals and perverts have fur.

Main Entry: Mike

Kind of Species: a sculptor, writer, and super pervert

Definition: my beloved candy man

Synonyms: cheer, complacency, contentment, coziness, comfort, diligence, dessert, enjoyment, gratification, green toenails, happiness, health, inspiration, intensity, pleasure, protection, radical, relaxation, rest, romantic, safety, security, satisfaction, sincerity, warmth, and well-being

And you say you have trouble with English?

I am also a little tired from all the exercises I did with you.

Exercises? That's a good euphemism. But remember your transversus abdominis.

I found there is a sculpture park and Noguchi Museum a minute away from work. Have you been there?

Years ago. It is excellent.

This made me excited.

I thought only I did that?

I don't usually go to Old Navy, but it was the most luxurious shopping I've ever had, and experiencing the fitting room with you...

What fun. I'm so happy you enjoyed it. A good show but I'm sorry I rushed you. I think I was bothered by the fact that our legs could be seen from the bottom of the door.

Thank you for the clothes. Thank you for the sweetest weekend as usual. I am also amazed at myself that I naturally, openly accept what we have and what we are going to have.

I am so content. I am so lucky to have you as my woman. I am not usually so relaxed and satisfied. A woman who takes care of me and makes my life easier is a rare find.

Living with you was what I always worried about.

It is always difficult to live together because you lower the intensity and the mundane and straightforward things take up your quality time. I love to buy you clothes, dressing and undressing you. Making love and music. I dream all the time of keeping my hands on you and touching you all over. Thank you for supporting my super perversions.

Kiki, Incredible emails. Made four shopping trips today. It's not easy keeping you fed. Then went to the studio to work on the new sculpture base so I can photograph the new sculpture. I laughed for five minutes before I saw your signature. I thought you signed Honey Bitch with Big Ass.

I was so sorry that you made four trips for shopping yesterday. We can go shopping on Sunday so that I can help you.

No. Part of me being your slave is to save you time so you can relax and give me super BJs.

Having a big appetite for your food is a big compliment to you.

No kidding.

I got a call from my friend in San Francisco; He said his future brother-in-law would be working at Dream-works that made the Shriek animation. I was glad when I pictured their happiness.

You must network more and use your Japanese connections.

I keep realizing how much I have. I have nothing but potential.

But to realize it, Wow. Why do you think I'm with you? I don't pursue dead ends.

But I'm getting smarter, and I'm becoming a woman with you.

You are already more than I can handle. I'm going to eat Viagra like jellybeans to keep up with you. Have mercy on me.

Another good news is I'll shave you, massage you, eat you, and hug you forever, if you like. I can't believe that you would get Viagra! Your salami never sleeps! Maybe we are so good together that we don't need your analysis and explanations.

What more can I ask? You are my best. You are my surprise, sex slave, woman, friend, and lover. I think I'm beginning to trust you. Don't miss the sunset. My Puerto Rican goddess said she would give me a good one. And the food will make you come. Love, Soon Your CM with tinted TN

Mike, I got this email from Dr. Neil. What would be good? Should I call him and make an appointment? Or we can visit him together? Or would you contact him? I want to visit him with you if you have time.

Let me speak to him first. We will have lunch with him.

Subject: RE: Improved website

Hi, Thanks for the feedback on my site. Come in and let's talk. I also have something new I would like to develop, and I think a website is indicated. Neil 212-826-0777

Honey Bitch, the wait was hours. The definitive prognosis is I need an operation on my sinuses and a special filter AC that also dehumidifies. Perhaps letters from two different doctors will help my AC case. The bottom line is that I like you and we get along. But it is nice to be appreciated. I dreamed I sneezed my eyeball from my head. I relived my mountain climbing accident.

You have a reason you were alive.

I reviewed the conversation you will have with Neil Zane. I think I'm getting sexually involved with you.

What does this mean? I wonder if this is the right time you can say it when we have a lot of records.

I want to tickle you until your nose bleeds. I woke up, and my tooth had become loose. I will see Neil tomorrow and try to prepare him for you.

I walk with light steps. I'll be strong to keep up with you. My legs are tired from exercising yesterday; it makes my body heavy today.

For two reasons: one, you did not drink enough water and two, you did not stretch enough after your workout.

How did the conversation with Dr. Neil go?

We meet with him for lunch on Tues. He wants a new site on sleep apnea. A temporary cessation of breathing that happens to some people while they are sleeping. Apnea Ape-ne-a A temporary suspension or absence of respiration.

We spend half of the time in your bed.

Your fault.

I don't have complaints, my roots have become more sensitive, perceptive, and absorb the nutrition and wine you give me, my leaves have learned how to enjoy the sun and direct my hands. And I have just found my red lips are about to open. I'll blossom more soon.

Prose like Poetry. The madness continues. I always feel a lot of pressure when I am about to leave the country again.

I am not out of love songs for you,

I have to have you sing them to me.

Curiously I'd rather like your hairs.

Birds do not nest in bare trees. We got the judge we wanted for the AC case. She is smart and fair. Good news maybe. No new plans for the weekend, just you and me together.

So, you may end the war over AC soon?

By the time I come back the judge will have ruled. But my prescience tells me that this is going to, mushroom into something more, give me a lot of stress and not be resolved for a long time. The coop micro-manager has turned this minor issue into a contest, and he considers any loss a blow to his power. His special interests are so entrenched I will need spelunking gear to go after him and the rubber stamp board.

I found it funny that you didn't understand my joke. When I said, "I think I'm becoming sexually involved with you." It's like nicknaming a 300-pound man Tiny. Or saying to you "I believe that you need something to stimulate your appetite."

I am still reading the book about computer programming; it's boring yet exciting.

And it is way beyond this Luddite. Just got home from a memorial for a friend. He was only 53 when he died. I'm Hungry and tired. Lots to tell you about. I have decided that you are more evolved since you do not like shiny objects.

I was pretty busy today, opening and closing several works. I keep thinking if I can handle the job, do it well, and still manage the heavy schedules.

DON'T CLING TOO TIGHTLY TO YOUR VISION OF PERFECTION IN YOUR WORK AND LIFE, OR IT CAN TRAP YOU IN DISAPPOINTMENT. DONE IS BETTER THAN PERFECT. LET GO AND DO NOT EMBRACE UNATTAINABLE STANDARDS.

I am happy I can give you pleasure in many ways, although I eat a lot! I feel like I am a baby that didn't have a life before. All the fear I had is gone, and I thought I would be shy and indecisive for the rest of my life. Most of all, you made me brave, you let me be myself. Everything with you is natural. (This is still strange to me.)

Such a beautiful letter- I can't touch it.

I love your eyelashes.

Although your blue eyes are sensitive to the light, the colors soften and enrich your masculinity. I love that I am the one who enjoys your movie-star eyelashes most.

I talked to my friend who just had a baby boy. This is her second baby, so I thought it would've been easier than her first one. She told me that she had a complication from contractions and I should think about having a baby by cesarean. What makes me sad is that she is moving to China soon. Either she is in China or Japan, and we don't live in the same country. We used to talk to each other often during her lunch break. Although we are having disparate ways of life, we look at each other and each other's life that we haven't had.

I love your smell.

Even though you are sweaty, even when I expect your fresh smell of soap after your shower, and when I am half-awake in the late morning, I love to have your smell. I love to put my face on your neck and your cheek. Smell of sweat, smell of your warmth, and the smell of authentic nature. But I hear your heart is beating faster and healthier than any other young people.

I love your heartbeat. I feel your aggressiveness, energy, and passion; besides I feel safer next to you. When you sleep, when you hug me, when we have a cup of coffee together, I feel more secure.

I took a walk down the whole Central Park following the bicycle path with my Dominican friend this morning. It took about three hours, but I felt so good with the smell of green nature, chatting, and watching people.

I found two ways to register your website. I am excited about opening you and your site to the world.

I love your water.

Since your stage of life is different from me, knowing your age was one of my fears. What kind of future can I expect with an old man?

I had the intuition that you would be an important part of my life, but I admit that it took time to overcome my fear. One day I watched an animation named "Madagascar." The story is about the animals of Central Park zoo. A giraffe loves a fat hippo. After lots of episodes, the giraffe is willing to give up his life, because he depends on a lot of pills to live, and he has left only about 18 hours left to live. Nevertheless, the hippo is impressed with his love. She accepts his love, even though the time they can be together is way too short. I cried, watching this animation that was supposed to be silly and funny.

I love lying in bed with you on lazy Sunday mornings. We rarely get up before noon. We have several records that I can't tell anybody about. What makes me pleased is I knock you out, so you have a deep sleep. This rainy day is happy to keep us in the bed, good to have a quiet day with you. When I am with you, my cold temperature becomes a radiator.

I will give you a challenging puzzle to make out.

Who is an obesity-hater?

Who is an infinite creative candy holder?

Who is a Brooklyn Buddhist, who is friends with a Puerto Rican goddess?

Who has prettier toenails than fingernails?

Who is a Luddite, who likes techies?

You can request more hints if you are confused.

I haven't seen the sun since you left. In Japan, there is a rainy season for about two weeks, during August. But I saw the news a few days ago about global warming. The Western part of the country is dried out, while the East is twice as rainy. My ordinary days are void of sweetness without you. I am a candy without sugar.

I love your craziness.

I appreciate and adore your craziness. If you were sane, if you were merely ordinary, you would not find me at all and not know about me just like everybody else. Your dignity, maturity, humanity, honesty, and humor enhance your iconoclastic impression. I appreciate the extraordinary chemistry between primitive candy man and conservative honey bitch over and above language, culture, intellect, sex, generation, and status.

I have to be satisfied with seeing the weather where you are. I can't picture you there, but it will be about your continuous diligence. Instead of touching you, I touch my plants that are growing very well. I didn't know you put something in my eyes since you always put something in my ears. You taught me the meaning of a nonsequita. Your knees are fucked, but your ass is fine especially when you wiggle it against me. Jump you soon.

Don't worry about me in case there is a hurricane. The house is built like a Nazi bunker. Drink more water.

I am meditating on a deck above the beach looking east into the vastness of the Atlantic Ocean. My beach shack is on a tiny island a few hundred miles from the mainland. The wind off the sea is a high twenty knots, and the salt spray floats across the waters and settles on everything a salty mist. The churning waters are a milky blue opaque and the Whitecaps run clear to the horizon. Swimming in the chop with only a mask and snorkel is like a sensory deprivation tank. You cannot see anything but the white water, which acts as a mirror reflecting your thoughts, and there is nothing but the vast sea surrounding you with neutral buoyancy. You breathe deeply and inhale fresh, clean air. There is life in every breath. This is the life of a Zen Buddhist. This is Bushido, the existence of the warrior. So, breathe deep and be grateful for the gift of life and all it entails as the sunset turns blood red.

Hi Honey Bun,

Remember me? I'd love to see your funny face again. The forecast says sunny on Sat. Could you come early in the afternoon about one o'clock? Then you could tan your tushie. And stay over if you like.

CM, you came home early.

I hope not. It never was a problem before.

I thought you would come late at night.

I got home at one a.m. after a six-hour delay.

I checked someone read your emails and I changed your password several times.

Great, that's why I'm not able to send anything, and my email is bent.

I wasn't sure if you could change your password.

Neither am I. Why would I want to change it? It worked perfectly until you messed with it.

My breast is still colorful with scratched marks. I will be more careful not to be colorful like you, although I cannot insist on not touching you. Because of our long weekend, I like these short weekdays. I am OK if you don't say you love me. I don't need more presents. But please touch me more.

Seeing Steve tomorrow for AC stuff then off to remove the stitches. Unbelievably, the cooperative manager hired an entire law firm instead of one lawyer to handle this little judgment. They now want to bill and ruin me by having me reimburse them for their ridiculously inflated legal expenses of $170,000 thousand dollars. The manager is using the cooperatives superior economic power, since it does not come out of his pocket, to destroy me economically. It will cost me thousands to defend myself. When I ran for the board of directors a few years ago my platform was transparency and, "The Coop Board of Directors, (read rubber stamps) and the Management, (read incompetence and greed) are like diapers." Do you think they hold a grudge?

The cooperative AC case reminds me of something my grandfather used to say all the time. "If you give a little person a little power, you see how little they are." You always say the right things. This will be such a crazy week, but at least I am moving forward. I like the concept of getting things done and the satisfaction of finishing. But I always think that when I just finish the next few jobs, I will be free. I have been invited to teach a course at New York University this spring. The name of the course is the book A Way to Live –Zen. Some bright person made the connection between good health and Zen Buddhism. It will be good to share. Well, **rather busy than bored.**

Still, I want to finish so I can begin anew again. I appreciate your efforts and thoughts in your emails. It is always heavenly holding you close to me.

So, you forgive me for changing your password? I will work with you, but you have to hug me first. Missing you was a meditation. I found myself weak, confusion between reason and emotion. It was such a great weekend. It was luxurious enough to forget how much I missed you. I could have a deep sleep, refreshing sunbathing, excellent meals, warm cuddles... I feel I have a heart when I am with you. The funny thing is that you let me spread my legs when I get the sun and put my hair down, this is the only time I can do these things except when I am alone. And you like the way I am.

No, I love the way you are.

Richard,

Kiki and I have been out shopping, shopping, shopping. I realized that even though there are two billion Asians I picked the only one who is independent, stubborn and an individual who continually asserts herself. But I must build her up even more so she can live with me and be my partner. She has become a healthier plant that is outgrowing the pot within which she has been planted. Unfortunately, the newly liberated are oft time confused, defensive and hypersensitive to anything that defines their status. All these qualities contribute toward a steadily deteriorating relationship because of assertive independence on her part that is acerbated by my decreasing energy level. I will call you tomorrow at the usual time. When are you coming back from Abu Dhabi to NYC? Love ya, M

Mike, I have called you multiple times over the last few days and no answer. It sounds like you have a Japanese Lolita. I'd love to have your problem. By the way, it is Stephen's birthday. What a symbiotic relationship we have, incredible overlapping of different skills and diametrically opposite mentalities that dovetail. Cheers, Richard.

Richard,

Am I cursed? I try to give the best woman I have ever been with everything. But instead of her focusing on making my life better, she shifts all of her priorities and energies to her studies. And when I am away, and she is home, she cannot even remember to water the plants and buy some cream for my coffee, even though I remind her from a thousand miles away. I guess it always comes down to a choice in any argument with your woman; **do you want to be right, or happy?** Although I love her with a terrible intensity, I am reminded of a poem by Hank and a song by Neil Young.

"There was a little girl, who had a little curl
right in the middle of her forehead,
and when she was good, she was very, very good,
But when she was bad she was horrid."
(Henry Wadsworth Longfellow)

"Love is a rose, but you better not pick it
It only grows when it's on the vine.
A handful of thorns and you'll know you've missed it
You lose your love when you say the word "mine."
(Neil Young)

Do all happy endings have a catch?

Hi Honey,

They are working on the terrace. So, come after six on Saturday. We may have to have dinners out this weekend maybe dinner in Queens on Sun. Everything is up in the air so stay loose. Dishwasher repairman never showed up or called. **Good news; the tax audit man allowed all my deductions.**

I love you, but I will not tell you how much. If I did I would have to touch you more, (Is that possible?)

Mike, I watched a movie that is about an old man's love story with his young student. The protagonist doesn't believe in love and finds love. I see many everyday things with us, but there is no dramatic difference like us. It may have beautiful scenes because it is a movie. When I think of you, you made more beautiful scenes and memories, even though you keep me in bed all the time. When I think about the time I had waited for you, our happy unity cannot make me bored. I laughed at the thoughts you showed me macho power, killing a fly. Of course, I love it!

Seeing you changed my mood as quickly as you got home. I feel I have been with you for a long time, but you make my heart beat.

Fantastic. It just blows me away when there's a correlation as strong as meeting someone like you. I have nothing more to say except, you are what I need, and what I want. You are excellent. It feels good to be in love so bad. I believe that we make each other happy because we both live in the now. Although I have been a student of Zen Buddhism for most of my life, I have never gone with a woman who was a Buddhist. So, I'm looking forward to biting you in the now. I think that I have focused too much on just a beautiful face in my search for a new honey. And now I have a woman who is exquisite inside and funny looking outside, but with a soul, complex depth, a dry, fast sense of humor, and sexy as hell. Is it possible that, at last, I have learned? You make me happy. I'm afraid of hugging you too hard. You know I have this strange prescience, and sometimes I doubt myself because it seems so just dreamed about.

CM, I have been thinking, since death is a part of life, I want at least to prepare for my death whether it is positive or not. I've become serious about our health and diet.

I think of my life. I think of you. I have been reborn since I met you. I had had a thirst all my life for knowledge and intelligence. I had lived all my life within naivety and ignorance of the world. It was a necessary fate to meet you. I have learned, grown and changed with you. My anxiety has gone, and I have gained composure and strength. Because of my status, it seems that I brought misfortunes to our relationship, but I am waiting for the moment that I can express what my repressed culture didn't allow me to say and tell obnoxious people to kiss my ass.

And express my happiness with you, my talent, and confidence. You are my best friend, lover, mentor, role model, and companion.

Kiki,

Having spent the three-day weekend with Stephen and Maggie started me thinking about success. **I have come to believe that success depends on growth and application. However, these are necessary, the paramount factor is change. So, compare those you know and are learning about, including yourself, about change and you realize why some succeed, and others fail. You will be incredibly lucky if you have grown and changed the most.** Life is action, so I want you to move in with me.

Smart lady

After coming back from a lovely party, Kiki said to me, "When I went into the room downstairs by their Christmas tree their daughter was tearing open the wrappings on all the presents that the people brought to the party and throwing the ones that were not for her in the corner."

"Well I'll tell Richard; she certainly should get a talking to."

"No Mike, don't say anything."

"Why not?"

"Because you can't say anything about a child to the parents, especially about an only child who can do no wrong. The parents always resent it, and you will louse up your friendship."

"Kiki, this is Richard, not just some acquaintance. If I go out wearing a silly hat people might laugh at me, but a friend has an obligation to verbally hold up a mirror and say, 'you look foolish in that hat.' And you can only know yourself through the eyes of another."

"What does that mean?"

"It means that you have to choose your friends wisely and listen to them, as you would see a mirror accuracy reflex your image, and Richard hears."

"I still do not think it's a good idea."

"Kiki, I told Richard about it, and he said, 'See I raised her right.'"

"I told you."

"But then I compounded the error."

"What did you do now?"

"Richard sent me an email with a photo of him and his child playing with a giant chess set. The subject was 'I'm teaching her.' I couldn't help myself to try for a double meaning joke and emailed back, 'Let's see you try to teach her that she is not the queen.' He wrote back, 'You don't like her, do you?'

"You have to be more sensitive to your jokes and stop trying to teach everyone."

"I know. But I taught at least fifty thousand children and saw them develop over many years, so I'm objective and professional. Most parents have no idea what they are doing because they learned most everything about raising a child from their parents and pass on the mistakes or overcompensate. That's why the world is so screwed up and why most families are so dysfunctional. I don't want Richard to have his hands full with her and have a future of aggravation as she grows up."

"Yes but parents do not know that they are dysfunctional and passing it on with their variations. In fact, they take joy in seeing that their child possesses their idiosyncrasies. You cannot help unless you are asked and even then, you have to modify your response. Remember what you told me, 'You cannot save anyone.'"

"But you don't fully understand. I only care deeply about a few people in my life. Everyone around those people either helps or hinders them, makes their lives easier or harder. So, if I see a situation that will contribute to making my friend work harder or aggravate more in the future, I have to say something now. All children are just, gimme, get me, buy me, and the payback is a little love, ego, and an unrealistic chance at immortality. So, if a child does not share or understand that it is not just about them, then when they get older they do not include their parents in love and stay totally self-centered forever."

"You cannot set parameters for other people or their children. Everyone has to go through their learning by themselves."

"Kiki, you have either come a long way, or you were always smarter than I initially thought."

"Yes, both, my big brain is not an ornament."

Relationships

Philosophies

Life Rewards Action.

Since I am old, all I have is the wisdom of a lifetime, and like all old retired educators, I have a tendency to lecture.

Nobody knows anything, and the societies' greetings prove it. "What's up? What's happening? What's going on?"

When you change the way you look at things, the things you look at change.

If you agree with my assertions and viewpoints, then they are completely original and authentic. If you do not agree, then they have been gleaned from other sources or someone else's opinions.

Uncontaminate your heart. You have to give yourself what no one else can give you and what your parents never gave you.

The first premise is that because we live in this age and society that everyone is crazy. You used to be able to tell the nuts because they walked in the streets talking to themselves. But now, with the advent of cell phones and tiny speaker wires, you cannot tell anymore. People are alone and continually searching for a mate because they look for someone who is sane. Since no one is sane, they gather a few friends around them, but continually are discontent and searching. The key is to find someone with a complimentary neurosis. Then you can dovetail and find symbiosis and compatibility.

I was going with a woman in a different country, where I worked at irregular intervals. It would take me a whole day of tension driven travel to get to this remote island. I had to get up in the middle of the night to catch the plane that would get me to the second half of the journey. Then a taxi, then a boat, another taxi and finally land in another country. When I was there, I always took her to dinner in the best restaurants on the island. Do you think she could have made dinner for me on the day that I came to her? Would it have been a gesture of reciprocity or just good manners to say "I'll have dinner for you when you arrive." When you have a friend, who is visiting you from another country, make them dinner the night that they land. They are stressed out, tired, need some down time and it is just the right thing to do. I stopped taking her out to dinner. If you have to tell someone how to reciprocate or even make life a little easier for you and turn out, then they do not have the awareness for a real relationship.

Think before you speak. For every action, there is a reaction, cause, and effect. Your words can produce change and modify behavior. If you cannot control your mouth, you lose control of your life. Language is like fire. It can either heat your home or burn it down. It is not enough to know what to say it is necessary to know how to say it.

"The most important relationship in life is the one you have with yourself. If you have that, then any relationship is a plus and not a must." Diane

What is the difference between men and government bonds? The bonds mature.

When you are happy, people will want to be around you and share your happiness, but when you are sad, people will avoid you.

We have all been hurt, but try to love again.

Do not focus on the hurt or you will continue to suffer the pain. Instead focus on the lesson that you learned, so you will not make the same mistake again, and you will grow and learn. (see blog Aug. 2017)

Gesture

Ask people to extend themselves, even slightly, at the onset of a relationship. It will teach you a lot about them immediately. Like all the rest of the people, you meet for friendship, romance or otherwise, you will see if they were "too busy." And even if they were not, you can observe if they seem possessive of their time especially if the time was not spent on or for them.

"Why didn't you tell me?

"Why didn't someone tell me?"

"I'm telling you now."

Want and Need

There is not an absolute correlation, but if you hold out for everything you often end up with nothing. Life and physics frequently require a trade-off and compromise. You have to give up something to gain something else. You have to give up weight if you want speed. You have to relinquish space if you want depth. You have to part with some desires if you want happiness. You have to give up some ego and make some concessions if you want a relationship. This exchange is especially useful concerning your desires and your essentials. You must prioritize and sharply differentiate between your wants and needs.

In seeking a meaningful relationship, we have to give up our vested interest in the judgments we already have and move our faith into the unexplored.

Sense of Humor

Exercise probably helps to sustain your life more than any other factor. It allows us to have more focus, energy, and relaxation because it reduces stress. The second most important factor in prolonging your life is probably a sense of humor. Laughing also deactivates stress hormones and aids the immune system. People with a developed sense of humor tend to be more creative and more adapt at solving the many problems that life gives us. It improves many cognitive functions. Most of all, it helps people get along with others.

Humor and Temperament

Two people sharing lives together, who both have a good sense of humor, are significantly happier than those couples with a poor sense of humor. Humor can act as an emotional release thereby releasing stress and promoting longevity. It also allows us to cultivate and keep friends, support groups, and perhaps even love, and love heals. You want to be with someone who makes you smile and laugh. To me, it is the definitive personally trait that makes being with someone over time possible.

Laugh and the world laughs with you;

Weep, and you weep alone;

For the sad old earth, must borrow its mirth,

But has trouble enough of its own.

Solitude by Ella Wheeler Wilcox

A smile from you can bring happiness to anyone, even if they don't like you. But a smile can also ingratiate you with someone, help you succeed, allow people to like you more, improve your love life and interpersonal relationships, etc. Most of all, a smile on your face can and will make you happier.

My friend has expectations of meeting a catholic who shares his main interests. He has to meet a roller skating nun. But why not, didn't Zigfreed and Roy, two gay lion tamers in Los Vegas meet?

My exceptionally intellectual friend Richard Mavrovich sent me an email with the subject line, "The difference." The message was an image of two panels shaped like the dashboard of a jet fighter. One-labeled WOMAN was covered with knobs, buttons, diodes, switches, and dials, complex and almost unfathomable. The MEN box had but a single switch, labeled on and off. The "message" certainly makes men look simpler than women. Perhaps it is true, since most women associate sex with family, children, new life, and new relationships, whereas men associate sex with life itself. For a man, being with a woman and making love, with all its intensity and intimacy, is a way of affirming a primal instinct of procreation and refuting death.

Philosophies

I know a lot of heavy people who have a multitude of excuses as to why they are fat. In the same respect, I know a lot of smart, attractive, independent individuals who have many reasons as to why they are alone. So many of us are working, sleeping, e-mailing, and eating, at the same time. Such a treadmill schedule leaves no time to allow for another person. As much as we say we want a relationship in our lives unless they can instantly dovetail with our pace, schedules, and timetables, it's to no avail. Also, most single women I meet are unrealistic and have impossible ideals about marriage and are very picky about men. More about what men want and expect later.

Superimposed on this agenda, are our preconceived ideas of what and how a relationship should, would, and could be. And so, instead of allowing a positive predisposition, we scrutinize to find fault, lack of chemistry and incompatibility. In the end, what we seem to want, in spite of our insistence that the other person is fun, individualistic, exciting, dynamic, caring, smart, etc., is a mirror image of ourselves.

Add to the above that we are not flexible and that we insist our perceptions are correct, mix in some educational and cultural variables and presto, we have a society of independent men and women who are seeking a mate and companionship but are alone, forever searching, and unfulfilled. But mainly we are alone because that is how we have gotten comfortable. We are slow to give up our space, time, money, and freedom for the compromises and sacrifices of a relationship and marriage. Everyone we meet has something wrong with them or does not conform to our preconceived idea of manners, rules, body type, health, sensitivity, correctness, or you name it. If we at least gave the person we met a few meetings or chances of interaction, we might be pleasantly surprised.

A key to relationships

A woman is with a man because she chooses to be. Women are more complicated, concerned, and committed to relationships to form a protective environment for raising children and the survival of the species. Men are more concerned and committed to sex. This is not because all men are chauvinistic. It is just hominid math. For thousands of years, nature needed a lot of wombs to keep the bands and family's going, but nowhere near as many penises to impregnate the wombs. So, man's nature is to have sex primarily for sensation's sake and climax with one or with many women. This made men more expendable, and they are programmed internally to be more insecure and vulnerable. These factors manifested themselves in the overcompensation and assertiveness that permeate the male ego today.

Our past genetics are the underpinnings of our discontent. A man can no longer define his masculinity by killing a lion or defending the entrance of the cave. Women can still procreate, but with a population of seven billion humans, this overpopulated planet is no longer dependent on her to continue the species. It is a fact that our genetics are the same as those of our early human ancestors from more than one hundred and forty thousand years ago. In effect, we are Stone Age physiologically humans living in the modern age of space.

So, what does this mean for a woman and what can she learn from these concrete facts? Keep it simple. If he is hungry, feed him, even if it is only a sandwich. If he is horny, give him a BJ and screw him. The results are a happy relationship with him being satisfied and content, and then the answer to anything a woman might ask him for is "yes." For a man the lesson is, listen and learn from your woman to become more evolved, complex and civilized. I have repeated these oversimplifications with many variations, several times, to emphasize this basic formula, because it works.

Feminists will argue that these viewpoints are unpalatable and chauvinistic. But I would claim that feminism has only been accepted because of an upper-middle class elite that has become liberated from daily drudgery because of men's labor saving appliances and capitalism. I ask the question; why have so many achieving women chronic uncertainty about their prospects for meeting and becoming involved with a man? The answer is because the feminist movement, with its Puritan residue, has denigrated masculinity and manhood with their many unjust assertions and gruesome statements like, "A woman needs a man like a fish needs a bicycle" or "Men are becoming obsolete."

A woman still needs a man because you can't take batteries home to meet your mother.

Intelligent, objective observation shows that obstructive traditions came about not because of men's hatred or enslavement of women, but arose because of the natural division of labor that protected women enabling them to raise children. Feminism notwithstanding, everybody understands that women and children come first. Because this is survival of the species or family, and men are not as precious. But that context can sometimes be exaggerated and unseemly when men are viewed as expendable, but the death of a woman is tragic. When an educated culture negates the fact that men are indispensable to the infrastructure that makes their lives possible, it seems startlingly immature and elitist. Is it any wonder then that women are perpetually stuck with boys and searching for a "real man"? Without strong men as models, either to circumvent or surrender to, women will never attain a centered sense of themselves as women. Both sexes have to learn from the strengths of each other and that the reality is that they need each other.

One example of how incredibly ill-advised women are, is the fact that a dating manual, The Rules, became a best seller in 1995, and is still being updated. The new dimwitted strategies now include more modern language like texting and cell phones, but still assert that making the man wait, rarely returning phone calls, and generally "freezing him out," will make him desperate. These strategies are supposed to "change the game, deprive the man from having the upper hand," and the authors agree, are effective in many circumstances. Surprise archaic ladies, men do not respond well to being punished, being played with, and unresponsive women. Without modern rapid communication, a man will move on. Note that this advice is given by two women who eventually got bad guys, unhappy marriages, and divorced. This manual is equivalent to taking, getting how to obtain wealth, advice from a homeless woman. Yet the book, and its astonishingly unintelligent recommendations, still sells.

It is any wonder, after reading the past few paragraphs, that the sperm count among men in western countries, including north America, and Australia, have declined more than 50% in the last 40 years. (Time August 7, 2017)

A real man never hurts a woman. Be careful if you make a woman cry because the universe counts her tears. The women came out of man's rib, not from his feet to be walked on, and not from his head to be superior, but from his side to be equal. Under his arm to be protected and next to his heart to be loved.

Be careful who you open up to. Only a few people genuinely care. The rest are curious or have hidden motives.

Some Men and Women Physical Differences

Relationships are made even more complicated between men and women because of the mental attitude as well as physiological. Men lose brain tissue, as much as three times faster than a woman. By midlife male brains, which are larger earlier in life; shrink to about the same size as female brains. An increase in metabolic activity compensates for some of the declines. This phenomenon may be one reason females live longer than males. However, it is not the size of the brain that determines intelligence, but the number of neuron connections. Females have thicker more developed left hemispheres of the brain and men have more developed right hemispheres. This is one reason why girls learn to speak earlier and have better fine motor control. Men are better at isolating problems in their attempts to solve them. Men have the ability to coordinate logic with emotion when they make decisions. This is due to men's increased hemispheric specialization. But with less communication between the two hemispheres men are more vulnerable to many health problems.

Acceptance

I was spending a weekend at a mountain resort. The main features of the hotel were its hiking trails in the daytime and its BBQ dinners in the evening. The dining was at large community tables. A stunning woman continually criticized the food, appearance, service, and a multiplicity of picayune subjects while eating at the community table. While it was true that the steak had a little too much fat, the place was a little drab, the service could be improved, the tables could be cleaner, and many other amenities could be criticized, on the whole, the hotel, for the price, was a reasonable resort.

I was near this woman when the hotel's manager spoke to her.

"Many of the guests have brought to my attention that you are not happy about many of our facilities and procedures. Your complaints have become excessive, and you are spoiling other people's vacation. If you are not satisfied here, we can refund your money and ask you to leave. Either you accept what we have to offer, without complaining, or go somewhere else. Please decide now so we can make arrangements."

The woman was apparently used to getting her way but pedantically gave in. The next day, over dinner at the community table, she continued her complaints against the hotel and the managers' actions. Before the dinner was over two of the hotel's staff brought her luggage to the table, and the manager escorted her to the waiting cab. She protested that it was a mistake; she was only... and complained all the way to the cab. She just didn't get it.

Many people in a relationship also don't get it. It is easy to complain, criticize, argue, expect the other person to help, solve problems, act unilaterally, and unreasonably think that your way is correct and you can do it better, etc. But this is not compatibility. This is stubbornness, self-centered, unreasonable behavior that angers a mate and destroys the relationship. Either you are part of the team and work totally toward mutual benefit, using only constructive criticism, respectful conversation, and positive ac-

tions, or you are an individual who should move on, work, and be alone.

To be fruitful and compatible in a relationship, accept it for what it is, not for what you want.

Men can live without affection, but not without sex, while women can live without sex, but not without affection. Ergo, to men there are no ugly women at closing time.

When women are in their homes, they are attached to their furniture. They run around it all day long and are always fussing over it. But when I am with a woman on a journey, I am the only piece of furniture she has available, and she cannot refrain from moving around me all day long and improving something about me.

Life is short, live it.

Love is rare, grab it.

Anger is bad, dump it.

Fear is awful, face it.

Memories are sweet, cherish them.

If you have been absent when I was struggling don't expect to be around after I achieve success.

Sunshine and Friend

Sunshine walked with a bounce. Her closely cropped head was an undirected challenge to the world, as her bounce was an attempt to be taller. She would rise in the morning full of life but irritated that she was not physically strong enough quickly enough. Only when her energy faded would she set her body to rest. She was pushed by a dormant cultural heritage that was awakening and she meandered for many years determined to find her direction.

It was about this time that Sunshine met Friend. Friend was thirteen hundred years old. He was born with a predisposition toward happiness. His world was not as full as Sunshine's because his path was narrow and his vision focused. One day, Sunshine and Friend met. Instantly, Friend knew that Sunshine was important to him. He had always known but had never been so close to the light, karma, and healing powers that Sunshine possessed. He wanted all the Sunshine he could get. Sunshine, however, would have nothing to do with Friend because he was always moving. Friend did something now that he never did before. He went off his path to follow and try to be with Sunshine. After a while, Sunshine got used to Friend. She had never known anyone as outward as Friend and secretly longed for his focused direction. Friend was sagacious and knew Sunshine's secret desires to climb higher and be connected. He also knew that no one ever changes, but he set out in spite of himself to try to help Sunshine become whatever she wanted. Not altruistically, because this was not his way, but selfishly, believing that if Sunshine became directed that they could travel in the same orbit together.

Friend showed Sunshine direction, strength, and affection, and in exchange received Sunshine's warmth and companionship. Both were jubilant, and they traveled over the earth together, touching unceasingly, and giving the other completeness that neither of them had experienced before.

Friend would have stayed with Sunshine forever, but the cultural seeds that were dormant within Sunshine began to grow. Sunshine began to resent Friend's inner-directed focus and human weaknesses, especially seeking unobtainable perfection. Friend was very stubborn and liked to be right all the time. In fact, Friend was right most of the time, because he was very smart and wondrously sophisticated. But Sunshine was also wise and very idiosyncratic. One significant day they drifted apart, both loving each other, both right, and both unable to change.

Relationship Stereotypes

On a chain of beautiful deserted islands, in the middle of nowhere, the following people are stranded:

Two Italian men and one Italian woman; Two French men and one French woman; Two German men and one German woman; Two Greek men and one Greek woman; Two English men and one English woman; Two Bulgarian men and one Bulgarian woman; Two Japanese men and one Japanese woman; Two Chinese men and one Chinese woman; Two Irish men and one Irish woman; Two American men and one American woman.

One month later on these stunning islands, in the middle of nowhere, the following things have occurred:

One Italian man killed the other Italian man for the Italian woman.

The two french men and the french woman are living happily together in a ménage a trois.

The two German men have a strict weekly schedule of alternating visits with the German woman.

The two Greek men are sleeping with each other, and the Greek woman is cleaning and cooking for them.

The two English men are waiting for someone to introduce them to the English woman.

The two Bulgarian men took one look at the Bulgarian woman and started swimming to the next Island.

The two Japanese have faxed Tokyo and are awaiting instructions.

The two Chinese men have set up a pharmacy/liquor store/restaurant/laundry, and have gotten the woman pregnant to supply employees for their store.

The two Irish men divided the island into North and South and set up a distillery. They do not remember if sex is in the picture because it gets somewhat foggy after several liters of coconut whiskey. However, they're satisfied because the English aren't having any fun.

The two American men are contemplating suicide, because the American woman will not shut up and complains relentlessly about her body, the true nature of feminism, what the sun is doing to her skin and hair, how she can do anything they can't do, the necessity of fulfillment, the equal division of household chores, how sand and palm trees make her look fat, how her last boyfriend respected her opinion and treated her better than they do, how her relationship with her mother is the cause of her problems, why didn't they bring a cell phone so they could call 911 and get rescued so she can get a facial and go shopping.

A Serious note

This book is sprinkled with stories, expressions, blogs, and attempts at wisdom, many taken from the syllabus of the course I teach at New York University, A WAY TO LIVE- ZEN. The paragraph below is taken from one of my blogs by the same name. If finding a new honey is your goal, if you need a relationship and cannot seem to take it from a dream idea to reality, perhaps this advice will help.

It is very romantic to believe, like the old troubadours suggested, that true love appears only without lust. The reality is that humankind exists only because those who are aggressive and pursue are compensated for their efforts. You might be tempted to look back on your younger years of amorousness and believe that passivity and fun and games were attractively romantic. The actuality is that you can never return to those good old days because there just never were any, ever, anywhere. More likely, you just did not know or have an awareness of passion or relationships. But now you have a need and desire for physical and spiritual love. You also have a choice to hone your screening devices by interaction, or passively accept what comes your way. Be flexible about nonessential parameters and concentrate on growth potential and self-improvement. Don't ignore your instincts, cultivate them, they can save you if you combine them with intellect. No one likes to be rejected, or do stupid things or fail. But learning requires effort, enthusiasm, assertion, and making mistakes.

My reality check bounced.

Change

The most difficult things to learn are new ways of acting and relating. Because before we acquire new actions we have to unlearn the patterns and procedures that we have already set up, disregard them and change, then learn something new. Can we extrapolate this creativity toward other aspects of our lives? Can we bring more imagination to our loves, friends, our health, and aspirations?

Just as a snake sheds its skin, we must shed our past over and over again. In life, we cannot avoid change, and we cannot prevent loss. Freedom and happiness are found in the flexibility and ease with which we move through change.

Choice

There are three types of people, positive, negative and neutral.

The trick is whom do you choose to interact with? Because of your job you may be forced to interact with negative and even nefarious acquaintances. Loneliness can force you to respond to neutral friends and lovers and allow you to have companionship. The positive links may be easy to spot but can be too dynamic and energy consuming. So, what do you do? First, you move away and put distance between you and the negative acquaintances with an eye on giving them up altogether. Try to improve your screening devices and give the negative up before you even interact with them. Refuse to let the meatballs into your space or life.

The neutral contacts and romances, in spite of their comforting and friendly interaction, are in reality taking up your time and preventing you from meeting positive people. Positive friends and lovers are the only ones' worth cultivating and keeping. If they are too dynamic for you, learn to follow their leads and learn something new. Friendships and relationships have to be cultivated. The best way is with manners, honesty, and reciprocity.

But most of all, you reverse the situation, become confident and one of the positive people. First, understand that our instinct is to view strangers as predators. We do not want to become victims. When meeting people, when trying to get a date, when selling something, first allow some warm up time and allow the other person some space so you can become more familiar with them. If someone says to you, Hi, you look good today." Just don't say, "Thanks." Say, "Yes and you look good too." Communicate.

Control

Appearance is important in everything and people act on prejudices rather than knowledge. So, look as good as you can and if you cannot be beautiful then be interesting looking. Show off your best features. Decide what about you looks best, and exaggerate it. Science research has proven that you are more attractive if your face is symmetrical. So, don't wear just one earring or piercing on one side of your face. If you are a woman, show your narrow waist. If you are a man, show your broad shoulders. Interestingly these are the factors that people see first when you are walking or standing. The way you carry yourself and your clothes broadcast who you aspire to be and who you are. Chew gum, pierce your nose, frown, tattoo your face, and you may limit any chance of success.

Your attitude and appearance especially clean and the best wardrobe you can afford will gain for you a better first and lasting impression. Looking as good as you can look, coupled with a smile and sense of humor will pay off faster than any other investment you can make.

Staying in shape physically and mentally is the most important aspect of your life. People judge you more by appearance than any other way. Physical attraction has always been a key-determining factor in mating. Get slimmer, be healthy, have more energy, take control, and you win. Everything else is secondary.

Increased physical activity and exercise are paramount to improving your mental power, emotional strength, and gaining more control. Think of how you learn to play a musical instrument or meditate. Practice, focus, intention, and control. All these leads to more pleasure, enjoyment, skill and satisfaction. Change, unlearning, and relearning new methods takes courage and determination. However, since life is action, you must start moving NOW for a new beginning.

Achievement

To live in the now, you must actively change your focus. Thinking, planning, having ideas, and dreaming are all constructive if directed toward a goal. You must refine your thinking. Make significant concrete plans toward your goal and start to act physically. Then, when an opportunity presents itself, you can incorporate the chance to aid in fulfilling your dreams and establishing a foundation for your actions. You only accomplish by performing and taking responsibility for your actions.

You cannot say, "Why didn't someone tell me?"

I'm telling you now.

Start, Life is Action.

Alternate names of chapters

A kiss from the heart.

All at once I love her.

Between adamant and acquiescent.

Birthday Spanking

Buy, buy, buy. I want dis, I want dat. I want dis, I want dat.

Cappuccino overdose

Cool as a moose and loose as a goose.

Covered Valentine.

Dating manners.

Dishonest people believe in words rather than reality.

Emotional testing service.

Fat birds don't fly.

Fool for love.

If you hold out for everything you get nothing.

King Kong died for our sins. Playing with me is like teasing King Kong.

Kissing frogs and catching princes

Looking for a honey

Love and Circumstance

Love daze

Neurogenic telepathy (reads your mind and controls your action.)

Overkill

Perfect Pervert

Prisoner of love

Privacy and power

Rocking the dream boat

Swinging on a star

Tell the truth and run.

The chase

The death of the sugar daddy.

The edge of forever

The Reassurance of Harmonious Communication.

Trading passion for glory.

Unplanned chastity, money, and sex

Waves of stone.

You can't keep a good Kamikaze down.

Young, rich and full of sugar.

Give this book to your boyfriend

Why you can't get a man or woman.

How to get a man.

Apology

In writing this book I tried to make fun of, laugh at, and abuse, as many races, creeds, religions, sexes, institutions, locations, accents, personalities, ethnic groups, governments, and established ideas as possible. However, this is tough to do in one book. I am sincerely apologizing to anyone or group I might have missed. Please forgive me for my insensitivity, and I will endeavor to rectify this condition in my next book. I always say, "If you can't laugh at yourself, make fun of other people."

Disclaimer

"Methinks madam doth protest too much." William Shakespeare

This publication is designed to provide competent and reliable information regarding the subject matter covered. However, it is sold with the understanding that the author and publisher are not engaged in rendering legal, political, financial, technical, medical, physiological, personal or other professional advice. Laws and practices often vary from state to state and if legal, financial, technical, psychological, medical, or other expert assistance is required; the services of a professional should be sought. The author and publisher expressly disclaim any liability that is incurred from the use or application of the contents of this book.

My words are not my own but of the universe. As freely as I have received, I give on to you.

Any resemblance to any event or any person, living or dead may be coincidental. Everything described has happened or was to have happened. None of the names have been changed to protect the innocent, as I have never known any innocent person. However, to avoid living persons being confused with the individuals mentioned in this project, it should be noted that all characters mentioned in this book are composite characters, and features and actions ascribed to them may actually be characteristics or actions of others.

This book is entirely fiction. Any resemblance to any persons living or dead is purely coincidental. Any resemblance to any place, incident or event is also by chance or coincidence. No character in this book is real. All names, places, events, and descriptions are fictitious, and any similarities to real life situations are probably literary devices used to create the illusion of actual life associations.

All the stories in this book are imaginary and fabricated. The history is fictional, and all conversations are manufactured from imagination and fantasies. Although written as factual all characters are illusory, and their conversations are purely speculative utterances.

All statements shown and quoted are inaccurate, speculative, and simulated and intended to be used only to enhance humor and irony. Accuracy or Completeness of information relating to any position, person or decisions does not necessarily reflect any experience and is, in fact, hypothetical and conjectural. Actual quotes are all suppositions and non-existent.

Time and events are not in chronological order and are condensed and synthesized. All occurrences that I have recorded are based on my perspective and personal experience. I have embellished some episodes and have succumbed to the exuberance of literary invention to create a more cohesive and faster-moving narrative.

This book and the articles contained herein provide reviews of emerging health and legal issues about the responsibilities of every form of relationship, interaction, and personal responsibility. It is not intended as a complete catchall absolute source of legal, health or interpersonal relationship advice but a barometer of recommendations that have been gleaned from a plethora of readings, numerous texts, and multiple life experiences.

I am informed through the actuary tables that I have just twenty years and three months to live. That's what I call a real deadline. I was going to write this book as an end all, "relationships," doctoral thesis, complete with an elaborate bibliography, exacting sources, and footnotes, a glossary, scientists quotes, research and experiments, credits and notes. I reevaluated and decided that there was not enough time left in my life. So, as a freethinker, I have taken advantage of the sharing capability of digital content, extracted from the Internet, and the universal access to information. I have rerecorded, paraphrased, creatively shared and summarized a plethora of communications and information, while adding my life experience and readings, to create a self-help book that will make the reader a healthier person when interacting, or searching, with and for, their new honey. Some may consider this fair use a violation, but only a sore-loser buggy-whip maker would even ask this question. As American sociologist William Cameron states: "Not everything that can be counted counts, and not everything that counts can be counted."

How can we change the world for the better if we do not share our learning and give of our intellect and ourselves?

The Secret Of Life

I use Zen philosophy as an umbrella to cover a multiplicity of life and love topics. I try to blur and write the fine line between jest and sermon. I attempt to help and challenge the pompous belief that we are indispensable to something or someone. Therefore, since all knowledge is related, there is no clear order other than the common themes of inspiration and self-improvement. You must clear your thinking and move to living in the Now. Before you read about the meaning of life, I give you this exercise. Imagine that you have a fatal diagnosis like cancer and have only two years to live. Write down how you would change your life. When you confront death, and concentrate on the functioning and fragility of your body, you can negate the inevitable and start to live and love in the now, where every moment counts toward your enlightenment.

The meaning of your life is all you see and touch. It must come from within and be defined by only you. Those who cling to life die, and those who defy death live. Throw out opinions, prejudices, and theories until there is nothing left. Then throw out the nothing.

If you cannot find the truth right where you are and in this book, where else do you expect to find it?

Life is action, suck out all the juice, and consider all the opportunities since this is not a dress rehearsal. Do whatever you want to do, with style, without hurting anyone else. Anything worth doing is worth overdoing. All you see, hear, touch, and love is all your life is ever going to be, so start now. Work like you don't need the money. Love like you've never been hurt. Dance like nobody's watching. Sing like nobody's listening. Live like it's Heaven on Earth. The most precious thing on the planet is water. Drink more water while you still can. It can be a fine line between enthusiasm and madness. Embrace the madness, since perception usually triumphs over reality.

Satoru

Why didn't you tell me?

Why didn't someone tell me?

"I'm telling you now."

THE END.

And hopefully a new beginning.

Dedication

This book is dedicated to all the wonderful women living on this tiny, fragile, lonely planet and their great gift and power, procreation. Especially to the women who have civilized me, helped me grow, and taught me so much of the knowledge that I use today. Women are the hope and continuance of our global civilization and conceivably the only ones who can fix this broken world.

www.ingramcontent.com/pod-product-compliance
Lightning Source LLC
Chambersburg PA
CBHW020728160426
43192CB00006B/145
9780985407841